Roseann Brennan

Mammy, I Don't Want to Die...

The Story of a Little Boy, Jake: His Life, Love & Legacy

This edition printed and bound in the Republic of Ireland by:
eprint
Unit 35, Coolmine Industrial Estate,
Blanchardstown,
Dublin 15.

Co-author: Kathryn Rogers.
Publisher: Orla Kelly
ISBN: 978-1-912328-07-9

*T*his book is dedicated to the most important people in my life: My husband Chris and my three beautiful children, Jake, Kaelem and Savannah. These four, wonderful people make me want to be a better person and make me proud to be a wife and mammy!

ACKNOWLEDGEMENTS

I have so many incredible people to thank, so buckle up, this going to be a long ride!

First, I must send heartfelt thanks to our amazing families. I've always said to Chris that I don't know how anyone else gets through a nightmare like this without families like ours.

To say that Jakie is loved and missed by so many people is an understatement. Thank you to every one of you, and I love you all so much.

So, thanks to my mam, Joan Hayes, step-dad Michael Nolan, my birth-mam Ann Hayes and her partner, Sean Byrne. Also, to the vast and extended Hayes and O'Shea family including my wonderful sisters Pamela Costello, Mary Hayes, Catherine Hayes, Angela O'Hara, Chantelle Rossiter, Margaret Dempsey and Bernie Hayes.

Thanks too to my incredible brothers Darren Hayes, Eamon (Ninja) Hayes, Michael (Yapper) Hayes, Jason Hayes and Jamie Hayes.

A special note of appreciation to their better halves – some of my favourite in-laws include Pamela Hayes, Kathleen Hayes, Ann Bolger, Tanya Hayes, Robert Costello, PJ Costello, Brian O'Sullivan, Pakie O'Hara, Leon Rossiter and Liamy Dempsey.

Many of Jakie's favourite playmates and babysitters are among our many lovely nieces and nephews: Sherice Costello, Kayla Costello, Cassie Costello, Donna Doyle, Megan O'Sullivan, Sasha O'Hara, Jaida O'Hara, Rihanna Farrell, Cheyenne Hayes, Becky Smith, CJ Hayes, Charlene Bolger-Hayes, Taylor-Rose Hayes, Lauren Rossiter, Abbie Rossiter, Jenny Dempsey and her partner Bryan Middleton, Sandra Williamson and husband James Williamson, Kelly O'Sullivan, Sinead O'Sullivan, Samantha George, Mason Costello, Bradley Costello, Paddy Doyle, Fintan Hayes, Jordan O'Sullivan, Nathan O'Sullivan, Kai O'Hara, Rhys

Hayes, Adam Hayes, JJ Hayes, Liam Dempsey and the much-missed Denis (Bocky) Dempsey RIP.

I'm blessed to have an amazing, loving, and sometimes crazy family and I love you all. Xxx

To every one of the Brennan and the Nolan families, you will never know how much you mean to us and how much all of you helped us in so many ways.

Special thanks to Chris's mam and dad, Bernadette and John Brennan, his grandparents Mary and James (Jessie) Nolan, his sister Alison Hirbod and brothers Michael Brennan, Eddie Brennan, Paul Nolan, sister-in-law Miriam Brennan and brother-in-law Shervin Hirbod. Thanks too to our nieces and nephew on this side of the family: Amy Brennan, Kayla Brennan, Abbie Brennan-Wall, Sophie Brennan-Wall, Taylor-Rae Hirbod and Nathan Hirbod.

I'm also blessed to have the best friends a girl could hope to have. Thank you for showing me what real friendship is. You've left your families at all times of the day and night and come running when we needed you. I was never short of a sympathetic ear at the end of the phone or a shoulder to cry on.

At times you've styled my hair to give me the boost I needed or reassured me until I had the courage to speak out at events for Jake's Legacy. And no one has ever had as many massages in their life as I've had from all of you! I love you all so much. Thank you for being in my life and thanks too to your incredibly families.

Thanks to Samantha McCullagh, James Hurley, Kyle Hurley, Amelia Hurley, Nicola Dunne, Ciara Hayes, Alanna Phelan, Dave Phelan, Yvonne Denieffe, Adrian Walsh, Mary Conroy, John Conroy, Shanice Conroy, Johnny Butler, Emily Flood, Emma Flood, Sylvia Rafter, Josephine Dewberry, Marzey Wall, Adriana Cahill, Kristen Campion, Claire Fortune and Margaret Leahy.

I want to say a special thanks to all the amazing family and friends who I call Jakie's Crew. You have stood by us every month, through all these years without fail. You mark Jakie's every milestone in rain, hail and snow.

I could never find enough words to truly express how grateful I am to you all. You've helped Chris, Kaelem, Savannah and me in countless ways, sometimes in practical ways like cleaning or cooking for the kids; or sometimes by being our emotional crutches and allowing us to cry.

Thank you for never leaving Jake out of a single occasion. He is part of all your homes and hearts so thank you all from the bottom of my heart. I hope ye all know that ye mean the world to me. Jakie's Crew are named above, and throughout the book, so I won't repeat the names here.

There are so many other good friends and neighbours around Kilkenny. You have helped us through our time of grief and have given up your free time for Jake's Legacy. It helps to know there are so many good people in this world. Thanks to all for being with us on the hard journey of surviving the loss of a beautiful child.

To Joanne Doran, Lisamarie Manual, Sharon O Neill, Shona Canham, Louise Fitzpatrick, Linda Morris, Kevin from Jesters Stage Academy, Zoe Cahill, John Delaney, Carla Keogh, Mary Phelan Waters, Anne Marie Cullen and your sorely missed husband Tony R.I.P.

To Rita Ní Mhaoileoin: You have shared the horrors of your child being struck by a car. Thank you so much for joining our protest at the Dáil and for your work as regional support for the Jake's Legacy Campaign in Clare.

Thanks to Yvonne and John Power - you were so kind to us during the worst of times - and to little Siofra who loved Jakie and was a great friend to Kaelem.

Many thanks too to my former employers, and good friends, at the Brog Maker in Kilkenny, Bobby Quinn, Breda Quinn, John Quinn and Carmel Quinn for all your help, generosity and friendship. I can't thank you all enough for all your kindnesses and your support. Thanks too to all wonderful staff of the Brog Maker who helped Bobby and Breda cater for all the mourners after Jakie's funeral and at the benefit night.

A big hug to Alan Gannon who wrote and sang beautiful songs for our Jakie in our time of loss. You touched my heart and helped me survive some very hard days. To see someone, who was once a stranger, show such love and compassion helped me to keep fighting. Thanks too to Assumpta, your lovely wife.

Thanks for your support, Noel Quigley, and for sleeping on the streets of Dublin with us for Jake's Legacy Thanks!

I've met some other incredible people who will always stick in my mind. Thanks to The Pink Ladies, a group of fabulous Dublin women of all ages, who turned up outside the Dáil on numerous times to support us and add lots of fun and laughter to the cause!

Other people who are owed our thanks and prayers are Sandy McSweeney, Bernie Stokes, Ruth O'Connell, Leanne Dreeling and Paige Casey.

To our friends and owners of Café Roma in Kilkenny, Maria Corduano, Daniela Corduano and Dominico Corduano: You started as my employers on my 16th birthday, and you ended up as friends. You have all done so much for me through everything and you are still there for me. I truly honour all your friendships.

A special mention to all at Authentic Turkish Barber in Kilkenny. Jake loved his visits to you with his dad, and I loved that you visited us so many times afterwards. I can see you were heartbroken over Jake's death.

Thanks to Jonathan and Claire Clement of Forget Me Not Florists. Four years on, and no matter what mad idea I present to you, John, you are there to help me and go way beyond the personal touch. I'm so glad you're my florist!

Special thanks to Tim Kiely of Poe Kiely Hogan Lanigan Solicitors in Kilkenny. Tim, thank you for going beyond the call of duty with me. I have your mobile number, which I have over-used, but you have always been so patient and so kind to me.

No other solicitor would have shown so much dedication to our cause and helped me as much as you have. Words could never express my gratitude but will have to do!

Thanks too to your deputy, solicitor Michael Lanigan. You did Jakie and my entire family justice the day of his inquest. You never held back. I honestly felt you voiced everything that I wanted to be said on the day.

I want to thank all the people who helped us on the worst day of our lives on Lintown Road on June 12, 2014. Thank you for giving your statements and thank you, to those who were called and agreed to go as witnesses to the inquest.

It's an incredibly brave thing to go on the stand and take an oath but you did it while one of the main witnesses, the driver, was represented by a doctor's cert.

Thank you, Karl Gleeson, Michael O'Keeffe, John Renehan, Josephine O'Riordan and Adrian Bouros. Chris, Kaelem and I are beyond grateful to you all.

Thanks to Johnston's Funeral Home in Kilkenny for treating Jake with such loving care. It's a very hard thing to place your baby in the care of someone else, but you treated him as you would one of your own precious family members. I knew you would mind him for me. Funeral director, Sammy, thank you for being so attentive to Jake and to us for the two days that he was at home. You were beyond professional, and you made our baby's final journey that little bit easier.

I want to thank the teachers of Presentation Primary School for your care of Jakie for the two years he was with you. Thanks to Jake's junior infant teacher, Catherine Millea, his senior infant teacher, Susanne White now Ryan and the principal Marie Kelly.

Jake loved school, and he loved his teachers and friends there. Special thanks to Jake's Miss White for the beautiful speech you gave at his funeral. I read it regularly, and it means a lot to me. It also means a lot to see you, Marie, every year at Jakie's anniversary mass. I just love that people in his life still remember him.

Thanks to Jakie's lovely classmates who planted a Cherry blossom tree and laid a special plaque in his memory so that he will be part of the school forever.

Thanks to all the amazing people who arranged benefits in Jakie's name including the members of the Darts Club, Castlecomer, my cousins, Edel Bolger and Rachel Bolger, and friends Marzey Wall, Sharon O'Neill and Claire Fortune.

I want to thank you all so, so much for the amount of time and work that you put into organising these nights and helping Chris to create our own memorial garden for Jake.

I love spending time in it and looking out on it every day. Now I also watch Kaelem and Savannah play in Jakie's garden instead of spending every day at his grave.

Thanks to party organisers, Party Dreamers in Kilkenny, for throwing your amazing party for Kaelem and Savannah from Jakie in heaven.

Thanks too to Jellietots Playcentre in Kilkenny which Jakie enjoyed so much when he was alive. You have been so good to Kaelem and Savannah since.

Our thanks too to the individuals behind road safety organisations like Love 30 and PARC Road Safety Group. Also, to Rod King of 20's Plenty in the UK and Donna Price of Irish Road Victims Association. You were so generous with your time and advice for Jake's Legacy. People like you change the world, so I hope you all keep up the good fight.

Thanks to everyone who gave us support on Road Safety Day including the Ormonde Hotel, Kilkenny, Lidl on Johnswell Road and Maria's Cakes Kilkenny who supplied wonderful cupcakes. Thanks to the Road Safety Authority who provided safety packs for all the children.

To Pat Moore Photography and Jellybean Julie for the lovely entertainment for the kids that day.

Thanks especially to Brian Carroll of Brian Carroll Road Transport Safety for your huge help during Road Safety Week. You were on hand for any advice we need and thanks too to all the speakers, sponsors and volunteers who helped us.

It meant so much to me, and I will be forever grateful to you all. It's so hard to remember everyone as my mind was a black fog at the time.

Please know I'm grateful to you all for your passion, love and support.

Thanks to Garda Frances Dunphy, our Family Liaison Officer for your kindness and compassion.

To Brian Cody and the all the incredible Kilkenny hurling team: you gave Jake's Legacy a big promotional boost when we needed it. You donated a signed jersey and invited us to your training session. You brought us out onto the pitch and held up Jakie's banners. We have treasured photos of Kaelem and Savannah with you all. Please know, that it meant a lot to us here at Jake's Legacy, to have the support of our champion county team.

And many, many thanks to GAA legend and hurling hero, Henry Shefflin, who so kindly agreed to launch my book. I can't begin to express my gratitude for your generosity.

Another big thank you to KCLR's Eimear Ní Bhraonáin for so kindly agreeing to host my book launch and for all your support with Jake's Legacy. Please know that I appreciate it!

I'd like to add more appreciation to Eamon Langton of the great Langton House Hotel for providing a wonderful venue for my book launch - thanks so much Eamon!

To all the other media who supported Jake's Legacy: My head was, and sometimes still is, all over the place so I can't remember all the names and organisations who helped. But I know everyone heard Jake's story because of you.

Thanks to RTE's Ray D'Arcy, Matt Cooper of Today FM, Sue Nun of KCLR; to the presenters and producers of Ireland AM, Claire Byrne Live, The Today Show, Primetime, RTE News and TV3 News.

To the Daily Mail, the Irish Times, the Irish Mirror, the Examiner, the Herald, the Sunday World, the Irish Daily Star, The Irish Independent and especially to Sean Keane, Sam Matthews and all the staff of our own Kilkenny People: Thank you so much for the help Jake's Legacy has received over the past four years.

More thanks to radio presenter Johnny Oosten of Community Radio Clare (CRCfm) for your kindness. You are another very kind heart that we have met on this road and one that I will treasure forever.

I have many medical people to thank, almost all of whom are among the incredible staff of St Luke's Hospital. I know you all did the best you could do for Jakie in his last minutes, and you also showed us huge kindness on the day.

I'd like to give a special mention to Nurse Laura Ramsbottom and to the paramedic team, Mick Kavanagh and Peter Reynolds, who did their utmost to save Jake's life.

I need to thank Dr Séamus MacSuibhne and his secretary, Maria Corby, along with senior clinical psychologists Claire Regan and Martin Doohan and all staff in the Department of Psychiatry at St Luke's. Thank you all for helping me build up the mental strength to retake control of my life.

I personally never thought I'd be a person needing acute psychiatric care, but I would urge anyone who feels mentally unwell to seek help. The help is out there. I'm living proof.

A sincere thank you to the Coroner Dr Brendan Doyle for your kindnesses. I saw that you understood the depth of our grief at the inquest. You showed so much empathy and compassion.

To all the staff at Newpark Family Resource Centre. You hold a special part of my heart because Jake loved to spend time at the homework club there. You made a small child very happy, and for that, I'll always be grateful.

Thank you all for the love you gave him and for agreeing to do a guard of honour at his funeral. I know it was hard to do. Also, thank you for creating a memorial to him outside the centre.

Grateful thanks to Sheila Donnelly, Perle Leahy, Tilda Fitzgerald, Lorraine Bowden, Marcella Cahill, Bernadette Brophy, Aishling Donnelly, Mary Donnelly, Tina Knox, Jenny Brett, Sarah Butler, Mairead Donovan, Peter Healy, Jacqueline Brophy, Evelyn

Phelan, Virginija Dzinina, Margaret Lanigan, Linda Hennessy, Louise Nolan and Helen Synnott.

Thank you so much to our parish priest Fr. Frank Purcell at St John's Church. You married us, you christened Jake, and you were there for us again when we laid Jake to his final rest.

Thank you for all your advice and for making sure that I gave Jakie the send-off that his little soul deserved. Thank you too for your beautiful words during Jake's funeral and later at his month's mind, and for making us renew our vows! Our parish is so lucky to have you.

There are some politicians to whom I owe a debt of gratitude.

Huge thanks to councillor Andrew McGuinness, who's a man unlike most politicians I've encountered. I can't begin to list everything you've done for Jake's Legacy, both as the former mayor of Kilkenny and as a friend.

I appreciate all your help, your time and above all, your passion which I know comes from the heart and from being a devoted parent yourself.

Thanks also to Andrew's father, John McGuinness, for going above and beyond the ordinary with your dogged support for Jake's Legacy. Thank you especially for that powerful speech you made advocating the bill for Jake's Law in the Dáil in February 2015.

Thanks to Councillor Joe Malone too for his incredible community spirit and for giving me so much of his time and sitting with me and advising me. You all give politicians a good name!

To the incredible Mary Lou McDonald: Thank you so much for being a woman of your word. You supported Jake's legacy on a professional level, and you supported me on a personal level.

We were so happy to have someone of your calibre represent our Jake in the Dáil. You are such a powerful and inspirational woman in so many ways, and I am forever in your debt.

To Gerry Adams: For the way you treated us and made it your business to give us a sympathetic ear and your time. Unlike some politicians, you never made me feel I should be honoured to receive your support. Instead, you said you felt honoured to bring forward the bill for Jake's Law.

Thank you, and thanks to all in the Sinn Fein Party who helped support Jake's Law

Thanks to all the politicians who sincerely supported Jake's Legacy and to all the County Councils nationwide who have implemented Jake's Law.

Many thanks to Gerry Conlon of eprint printers for getting this book into my hands and to Orla Kelly Publishing who got my book online and available all over the world!

Thanks to my ghostwriter, Kathryn Rogers. She has been an amazing person in more ways than one. She will never know how much I appreciate having her with me for this experience.

I was petrified to begin this book, but when I spoke to her, I knew she was the right person for me. Moreover, I felt she was the only person who would do justice to Jakie's story.

I feel so comfortable with her, and she took me on as a friend, not just a client. I spoke to many writers before her, but none of them understood me as she did.

I must end it here as I could go on forever, but I can't finish without thanking the kindness of strangers.

We received support from so many people we never met in Ireland, England and even beyond. We received letters, flowers, little gifts and words of kindness which meant so much to us.

There were days when I was ready to give up, and something would arrive through the letterbox, and the message that came with it would lift my spirits and remind me how much good there is in the world.

To all our followers on Jake's Legacy, you'll never know how much you have helped us with the lovely comments, likes, shares and support over the last few years.

You might think that 'liking' a post on Jake's Legacy isn't much, but it means so much as you're letting us know that you stand by us in this fight to save other children's lives.

It also makes me happy to think that so many people are getting to know about Jakie. I only just wish he had the chance to get to know you all. Whether you 'like' our posts or not, I am forever grateful to everyone following Jake's Legacy.

Mostly, thank you to everyone – friends, family and people who we've never met - who reached out to me, my family and Jake's Legacy and showed that you cared.

All my love,

Jakie's Mammy

xxx

Contents

PROLOGUE   1
1. ROSIE AND CHRIS   3
2. JAKE'S BIRTH   21
3. OUR CHEERIOS HEAD   34
4. AND KAELEM MAKES TWO   46
5. PRINCE JAKE'S WEDDING   58
6. A SCHOLAR AND A GENTLEMAN   69
7. LITTLE SISSY, SAVANNAH   78
8. BEST DAY EVER   88
9. THE PREMONITION   103
10. MAMMY, I DON'T WANT TO DIE   116
11. DENIAL AND FURY   133
12. BABY'S FINAL REST   143
13. OUR ANGEL JAKIE   159
14. MARRIAGE ON THE ROCKS   169
15. JAKE'S LEGACY   177
16. 'MENTAL' PATIENT ROSIE   207
17. JUSTICE FOR JAKIE   220
18. LOVE, LOATHING AND JAKE'S INQUEST   230
19. GARDA BLUES   241
20. MY BROWN-EYED BOY   260
21. SUICIDE ATTEMPT SHOCK   270
22. TEARS, TRAUMA AND THERAPY   282
23. TRUE FRIENDS   297
24. A NEW START   309
MY GOODBYE LETTER TO JAKIE   321
EPILOGUE   323
THE DRIVER   326
LIFE WITHOUT MY MORNING SUN   328
ABOUT THE AUTHOR   329
PRAISE FOR THIS BOOK   330

Jake, you may be gone from my arms,
but never from my heart…

PROLOGUE

Everything becomes confused and surreal. Voices sound muted, and people seem like a distant blur. In my memory, everything moves in slow motion.

In parts, my recollections are shadowy at best and at other times, I have memories that haunt me in cinematic detail. When I try to tell the story of the horror, I feel like I'm back there; it seems like it's happening all over again.

I have a vivid memory of opening my eyes and seeing a shadow; something falling from the sky. It's so fleeting that I can't be sure of the height, but I know it's Jake.

There's no mistaking the sound that follows: a thunk, thunk, thunk, the noise of something being churned by car wheels. It's the sound of my baby being tumbled under that car like a rag-doll in the drum of a washing machine.

I have no memory of running through a garden strewn with toys or running past the parked car in the drive. I can only explain that it's like I open my eyes again, and Jake is there.

I'm outside our neighbour's house to our right and Jakie is on the road. He's standing, swaying. We're facing each other.

And he comes to me. He's limping, with a strange, twisted gait; a wounded pup. I can see his snow-white pallor even as I run to him.

His legs fold as I reach him; he collapses into me, and I fall to my knees supporting him.

"I'm sorry, Mammy," he says.

He thinks he's in trouble because he's been hit by the car. "Baby, you're okay; that wasn't your fault. You did nothing wrong; you did nothing wrong."

I'm in a soundproof bubble with Jake. The world around is muffled, and it's just my baby and me inside. Outside, I catch a glimpse of Christopher. He's running and running towards the end of the street. He's banging on the windows of a moving car with his fists.

"Why didn't you stop?" he screams from very far away. "Why didn't you f**king stop?"

It's all background noise because Jakie and I are in our bubble. I hold him to me; my body is quaking with terror and wracked by sobs.

"You're okay Baby; you're okay; relax Baby, I have you."

My mind is spinning, trying to absorb what's happening; trying to work out what happened.

Jake was on his feet. He must be okay; he stood up. I must be wrong. That couldn't have been Jake in the sky; that rumble from under the car had to be something else.

I talk and try to reassure him; try to be soothing.

"You're okay Baby; you're okay; relax Baby, I have you."

But he can feel me shake and hear me hyperventilate. There's a ball of fear lodged in my throat, threatening to choke me.

Then he says the words that make the blood in my veins run cold.

"Mammy, I don't want to die…"

1. ROSIE AND CHRIS

Three months after we met, Chris and I sat on the edge of the bed, hearts pounding, heads racing, awaiting the results of the pregnancy test in my hand. Outside the traffic rumbled by, birds sang, and we could hear my mother moving about in the kitchen below.

Life went on, but we hardly dared to blink or breathe, as we counted down the minutes to a result that could change everything. One blue line signified that our day would go on as normal; two blue lines meant that our lives would change forever.

Our relationship was one that certainly fell under the category of 'whirlwind romance'. That day it was hard to believe it was only twelve short weeks since Chris and I got together. It seemed like a lifetime ago. I could hardly remember a time when he wasn't the most important person in my life.

We met through my matchmaking friend, Marzey Wall, who was seeing a guy called Eddie Brennan. She kept telling me about Eddie's younger brother, Chris, who was single; she thought he was perfect for me.

"You have to come and meet him," she'd say. "Seriously, Ro, you'd love him. He's good looking and everything. Honestly, he is!"

But I wasn't looking for anyone, especially her boyfriend's brother. Things would get awkward if I didn't like him or I had to dump him. I'd also tried the occasional blind date before, and they all turned out to be disasters.

"No thanks, Marzey," I told her. "I couldn't care less what he looks like. I don't want to go out with anyone."

I'd been tied down in a silly relationship for five years during my teenage years, and since then, I'd rediscovered the fun of being single. Now, aged 22, I didn't want to be in a couple.

They called me 'the party sister' in my family, and I have seven sisters, so there was a lot of competition for the title.

It was early 2007, and Mika was flying high in the charts with Grace Kelly. Rihanna was about to reach stratospheric heights with Umbrella and Snow Patrol were still basking in the glow of their mega-hit Chasing Cars from a few months earlier.

My social life was curtailed because my job meant that I had to work almost every weekend. My original ambition after the Leaving Cert was to work and with that in mind, I studied childcare at Ormonde College in Kilkenny.

After qualifying, I went for an interview for a job in a creche and for a waitress job in The Brog Maker in Kilkenny.

The waitressing job paid more and had the added benefit of tips, so I decided to shelve my career in childcare before it even started.

Getting a weekend night off as a waitress was like finding buried treasure. So, I was in the middle of a rare Saturday night in Morrissey's bar when Marzey arrived with the fellow, Chris, that she'd been talking about.

The attraction for me was instant. I thought Chris was so handsome and has such a perfect baby face, that he could have walked out of a boy band video.

I liked everything I saw, from his poster boy looks to his expertly spiked brown hair, to his soft green eyes and his shy smile.

It wasn't the most promising start to a love story. We never exchanged a single word that night. He talked with my other friends, but he never spoke to me. He claims that he never knew that Marzey had ideas about fixing him up with me.

"You're terribly quiet!" I remarked, teasing him at one stage. "Isn't he very quiet altogether, Marzey?"

He ignored me. I was a bit drunk and giddy, and he was quiet and sober. I never expected to see him again after that first dismal meeting.

Weeks later, I went to The Venue Club, and while I watched my girlfriends up on the dance floor, someone tapped me on the shoulder. I turned to see my silent heartthrob.

"Well!" is all he said to me.

"Oh, it speaks!" I gasped, clutching my heart in feigned astonishment. "You wouldn't talk to me the last time I saw you!"

He could see that I was delighted to see him. I didn't know that he had been watching me and that he made his move as soon as my girlfriends disappeared onto the dance floor.

He didn't seem to be in any hurry to return to his friends, and he was all chat this time.

"I thought you must have fancied one of my friends. You talked to everyone except me," I said.

My heart skipped when he looked me in the eye and replied: "No, it was you straight away."

When we got to know each other better, he insisted he fell for me the instant he saw me across the crowded Morrissey's Bar.

"I saw your long dark hair and that tight red dress and that was it for me," he said. "But I didn't think there was any way you'd feel the same about me. I thought I was too quiet. I didn't think we'd click."

I learnt that he was living with his parents, Bernie and John Brennan, in Castlecomer, about 15 minutes outside Kilkenny. He was working on the building sites as a labourer at the time.

All too soon the club was closing. Chris said he had to meet a few guys because they had arranged to share a taxi back to Castlecomer. I lied and said that all the girls were going that way anyway because we wanted to go to Supermacs.

It was just an excuse to spend more time with him.

I herded the girls in the direction of Supermacs, and as we went our separate ways, he gave me a chaste kiss on the cheek. I knew already that I liked him and that I didn't want to be single anymore.

Work schedules and other commitments conspired to keep us apart for the next two weeks. I worried that he'd lose interest and meet someone else, but he kept in touch by texting and phoning. We got to know each other a little better.

I was still so nervous meeting him for our first real date that my heart felt like it was dancing in my chest. Chris said he'd meet me at the end of my road and we'd go for lunch. Our first date was March 3, 2007.

I could see him standing there, watching me walk down Ballybough Street at the appointed hour. I've never felt so self-conscious in my life. I was paranoid about how I was walking and was relieved when he closed the gap by strolling towards me. He looked as handsome as I remembered, and he kissed me on the lips this time.

Before this, I'd never met a guy on a first date that didn't involve alcohol. We went for a sober lunch in Matt the Miller's on John Street. It wasn't an ideal date because my work shift started at 4.00pm, but it was the only time we could find.

My stomach was locked with anxiety, and my mouth was dry. If Chris had looked up from his menu, he'd have seen mine shake from the tremor in my hand.

The last thing I wanted was something to eat, but this was a lunch date, and I knew it would look odd if I didn't eat something.

My first thought was to choose something that wasn't messy. A toasted sandwich seemed like such a safe bet.

Of course, I ended up with a toasted sandwich made in hell. Tomato fell from it in wet plops, and strings of melted cheese stretched like tightropes from my mouth to the plate. I was dying of embarrassment as I tried to eat.

But Chris never appeared to notice and afterwards, he took me for a romantic stroll down along the river.

We discovered that we shared similar tastes in film and music; I hated chick-flicks and loved action movies, and so did he. We agreed that Snow Patrol was our favourite band in the world. We held hands, talked easily, and my anxieties melted away.

And that was it for me. I was hooked on this guy. I didn't want to leave him and go to work that day, but I had to.

My heart leapt when I received a phone text from him later that evening. It was an invite to his house after work to watch a DVD. It might as well have been an invite to a romantic dinner in Paris because it made me so happy.

Our first proper kiss took place in front of that DVD. It was some Die Hard film, but I don't think either of us was too interested in the movie.

We fell hard for each other very fast. Christopher didn't know how gorgeous he was; he still doesn't. I could see that he was soft-hearted, genuine and kind. We fell in love very fast.

I'd go so far to say that we were even infatuated with each other. I spent my days thinking of Chris, and when we were apart, I spent my nights dreaming of him. I was always counting down the hours when I could see him again.

He always says he fell for me because I'm perfect. I know I'm not, and he knows I'm not, but that's the kind of thing he says. I used to be paranoid about my pointy chin, but he brushed off all my insecurities.

"That's MY chin, and I love it!" he'd say.

He hates to hear me moan about any of my many flaws. He throws his eyes to heaven if I complain about the few stretch marks I have.

"That's part of our life together, so what do you want to get rid of them?" he says.

He stopped me getting hung up on my looks. From the start, he made me feel beautiful and good about myself. I can appear in a tracksuit wearing no make-up and I know I look awful, but he'll still say: "You're gorgeous, Baby."

Back then, we were always waiting for one of us to finish work so that I could drive out to his house, or he could come to mine. I was the only one of us driving at the time, and I could still tell you the position of every mossy stone on the Castlecomer Road.

We'd spend hours together just talking. That's one of the reasons Chris says that he fell for me. He felt he could speak to me about anything and we didn't need to go out drinking or socialising; we were happy sitting in together chatting for hours.

He also says he admires me for not being afraid to speak my mind in front of anyone. He likes that I treat everyone the same and that I'm not intimidated by authority. When there's a battle to be fought, he'll send me to do it.

"There's no better woman," he says.

Home for me back then was with my mother, Joan Hayes, and my step-dad, Mick Nolan at 19, Ballybough Street.

It's a modest house in a row of terraced houses located on the edge of town, across the road from Kilkenny's army barracks. Reared in a family of seven sisters and four brothers, I moved out when I was 17, but I moved back about a year before I met Chris.

Chris fitted into my big and complicated family life with ease. He and Mick are cousins, so my step-dad knew all the generations of his family. Mammy fell in love with Chris almost as fast as I did, and he called her 'Mother' from the first time he met her.

My nieces, who were around 15 then, were big fans of Chris and used to giggle and make eyes at him behind his back. The younger nieces and nephews adored him because he enjoyed taking them to the beach at Tramore as much as I did.

We were only together a couple of weeks when I celebrated my 23rd birthday. Chris surprised me by arranging red rose petals spelling 'I love you' on his bed. He had a bottle of bubbly which he served to me with a tea towel draped over his arm like a posh waiter.

If anyone else had said 'I love you' after two weeks, I'd have called him a freak, and I'd have run for the hills. But with Chris, it was like we were together forever.

We lived a chaotic existence because we were always moving between our parents' two homes. I'd stay in Chris's house for two days if he wasn't working and he might stay at mine on other days.

On a couple of occasions, I'd forget to pack the contraceptive pill. I was never worried about missing a pill or two. I was never great at remembering to take tablets anyway. I had been careless in my previous relationship too and never got caught.

We knew what could happen, but the chances of getting pregnant seemed slim. I wasn't concerned.

Three months into our relationship, however, I got up early for a hair appointment and felt the strangest sensation. I had to steady myself at the bathroom sink because I felt so light-headed and sick.

I hadn't missed a period because I didn't always have one. I never had a regular cycle. But I'd never had that feeling before. I bought a pregnancy test to rule it out more than anything. Still, as we sat on my bed, looking at each other and the testing kit, we were petrified.

"What are we going to do if this is positive?" I asked. "We're together three months; we hardly know each other."

Chris never hesitated.

"I don't care," he said. "Whatever happens between us, I'm going to love this child, and I'll be a good father to it."

"Yes, but what if we break up?"

Everything was going through my mind.

"It's still my child, Ro. Don't worry; we'll be okay."

I slipped into the downstairs bathroom to take the test and returned to my room where we waited, hardly breathing, for the result.

Finally, like magic, a single blue line appeared in the display window. We weren't pregnant. There was a big sigh of relief.

At the same time, somewhere, deep inside of me, I felt a little disappointment too. The feeling took me by surprise.

Then Chris added: "You know, I wouldn't have minded if you were pregnant. I think I would have liked it."

I was able to admit that I had mixed feelings about the result of the pregnancy test too.

"It would have been a shock, but I wouldn't have been unhappy about it," I said.

We had a lengthy discussion about it and, mad as it seems, we said we'd try and have a baby. As I said, we were infatuated with each other.

Making a baby together suddenly seemed like the best idea ever. As far as we were concerned, we were going to be a team, forever. We decided we could make the sacrifices. Our social life would be over, and money would be tight. But Chris could work to keep the baby and me when I had to take time off work.

I always knew I wanted to be a mother. I loved children. What convinced me most though, was the fact that I knew Chris would make a great dad.

I'd seen him with my nieces and nephews, and he was so good with them. I'd watched him with his niece, Abbie, a toddler, and he minded her, changed her nappy and got her bottle without a problem. I'd seen how his parents doted over their grandchild, Abbie, too.

I felt sure that Christopher Brennan would never turn his back on his child. They were good people, and I knew in my heart that he, and they, would always do the best for our child. We were going to have a baby and live happily ever after.

Even when I told two of my sisters about our plans for a baby, they didn't try to discourage me. No one said: "My God, you hardly know this guy; what are you thinking?"

Then three weeks later, I felt uncomfortable while I was shopping with my older sister, Catherine.

"Why are my boobs killing me all of a sudden?" I asked.

"Oh my God, Rosie you're pregnant."

"No, I'm not. I told you I did a test three weeks ago."

"I'm telling you, you're pregnant."

"Don't be daft. I'm not. We're only trying three weeks. Even if I was. I wouldn't feel anything yet."

She couldn't help herself. She ran into the next pharmacy to buy a test and insisted that I do it right away.

To get her off my back, I agreed to take the test in the toilets in the Market Cross Shopping Centre.

We'd never get any shopping done with her nagging me.

I washed my hands while she concentrated on the testing strip. My sister is a messer at the best of time so when she shrieked, I didn't take much notice.

"Rosie, you're pregnant!"

"Ca, would you stop it? I know I'm not."

"You are, look!"

I looked. There was no doubt about it; there were two clear blue lines in the tester window.

I had this sudden rush of complete terror. The idea of a baby had all been a lovely pipe dream. It was this warm and fuzzy feeling and a prospect that could happen, sometime in the remote future. Not in three weeks.

That couldn't happen, could it? I could hardly think straight for the blood pounding in my heart.

My hands shook as I reread the instructions and double-checked the result. No doubt about it. Two blue lines equalled a positive test.

"I'll buy another test," I said.

It was a mistake. I was sure of it. It had to be. I stared at myself wide-eyed and terrified in the mirror.

We rang my sister Pamela and consulted with her. She looked up information on the reliability of pregnancy tests.

"It says here that a test can give a false negative, but you'll never get a test that gives you a false positive," she said.

I still took three tests before I broke the news to Chris. We were staying at his nanny's house in Castlecomer for a few months while she was away in England.

He hugged me and said he couldn't be happier, but I knew he was as scared as me.

We thought we had months, even years of trying before we'd have a baby. We never thought we'd be facing the prospect of being parents in three weeks.

Weeks later, my best friend Samantha McCullagh accompanied me to an early antenatal appointment because Chris had to work. We believed the baby was due around May, but the doctor disagreed.

"Your baby is too big," he said. "The pregnancy is more advanced than that. I'm changing your due date to March 28."

Samantha and I looked at each other and burst out laughing. The due date was my 24th birthday.

It turned out that the pregnancy test that I'd taken in my mother's house gave a false result. I'd already been six weeks pregnant the day that we decided that we wanted to try for a baby.

A few months later, I also discovered that I was wrong about Chris's birthday.

Chris led me to believe that he was turning 23 on November 24 and that he was only a couple of months younger than me.

I was well into the pregnancy when I discovered that he was only 20 and that he would be 21 on his next birthday. I was in complete shock. I realised that for a few months of the year, I was three whole years older than him.

Getting my head around it was hard. I was always going on that I'd never go out with a guy who was younger than me. It was something that I would have said a million times. Chris heard that and decided that he'd better keep his real age to himself.

The truth is I fell for Chris the minute he walked through the door of Morrissey's Bar that night. I didn't care what age he was.

My sisters thought it was hilarious though and had great craic calling me 'the cradle snatcher'.

Chris celebrated his 21st at Shortall's Bar in Castlecomer accompanied by his far older girlfriend with a bump.

I won't claim that it was all hand-holding and Hallmark moments between us in those early days. We had our rows, and we were on and off many times. We fell in love so fast and furiously, that when we hurt each other, we felt it intensely. The slightest thing, like Chris using the wrong tone of voice, became a whole big drama.

"Oh my God, I can't believe you're talking to me like that. You're not the person I thought you were!"

I'd never give in after a row. I always hated to be the one to crack and call him first. It used to drive him mad, so he started doing things like hiding my work shoes, so I'd have to ring and ask him where they were. He did hide my shoes, by the way.

"He's such a baby!" I'd wail to Samantha. "But is it any wonder? He's only 21. I knew I should never go out with someone younger!"

It didn't take me long to learn how to get my own way though. I can get around Chris for anything now.

Jakie Baby, you got that skill from me.

These days if things aren't going my way with Chris, I give in and say, "Okay, you're right." I look sad and add a little sigh of regret, but I won't make a big deal of it.

It usually only takes a few seconds.

"Stop now; you're making me feel bad," he says.

"No, no, you're right, Chris. I don't need it."

"Ah Roseann, stop. I'm sorry. If you want it, you should have it. Go on, get it."

He's the biggest softie so I know I can get around him for anything.

Chris is a real romantic at heart. It's the little things he does, like coming home to find that he's put a lit candle on the coffee table and ordered a takeaway.

He's the best, but even after all these years, I still feel like killing him sometimes.

There was no hiding my pregnancy with Jake. My bump appeared early and grew out in front of me at an enormous rate.

You wanted to be centre stage from the start, didn't you Jakie Baby?

From the back, I looked normal, but when I turned, the bump stuck out so far that it was like moving the stern of a ship.

I remember a carload of young lads stopped at traffic lights behind me one night. I was wearing leggings and high heels, and they started wolf-whistling out the window.

Then I turned, and they saw the massive bump swinging around towards them. The guys stopped wolf-whistling and cracked up laughing instead.

I never spent a night in hospital in my life until I was pregnant with Jake. Then I was in and out of the hospital with kidney infections, soaring blood pressure and suspected pre-eclampsia.

Chris was at his Christmas works do one night when I felt very ill with another kidney infection. I felt this terrible pressure to pee but struggled to go up and down the stairs to the bathroom as I found it increasingly hard to breathe.

It got so bad that any dignity went out the window and I sat on a potty in the bedroom with a duvet wrapped around me. As the hours wore on, I felt worse and worse, and at 3.00am, in desperation, I rang the out-of-hours doctors' service, Caredoc.

Exhausted, I explained that I didn't want to drive ten minutes to the Waterford Road clinic unless they could prescribe something for me. I knew that being pregnant, they would be cautious about writing a prescription, but the doctor insisted that I should drive out to see him.

My breathing was so bad that I could hardly talk in the doctor's surgery. I had stabbing pain in my back and sides from the kidney infection.

My jaw dropped when he advised me to go home and inhale the steam of a boiling kettle until my breathing improved. He couldn't have told me that over the phone?

I hadn't enough breath left to tell him what I wanted him to do with his kettle of boiling water.

Catherine called to see me the next morning, took one look and said: "Let's go, we're going to the hospital."

The hospital admitted me, put me on an IV for the kidney infection but ignored the fact that I could hardly breathe.

"Once we clear up the infection, you'll feel fine," they said.

I knew my breathing problems were nothing to do with a kidney infection, but they wouldn't give me an x-ray while I was pregnant.

A doctor finally listened to my lungs with a stethoscope, and he called over a colleague who did the same. They finally agreed to start treating me for pneumonia. It was the sickest I'd ever felt in my life.

It was after Christmas and right in the middle of another hellish kidney infection that Chris proposed.

We had discussed an engagement, but I thought it was kind of cheesy getting engaged while I was pregnant. Chris didn't understand my reluctance.

"I want to marry you, so what's wrong with getting engaged?" he asked.

I didn't see the point. I didn't like the idea of getting engaged while I was pregnant, and I wasn't interested in a diamond ring either.

I prefer big, bold, costume jewellery, not dainty diamonds. I begged Chris, not to buy a ring that I wouldn't appreciate. An engagement ring would be wasted on me.

"Wait until after our baby was born; we can get engaged then," I urged.

Then one weekend in January 2008, I realised he was about to propose. I had woken that morning feeling like I was coming down with a kidney infection again.

I may have been sick, but I wasn't blind and deaf. There were these hushed conversations in the house that stopped dead as soon as I walked in.

Chris finds it very hard to keep a secret, and so does everyone else in my family. I'm the only one who plans surprises because I'm the only one who can keep a secret.

My sisters confirmed my sneaking suspicions with ever-so-casual remarks that they'd see me later.

"Oh, we may drop by this evening" and "sure, we'll call in for a drink tonight." That sort of thing. I knew the proposal was taking place that night and that he'd invited everyone.

As the day went on, I was feeling sicker and sicker. I couldn't exactly turn around and tell him to cancel the proposal that I wasn't supposed to know about.

I hadn't even the energy to go up and change or wash my hair or do anything in preparation. I was lying prostrate on the couch, and I thought to myself: "Surely to God, Chris can see how bad I am, and he'll cancel everything."

But Chris doesn't like to disappoint people. He's also single-minded when he wants to be, and he was thinking: "It's time I got this ring on her."

So, I was lying on the couch, feeling miserable, looking wrecked, and hugging a hot-water bottle when everyone dropped into the house at the same time. The big moment came. Chris dropped down on one knee, and there was a hush in the room.

"Ro, I know you don't want me to ask you to marry me when you're pregnant, but I know I want to spend the rest of my life with you. Will you marry me?" he asked.

He had tears in his eyes, but I started laughing because that's what I do at the most inappropriate times. Then I saw the ring, a lovely big, glitzy, fake ring, and I was happy. I knew that he got me.

It meant even more that he got down on one knee and proposed to me in front of all those people who were now clapping, cheering and jeering.

He was such a shy person then. He still is to some extent. We weren't together even a year, so it was an ordeal for him to do what he did in front of all the people I love.

I didn't find out until later, but he had also asked Mammy for my hand in marriage. That meant a lot to her too.

Everyone else toasted the engagement with champagne that he'd bought for the occasion. I got back to feeling sick and sorry for myself.

I asked him later why he didn't postpone the proposal.

"Roseann, how could I call it off?" he reasoned. "I had everyone told, and they were all there."

I still laugh about it. The romance of it, proposing to your heavily pregnant girlfriend while she's lying on the couch dying of a kidney infection.

Yes, he could have brought me to a fancy restaurant another night and proposed to me like a normal boyfriend.

But there would have been no one to see him going down on one knee except strangers. It made it so much better that everyone we loved was there for my 'surprise' engagement.

I remember his earnest and handsome face that night, and I can still see the tears in those green eyes.

The truth is, I loved the proposal; I loved the ring, and I loved him.

2. JAKE'S BIRTH

Jakie Baby. My beautiful, perfect little Jakie. They placed him against my breast, my skin touching his, moments after he was born.

I see him so clearly now, his fists flailing and legs jerking, raging that they've evicted him from his cosy little nest inside me.

You never did like change, did you Jakie?

I see Christopher's face too, a red-hot mess of tears and sweat. He's crying, smiling, sobbing and laughing at the same time. Jake's dad can't always find the words to express himself, but torrents of emotion pour from his eyes.

"He's perfect, just perfect," I heard him say, over and over, reassuring himself, as much as me, after the terror of the previous hours.

My poor Christopher was a baby himself. A few months earlier he was a carefree lad at his 21st party, now he was a dazed dad in a delivery room, with a newborn son.

But he never wanted it any other way, did he Jakie? Chris was born to be a daddy.

I remember Chris, gazing at his son in my arms, stroking those curled fingers and plump cheeks in both shock and awe.

The delivery room had a relaxed air now with nurses bustling around us, cleaning up. They smiled and cooed over Jake, telling him, telling us, what a gorgeous baby he was. All 8lbs 14oz of him.

Drenched in blood and sweat and tears, I stared at our baby, watching him, warily, like he was some strange curiosity.

I smiled with my delighted-new-mammy face and agreed with the nurses that he was a beautiful baby.

But mostly, I watched him and waited. I waited for that sensation, that rush of deep love, that all-powerful sense of bonding that every mother feels for her newborn.

I waited.

But I felt nothing except relief as someone finally swept our baby away to clean him, dress him and keep him warm; to do the things I knew I should be doing.

It was 8.18pm on Wednesday, April 2, 2008, when Jake arrived in this world.

I have no memories of what kind of a day it was. I had been in St Luke's Hospital in Kilkenny for a week before Jake's birth because of soaring blood pressure.

Every day in the hospital seemed long, grey and dreary.

The doctors kept testing for preeclampsia. They jabbed me with so many needles that I felt like a living pincushion

I sat in a hospital bed as Jake's due date of March 28, my 24th birthday, slipped by with no sign of his appearance.

By March 31, I was stir crazy and relieved when my doctor announced it was time that Jake was born.

"We're going to have to induce, Roseann," said the doctor. "It'll be safer for both of you because we're finding it difficult to get your blood pressure under control."

So, they began the process of removing Jake from that warm and snug cocoon in my belly.

First, they inserted prostaglandin gel to open the cervix and kickstart the contractions.

As I felt the pains coming from deep inside me, I grabbed my older sister's arm in excitement and dread.

"God, Ca, it's working already," I said. "The contractions have started. I think I'm going to go tonight."

Chris, Catherine and I spent the next several hours looking at each other. There was no sign of Jake budging. That evening the doctor confirmed the cervix hadn't dilated at all. It was false labour.

Catherine and Chris went home while the nurse injected me with pethidine for the pain, knocking me out for the night.

The next morning, they sent for a procedure called membrane sweeping to start labour. This is where they manually separate the membranes of the amniotic sac from the cervix.

Chris had to work that morning, so Catherine came with me. Ca is a woman who has given birth to six kids, and her eyes were out on stalks as the doctor got to work.

"Even I'm feeling a bit queasy after that," she admitted afterwards. "I've never seen that before."

The doctor prescribed another dose of prostaglandin gel.

"We need to bring this baby along," he said.

It was a phrase that I was going to hear a lot over the coming days. They gave me the second dose, and the pains started up again.

By now I was really getting fed up with it all. Women arrived into the labour ward long after me, went down to the delivery room, had their babies and went home. I was still there, and nothing was happening.

Twelve hours later, there was still no stir out of Jakie. Once again, it was false labour. The nurse gave me another pethidine injection to sleep.

"You're going to need your sleep because one way or another, you'll be having this baby tomorrow," she said.

I didn't believe her. I was beginning to think this baby was never coming out.

The next morning at 10.00am, they brought me down for another fun procedure. This time they artificially ruptured the membranes to break my waters.

Shortly after, the contractions started for real. Now, they promised, my baby was on his way.

Hours later, Jake was still dragging his heels, and the doctor wasn't happy with the progress.

"The cervix is dilating too slowly," said the doctor. "We're going to hurry things up."

They inserted an oxytocin drip into a vein in my arm. Soon I was gripped by intense contractions with virtually no break between them.

"This baby must be coming any minute now," I gasped at Chris. "This is unbelievable!"

Two hours of grinding pain later, they said the labour still wasn't progressing. They increased the oxytocin dose and up shot the pain levels too. I didn't think it was possible to feel any worse.

At a previous check-up, the hospital had also discovered another potential complication.

They found that I had Group B strep, which are normal bacteria that exists in about 25% of healthy women. Usually, there is only a very slight risk of the baby contracting it from the mother.

However, having kidney infections is an indicator that the baby is at higher risk. They told me that he could develop nasties like sepsis, pneumonia or meningitis.

It meant that I had an IV for antibiotics in one arm while the oxytocin was going into the other throughout the labour.

Only one birth partner was allowed in the delivery room at a time, so Chris and Catherine were taking turns.

Ca is eight years older than me. We're very close, and I couldn't have got through that day without her. When it felt like I was being sawn in two, she held my hand, watched the contractions on the monitors and did her best to calm me.

"You've got this Ro," she'd say. "This contraction isn't as bad as the last. It's coming down now. Keep breathing. It's almost over."

Of course, I knew she was lying through her teeth. I'd given her the same bullshit when I'd been in the delivery room with her for two of her babies.

But she talked me through some of the worst times when I thought I was going to die from the pain. The nurses were coming in and out and doing their best, but they were too busy to do handholding and reassurances.

Poor Chris didn't know what to do or say. He was wild-eyed and was sweating nearly as much as me. He hadn't a clue what to expect next. I'd seen babies being born before, but a delivery room was a whole new, terrifying world to Chris.

As the pain levels rose, so did my levels of anxiety and it soon got to the stage I couldn't do without my sister. Chris was just going to have to stay outside.

"Please don't leave me, Ca!" I wailed. "I love him, but he doesn't know what to do."

One of the many kind nurses in St Lukes took pity on me.

"Look, stop worrying," she said squeezing my hand. "If it makes you feel better, we'll let the two of them stay with you."

It made me feel better for a few minutes at least.

Okay, I have this now. I have Ca, and I have Chris. I can do this.

I grabbed the mouthpiece and sucked on the gas as hard as I could.

The doctors recommend an epidural for pain management when they prescribe oxytocin. But I'd heard all the horror stories from my sisters about how it slows down the labour and about the back pain it inflicts afterwards.

"No, I'll stick with what I have, thanks," I insisted. "I'm bad enough as it is. I'm not having the epidural too."

But by early that evening, my blood pressure started going through the roof, and I had no choice in the matter.

"Roseann, we know you don't want it, but for your own health and safety we have to give you the epidural," said the doctor. "It's the most effective way to bring down your blood pressure. "

They turned up the dial on the oxytocin again and inserted the epidural, but then they turned it off again as Jake started to come.

Thank God, I thought, it must be nearly over.

"Okay, Roseann, this is all good, you're ready to start pushing now," the nurse said.

So I pushed. And I pushed and pushed and pushed.

It generally takes thirty minutes to one hour for delivery once the pushing starts. But a full hour later, Jake was no closer to emerging, and I was exhausted, terrified and screaming in pain.

"Any minute now Roseann, you're doing really well. I know this is terrible but any minute now," they promised.

Catherine said she'd leave and wait outside now that it seemed the birth was imminent.

"This is a moment for you and Chris to share," she said.

I didn't care who was there. I didn't care if I had it in the middle of a busy train station; I just wanted it to be over.

Chris was doing his best to encourage me.

"You can do this, Ro! You can do this!" he kept saying.

"I CAN'T do this! I CAN'T do this!" I screamed back. But the language I used wasn't quite so polite. I've never sworn so much in my life.

"Why isn't he coming out? Do something!" I screamed at the medical staff.

Somewhere in a fog of pain, I heard one of the nurses mention the word "section".

"A section? Am I having a section?" I cried, trying to search the faces of the medics around me.

I didn't know what was going on. I only wanted this to end. I was being torn in two from the inside out.

"It's going to take too long to prep you for a section," said a doctor. "But don't worry, Roseann, we're getting this baby out now."

They went in with the vacuum extraction and then the forceps, physically trying to tug Jake out of the birth canal. He still wasn't budging.

"Do something, get this baby out of me!" I screamed.

Then I wished I hadn't said that. They went for the final option, which was to cut him out of me.

They had turned off the epidural before it had even started so I felt and heard every slice of the scalpel as they carried out an episiotomy. I tried to back up the bed to escape from them. Chris was horrified but powerless to help.

Jake was out in the world at last.

"It's a boy, isn't it?" I gasped as soon as the pain receded, and I could breathe again.

"It's a boy, all right, and a fine sized boy too," someone said.

"His name is Jake," I managed to tell everyone.

I'd been right all along; I predicted all through the pregnancy that I was having a boy. I couldn't confirm it because Chris didn't want us to know the sex of the baby in advance.

On the few occasions that Chris couldn't make the antenatal appointments, I tried to find out behind his back. But every time they did a scan, Jake was turned the wrong way.

It was Chris's mother, Bernie, who suggested the name, Jake. Everyone jokes that she got the name from a 1980s detective series called Jake and the Fatman.

I didn't care where the name came from. I loved it the minute she suggested it.

I decided at six months pregnant that was my baby's name. And now my long-awaited Jake was here at last.

Seconds after Jake was born, Chris's face turned into a picture of fear.

"He's not crying! Why's he not crying?" he panicked.

But I could see the nurses were already clearing our baby's airways, and seconds later Jake's first cries rang out around the room.

When I heard Catherine's babies' cries for the first time, I felt this huge rush of emotion. This was my own baby, so I was expecting an even bigger rush.

But I felt nothing.

They placed Jake on my chest. Still nothing. Where were those wonderful feelings that everyone talks about? Where were those feelings of maternal bliss?

I started to feel nervous. I was looking at my baby for the first time, and I felt nothing.

I kept smiling and accepting the congratulations and agreeing that he was a beautiful baby. I also made sure to apologise to everyone.

"I'm so sorry for what I said to you and for being rude," I said to any member of hospital staff that I saw. I must have sworn at the entire maternity department by the time Jake arrived.

The nurses in St Luke's are an understanding lot though.

"You poor Divil, you're perfectly entitled to let a few 'f's out of you after what you've been through," said one nurse, patting me on the hand.

Another nurse suggested it was time to get our baby clothes and dress the baby.

"We don't want baby Jake to get cold, now do we?" she said cheerily as she tickled his tummy.

I left it to Chris even though I could see he was struggling to dress this fragile creature. Chris looked terrified as he had never handled such a small baby. Then Catherine arrived and stepped in to help.

Once I was back in the ward, visitors poured in to admire our newborn.

My friends Samantha and Mary Conroy and my sisters Angela, Mary, Catherine and Pamela were among them. My sister-in-law Kathleen came armed with a big tray of sandwiches. I was happy to surrender Jake to everyone else's care.

Mary Conroy gasped at first when she saw him.

"Oh my God, the size of him, he's taking up the whole cot!" she exclaimed.

To this day, I think they weighed him wrong. They said Jake was 8lbs 14oz and yet he seemed so much bigger than his brother Kaelem whose birth weight was far heavier.

Every time Chris took Jake in his arms that night, his eyes welled up again. He sat there holding his baby with tears rolling down his face. I wondered why I couldn't feel what Chris was feeling?

I wondered if I was some kind of monster when I didn't even want to hold my own baby.

I'd already decided I wasn't going to breastfeed. I'd spent too much time in the hospital with this pregnancy, and I'd seen too many women in tears, struggling with breastfeeding. It turned me off the idea altogether.

Surrounded by so many willing hands, it was easy to delegate Jake's first bottle feeds too.

But it was late, and soon the nurse started ushering everyone out. My sisters spent a few final minutes fussing, making sure I was okay, and snuggling Jake and kissing him goodnight.

"I'm grand, go on home," I assured them. "No, don't give him here, just put him in the cot for me, thanks."

Even though I thought I did a good job at hiding it, Samantha knew there was something wrong.

"Are you sure you're okay, Ro?" she asked, her eyes full of concern.

But I had my delighted-new-mammy face on again and insisted: "I'm fine! I couldn't be happier. Go home!"

The nurse looked in as Chris kissed me goodnight and she said she'd leave the baby with me for a while longer.

Suddenly, everyone was gone. It was just Jake and me in a sterile hospital room.

I had done nothing with him since he was born. Everyone else had cleaned, dressed, or fed him. They cuddled him and kissed him and placed him swaddled in a white blanket in the cot beside me. I could hardly bear to touch him.

I stared at this tiny, creature and still felt no joy, no emotional attachment at all to him. I was terrified. I'd felt more maternal instinct towards complete strangers' babies.

And this nagging voice kept running through my head.

This is it; this is it for the rest of your life. This baby is going to need you 24/7. You are responsible for this baby forever now.

I felt so sick, so guilty. I knew I must be a bad mother. God, what was wrong with me that I didn't even want to pick him up?

I loved babies. I had all these dreams that I was going to be like my mammy; someone who was warm, caring, and comforting; everything a mammy should be. Instead, I was already the worst mother in the world.

As I watched the tiny stranger fast asleep in the cot beside me, he started to stir, and his fists began to pump the air. I thought I saw his russet complexion redden even more.

Then he started to make this odd rasping sound. It took me a second or two to realise that he was choking. My baby couldn't breathe.

In an instant, I lunged for the cot. I snatched Jake out from under the blankets, pulled him to me and frantically checked his mouth for an obstruction.

The motion of yanking him from the cot may have cleared his airways because that terrifying rasp disappeared; I realised he was breathing easily again.

I took a deep breath. My heart was thumping, and adrenaline was coursing through my veins.

It was then that it came to me, that feeling I was expecting in the delivery room. That rush. The feeling in my heart was something that I never felt before. Total elation. This primal sense of possessiveness. My baby.

MY baby.

I held him to me as if there were wolves around the bed baying for his blood. It was Jakie and me against the world. What on earth had I been worried about? Of course, I loved him. Loved him madly, truly, deeply.

"I am so silly, baby, so silly," I whispered, rocking him in my arms that night. "I'm going to make you proud of me. Whatever happens in this world, you're my baby, and I'm your mammy. I'm going to love and mind you more than any mammy ever loved a baby."

It took that scare to wake me from a nightmare. But now nothing else mattered in the world except my little Jakie.

Look at him, I thought, how could anyone not love everything about him? He was perfect, from that little face to those pudgy little toes.

Jakie Baby, I knew I was your mammy, and it felt incredible.

I held that child to me with a ferocity that I'd never known before. I never ever wanted to let my baby go again.

3. OUR CHEERIOS HEAD

I loved to gaze at Jakie's little face. I remember sitting by his cot in Mammy's house, running my fingers through his silky, black hair and stroking his brow and cheeks.

I marvelled over everything about him from his rosebud lips, that tiny snub nose, and those chubby little hands and feet.

And sometimes I'd stare hard until I could discern the reassuring rise and fall of his chest, or I'd lean into the cot to make sure I could hear him breathe.

Jakie, you have no idea how many hours I spent watching over you as you slept.

I didn't want to go out at night anymore because I couldn't bear being apart from him.

Sometimes it was a struggle to leave him out of my arms to place him down in the cot. It was an astonishing 180-degree turn for a woman who liked to party all night not long before.

Chris was as bad as I was and insisted on getting up to do the night feeds with me. We were a mix of anxiety and obsession in the early days. Neither of us could take our eyes off him.

Of course, by the time the second and third babies came, we argued that it was each other's turn to do the night feed. But back then, we were young, innocent and in awe of our perfect baby.

A week after we got home from the hospital, I was a bridesmaid at my sister Angela's wedding. At first, she asked me to be her maid of honour, but as the pregnancy with Jake progressed, I had to step back.

I couldn't be the chief bridesmaid when I didn't even know if I'd make the wedding.

Anyway, I wasn't much help to Angela because I was in the hospital half the time in the run-up to her big day.

The night before the wedding, all the girls came to stay in Mammy's house, and doting women surrounded Jake.

The bridesmaids were wearing long, black gowns and it was a relief when I tried on the dress and discovered it fitted.

Everything was going smoothly until late that night when I started experiencing a lot of pain from the episiotomy. Everyone exchanged nervous glances. Angela didn't need a bridesmaid going down the night before her wedding.

The sisters frog-marched me to the out-of-hours doctors' service, Caredoc. It turned out that the stitches were tightening and causing the pain.

"All very normal, part of the healing process," the doctor said.

I cringed as he admired the handiwork of the surgeon, but he gave me lots of painkillers, and we all trouped home again.

The next morning Chris arrived to collect Jake as we left to get our hair and make-up done. Chris's mother Bernie had kindly offered to mind the baby for the day of the wedding.

I placed Jake into his baby car seat, strapped into the back of our car. Bernie was great with babies, so I had no concerns.

It was great to have a full day off again with no real responsibilities. It felt like I was single again.

I was going to get my hair done, slap on some make-up, wear a fancy dress and head for a big party. It was my first, proper night out in months. There was even going to be drink or two involved which was a real novelty.

I was a bit shaky about leaving Jake for the first time, but I knew he was in the best of hands.

"Enjoy it, Rosie," I thought. "You won't get this the chance again for a long time!"

Then Christopher drove off in the car with Jake and without any warning, I burst into tears.

Instead of Runaway Bride, it was almost Runaway Bridesmaid because I had to fight the urge to chase after the car. My sisters ran to hug me and comfort me.

"Aah, Rosie, you're a mammy!" my sister Pamela laughed.

I couldn't stop crying; the tears continued even when I was in hair and make-up.

"What's wrong with me?" I bawled, as my sisters cracked up laughing.

Even with the extra painkillers, I was still in agony from the episiotomy. Most women at the wedding carried sparkly handbags under their arms, but I had a big, fluffy pillow.

That pillow made its way from seat to seat around the wedding reception, as I told anyone who'd listen to me about my perfect baby.

I'd turned into a baby bore. Everything in my life was about Jake now.

Our nomadic lifestyle ended once Jake was born. Home became the back bedroom in Mammy's house. It was a big room with plenty of space for the baby's cot. Chris still lived between the two houses.

We christened our baby, Jake Michael John Brennan when he was 6-months-old. The name 'Michael' was in honour of my dad and my stepfather, while 'John' was after Chris's dad.

We chose my sister, Pamela and one of Christopher's older brothers, Michael, as Jake's godparents.

Jake had yellow jaundice when he was born, so we had to take extra care with him. The doctors said we had to expose him to sunlight several times a day and to feed him every three hours.

Months and months later, I was still giving him bottles every three hours. Everyone said he should be sleeping through the night by now, but Jake loved his food and always woke for his bottle.

By the time he was 10-months-old, he had turned into a little chunk of a baby who was able to hold the bottle and feed himself.

He still woke up on cue, every three hours, looking for his bottle. I was like a zombie with exhaustion by then.

Around that time, I was in a doctor's waiting room with Jake, and I started chatting with an older woman beside me. She asked if Jake was sleeping. I said he was, apart from wanting three bottles a night.

"Listen, if someone kept bringing you nice drinks in bed whenever you wanted, wouldn't you keep waking for them?" she asked.

It was a light bulb moment; I hadn't thought about it that way before. I hadn't thought straight about anything in a while because I was so tired.

She said he was well able to sleep through the night without feeding. I'd just given him a bad habit.

"Next time he wakes up in the night looking for a feed, give him water," she advised.

I started bringing Jake water when he woke at night. There were the inevitable tears and tantrums, but I didn't give in. Thanks to a chance meeting in a doctor's waiting room, Chris and I started getting a full night's sleep again.

Even though he put on weight from too much feeding, Jake got sick a lot, and he would shed the pounds again.

Doctors prescribed him with course after course of antibiotics for non-stop chest infections. I hated those medicines; I knew they weren't good for him and I was afraid there was something more sinister underlying the chest infections.

Finally, when he was around two, they diagnosed him with asthma. From then on, at the first sign of a cough, I'd give him his inhaler, and he stopped using antibiotics.

I was still worried because he had to take inhalers on average for two weeks of every month. But his father was asthmatic and grew out of it, so I hoped that Jake would be the same. He improved as he got older, but we'll never know if he would have grown out of it.

Despite some setbacks, Jake was the jolliest baby you could ask for. He was a funny, sunny child who reached all his milestones early.

He sprouted his first teeth at three months, crawled at eight months and ran around before his first birthday. He pulled everything down around him, but he was an easy, good-humoured baby.

He was such a placid and happy child that I could bring him everywhere with me. He was always on my hip. Even before he could talk, and he was able to speak from a young age, he loved going out.

It was no trouble to bring him anywhere. Samantha and I could sit in a restaurant without any embarrassing toddler tantrums.

He had the full-time devotion of grandparents and parents, so he was more advanced than most babies his age.

Jake was the sun that our lives revolved around, and he was showered with affection and attention from the start.

Mammy and Mick had the upstairs bedroom at the front while we had the bedroom at the back of the house. When Jake woke up in our room, the first thing on his mind was getting into his grandparents' bedroom.

"I want Nanny and Granddad," he'd said.

"Leave them alone Jakie. They're asleep."

"NANNY? NANNY?" he'd call at the top of his voice.

My mother would wake in seconds.

"YES, JAKIE?" she'd call back.

"See Mammy, Nanny's awake!" he'd say, triumphantly.

He'd knock on their door then. He always knocked. It didn't matter what age he was; he'd never burst into their room. He knew to wait for the invitation that always came.

"Come in Jakie, love, come into bed with us."

"Mammy said you were asleep, but I knew you weren't!" he'd say, clambering into bed with them.

His other game was to pretend to be the postman calling.

"POSTMAN!" he'd yell outside their door.

"Come on in Mr Postman," Mammy would reply.

"Post for you Nanny and post for you Granddad!" he'd tell them before tumbling into their bed.

When Jakie was 18-months-old, Mam and Mick moved to the downstairs room. Mammy was getting over a heart bypass operation, and she claimed it suited her to sleep nearer the bathroom.

"Sure, I'm bet going up and down those stairs," she said.

It was no coincidence that Mammy's decision to move downstairs came as we were thinking of moving out. We felt that it was time that Jake had his own room.

Everyone earmarked the room downstairs as Jake's first bedroom. I prepared the place for him by painting the walls and making it into a playroom; all his toys were there.

But I was very reluctant to let him sleep on a separate floor. It seemed too far away from us.

I'm sure that Mammy and Mick moved downstairs only so that we didn't have to move out. Still, they never let on that was the case.

We put a toddler bed into Jake's new room, but he was still so small that we let him continue to sleep in his cot.

Within days, Jake started escaping his cot and re-appearing in our room at all hours. Chris rushed to install a gate at the top of the stairs, but we couldn't figure out how our mini-Houdini was getting out.

The cot railings were quite a height, and we never heard any sound of a thump as he landed on the floor.

One morning, he arrived into our room unusually early, so we put him straight back to bed.

"No, Baby, it's sleep time," we told him, placing him firmly back in the cot. He didn't accept this at all. We knew another great escape would follow.

So, we watched him through a crack in the door.

First, we saw him stretch his arm and shoulder out through the bars of the cot. He panted with exertion as he stretched and stretched his arm until he got a grip of the blankets on the toddler bed in the room.

We never dreamt he could reach that far.

Then we saw him tug the toddler bed over to his cot. Then he simply clambered over the cot railings and landed with a bounce on the soft mattress on the other side.

Finally, he pushed the cot back from the bed with his feet, and he slid from the bed to the floor and to freedom.

We noticed the bed had moved, but we never connected it to Jake's escapes. I thought that he had been trying to get at his toys or his teddies, so I pushed the bed back without thinking.

We hadn't realised what he could do when he put his mind to it. Jake had it all worked out at 18-months-old.

We also had a nightmare keeping him out of my mother and stepdad's kitchen which was open to the living room.

We tried to block his access by overturning a coffee table and building an obstacle course around it. He still managed to burrow his way in because two of his favourite things were usually there: Granddad and food.

"Num-nums, Granddad!" he'd say as he popped up behind him.

For much of his day, Jake lived like a royal, sitting in his high chair, picking at his favourite Cheerios cereal and ordering everyone around.

"Our little Cheerios head," Chris used to call him.

His great obsession was Peppa Pig. We had a TV package with children's channels, and Peppa Pig seemed to be on around the clock. But once Peppa Pig disappeared off the TV, his whole attention swung to 'Granddad!'

'Granddad, out!' he'd instruct when he wanted to go for a walk.

'Granddad, fish!" he'd order when he wanted to feed the giant goldfish. It was normal size, to begin with, but it grew to vast proportions because Jake never stopped feeding it.

Or he might demand: "Granddad, dogs!" so that Granddad would lift him onto the sink to watch the dogs out the back garden.

Jakie took over the house, and Mammy and Mick let him.

We tried to give Nanny and Granddad some peace watching telly. Chris even installed a portable TV in Jake's room, so he could watch his cartoons without disturbing them.

When we were growing up, we were never allowed to disturb Mammy during her favourite soaps. But Jakie could toddle in and demand Peppa Pig at any time.

A serial killer could be on the loose on Coronation Street, and Mammy would change the channel without hesitation.

"Nanny's watching her programme, Jakie," I'd scold. "Leave Nanny to watch her TV."

But I was the one who'd get berated.

"Leave the child alone, Roseann; leave him watch his Peppa Pig!" she'd say. "Now, Pet, sit up here beside Nanny. Granddad, get up and get Jakie a biscuit and some milk."

The other big obsession in his life was Dora. Every night we had to read the book, Dora. There must be 50 Dora books, and I read every single one of them to him. I knew them all off by heart.

Jake's favourite night-time routine included getting his kisses from Nanny and Granddad. They often went to bed at about 7.00pm where they watched TV.

Jake loved getting between them and scooting underneath the blankets until he thought we couldn't see him.

42

I'd have to call into the room and ask, "Did Jake come in and get his kisses?"

They'd dutifully reply: "No Jake didn't come in here. We didn't see him at all."

"Are you sure, because he said he was coming in here?" I'd ask.

This exchange went on until we heard the little giggle and he popped out from under the blankets. They still laugh thinking about those days.

Mick reminded me the other day of how he used to stand on the arm of the chair in their living room. Jake would say "Granddad, watch this! One...two...three" and then he'd jump off.

Then he'd look up at everyone to gauge the reaction. Looking back, he had the bug for performing from an early age. He craved applause.

When he got praised, he'd shuffle off, head down, looking bashful, but you could tell how much he loved the attention.

He was spoiled rotten between two pairs of doting grandparents. He only had to flash that angelic smile of his, and he had two grannies and granddads wrapped around his little finger.

Mammy cried as much as Jakie the day we moved out. He was 3-years-old by then. We were expecting our second child and planning to get married. It was time to get our own place.

Mam understood, but she shook her head when she looked in at Jakie's empty little room.

"You could fit two kids in there," she insisted.

We moved into the Sycamores estate in Kilkenny first, and Jake hated the move. He hated change; he really did.

He was distraught leaving Nanny and Granddad's house; we had stopped staying with Chris's parents in Castlecomer too. He wasn't seeing much of either of his beloved nannies now, and he wasn't impressed.

"How am I going to get my goodnight kisses anymore?" he sobbed.

We tried to console him by promising that we'd kiss him every night instead.

I'd kiss him for Nanny Joan, Granddad Micky and for my dad, Granddad Hayes, who's in heaven. Chris would do it for Nanny and Granddad Brennan. The goodnight kisses became part of a sacred ritual performance every single night.

Still, he pined for his old bedroom in Nanny and Granddad's house. He hated his new bedroom. It was the wrong colour, wrong size; everything was wrong.

One day he got really thick about it all. He was fed up, and he wasn't standing for it anymore.

"I'm going back to Nanny Joan and Granddad Micky's house, and that's it!" he yelled.

Then he marched upstairs where he had a little Mickey Mouse bag, and he packed a pair of boxers and a pair of pyjamas. He put the bag on his back and told me again that he was leaving.

"Go on so," I said, cleaning the kitchen worktop and pretending that I wasn't bothered in the slightest.

I never thought he'd go. But he stormed right out the front door and went off down the path with the bag on his back. I couldn't believe that he'd gone. I had to run out and catch him.

"Come back here to me, Jakie," I said, bending to look into his tear-filled eyes. "You know if you leave me, I'm going to be very upset? I'll be crying because you left me all on my own. Do you love Nanny and Granddad more than Daddy and me?"

"No, Mammy," he said, with his bottom lip wobbling. "But I miss my bedroom in Nanny and Granddad's house."

We kept returning to Ballybough Street until he was reassured that Nanny, Granddad, and his old room, were still part of his life.

His grandparents loved the story about the time he nearly ran away, so he recounted the tale all the time.

"Do you remember when I packed my bag and came back to stay with you?" he'd say.

He remained fiercely possessive about his old room and didn't want anyone else using it. Every time we went back to Nanny Joan's, he made sure that everyone, including my sisters, knew it was still HIS room.

No one else could move in there.

"I still have my bedroom upstairs," he'd remind them. "Nanny, isn't that my bedroom?"

"Yes, Jakie that's your bedroom. Don't worry; I'm minding it for you."

Nanny Joan and Granddad Mick love all their grandchildren, but there's a big hole in their lives without Jake.

He was such a sweet, gentle, considerate child who left a hole in a lot of hearts.

Jakie's bedroom is still there though, and they've laid out some of his clothes and toys inside.

And don't worry, Jakie Baby, Nanny says that she's minding that room for you, forever.

4. AND KAELEM MAKES TWO

Chris's plans for our future were in tatters by the time we moved from my mammy's house. He wanted to do the sensible thing and find a house and then get married before we had a second child.

But I do everything backwards, and I was already eight months pregnant.

Some of the blame lies with my sister-in-law, Pamela, because she was feeling broody for a second child. She's married to my brother Darren, and their daughter Rihanna is the same age as Jake.

"It's the right time to have another baby," she said. "If we leave it until Rihanna gets much older, the age gap gets too big. It's nice when children can grow up together."

Jake was two-years-old at this stage, and I decided that Pamela was right. Why were we putting off having a second child? I was feeling broody too, and I didn't see the point in delaying.

"Wouldn't it be lovely if we had our babies at the same time?" I mused. "They'd be playmates for each other just like Jake and Rihanna are."

Pamela and I had it all worked out in our heads, but Chris had other ideas.

"Look, it makes sense to get our own place and get married first," he insisted. "We can't go on living in your mother's place with a second child."

I wasn't giving up though, and as I said, I have a habit of getting my own way.

"We can't afford a wedding if we're getting our own house," I argued. "We'll find a house, but there's no reason that we shouldn't try and get pregnant in the meantime."

If Jake had been involved in the discussion, he would have been on my side. Jake felt deprived without a brother or sister. He and Rihanna were small, but they wanted to know why they were the only cousins who didn't have siblings.

Chris gave in and agreed to try for a baby around the time we brought Jake to Disneyland in Paris in September 2010.

My sister Pamela and her husband, Robert, came too with their daughters, Kayla and Sherice. I was ovulating that weekend, and Pamela made sure that we didn't waste a baby-making opportunity.

"You and Chris relax for a while," she winked. "We'll take Jake to see the Disney Princess."

Disneyland was a huge success. Jake, even though he was only two years old, cherished the memories all his short life, and our second baby may well have been conceived there.

Jake was ecstatic with the news that he was getting a sibling at last. He decided he wanted a brother, but I was convinced that we were having a girl.

Once again, Chris was against finding out the gender of the baby before the birth. That was fine; I didn't need confirmation of what I already knew. I bought some cute girly clothes and had a list of girls' names prepared.

"It's completely different to the time I had Jake," I told everyone. "I'm not getting those kidney infections that I had with Jake, and my bump is half the size compared with the first time."

Unfortunately, the blood pressure problems returned during the fourth month of the pregnancy. I've been on medication ever since because it never went back to normal again.

My doctor worried about pre-eclampsia throughout the pregnancy again, so I ended up spending time in and out of the hospital.

It was a very turbulent time for poor Jakie. He was upset by all my sudden disappearances into the hospital. He was still out of sorts anyway after leaving his nanny's house and moving into the first home we called our own.

Our new home in the Sycamores estate in Kilkenny was a spacious detached house. It was the perfect place for a heavily pregnant woman as it was located beside St Luke's Hospital and its labour ward.

Chris was able to run home for a sandwich during the labour, and none of the family had to pay for hospital parking because they could park outside our house.

My labour with Jake was so traumatic that I didn't believe having a baby could be as bad ever again. But history has a habit of repeating itself.

The baby was induced again and then got stuck in the birth canal again. Our second son was born after another emergency episiotomy at 9.40am on May 1, 2011.

The birth of a strapping 9lb 6oz boy took me by surprise. I had a list of girls' names ready but nothing in mind for a boy.

I thought about Callum and toyed with Kaelum but my sister, Pamela, came up with the spelling Kaelem. By noon that day, we settled on Kaelem as our second boy's name.

Jake was thrilled that he had a brother and was even more impressed that the baby bought him a toy which taught him to spell words.

Number one son adapted better than we expected to another small person in the house.

In fact, he was all over his new baby brother in the early weeks. He wanted to hold him, feed him, carry him and show him off to all the cousins.

There was no resentment or aggression towards this little interloper, apart from the fact that Jake regressed into baby mode.

We laughed when he started demanding bottle feeds and to be "carried like a baby". One day I tried to calm Kaelem with a dodie, but Jake snatched it from his mouth and stuffed it in his own.

But apart from a few minor things like that, Jake made a smooth transition from only child to big brother.

He still wasn't happy living in our new house, and soon I wasn't either. He wanted to go back to his Nanny's house, but I just wanted to live closer to her.

There was a lot to love about our first home. It had a large garden both front and back, a big bay window to the front and big high ceilings. It was airy and bright, and we also had a lovely landlord.

But it was an older property without modern insulation or double-glazed windows. We soon discovered it was a cold house to live in and was going to cost us a fortune to heat.

But the main reason I didn't settle there was because I was on the far side of the city from my family.

I'm a home-bird at heart. I wanted to be able to take out the buggy and walk over to my mother's or my sisters' houses, and we were too far away for that.

Within a few months, a house on Lintown Grove, near my mother's, came on the rental market. I drove over and checked out the housing estate before even making an appointment to look at the property.

The location seemed perfect for us. The house for rent, number 15, was near the end of the cul-de-sac.

It was part of a row of modern, terraced and semi-detached houses which occupied one side of the cul-de-sac. It was a red-brick faced, semi-detached house, typical of lots of homes in modern estates.

It had a dark green door with oval glass set in the centre of the house in a small arched porch.

Facing the houses, across a wide tarmacadam road, was a small green area with newly planted trees. Beyond this, was a wall topped with high railings which separated Lintown Grove from the busy Johnswell Road on the other side.

Only a handful of homes lay beyond number 15, so very few cars would pass our door. It seemed like a quiet road and such a safe environment for kids.

We made an appointment to view the house and saw that it was modern and bright with a big back garden. The immaculate kitchen looked out over the garden at the front of the house.

We met with the landlady, Ingrid, and we signed a lease for the rent. Shortly afterwards, we moved into what we believed was our dream home.

But the only place Jake wanted to move to was back to his nanny's.

The novelty of a baby brother wore off too around that time. He expected his brother to arrive ready to play like Kayla or Rihanna. He soon got fed up with helping to feed him and lost all interest in holding him.

"Babies are boring; they just sleep all the time," he complained.

Kaelem's crying irritated him, especially when Jake was trying to listen to his cartoons.

"Kaelem's tired Mammy, he needs to go to bed," he'd tell me.

But there was a dramatic change in Jake as soon as his little brother started crawling or toddling everywhere after his big brother. Then Jake decided that having a hero-worshipping little brother was great fun.

Overnight, he became Kaelem's mentor, teacher and chief advisor. You could hear the teacher-and-student conversation going on between them all the time.

"See this, Kaelem? You just hold it like this, and you do this. See, like this. No, Kaelem, like this. Okay, I'll show you again."

We'd wake in the morning, and we'd hear Jake busy reading storybooks to Kaelem. He wasn't even in school himself at the time, but he knew the story, and he'd follow it from the pictures.

"Now Kaelem, will I read you this one or this one? Okay, this one. Once upon a time…no, Kaelem, don't turn the page yet. I'm reading. I'm telling a story…Once upon a time…Kaelem stop…"

He was brilliant with the baby; he never forgot the golden rule about toys even though he was only a toddler himself.

"If it fits in my mouth, I can't give it to him, right Mammy? So, look, see, this doesn't fit in my mouth, so I can give it to Kaelem, right?"

Of course, there were endless rows and plenty of sibling rivalry. When I was trying to dress them, I had to put one leg from each of them into their trousers to stop a row about who I was dressing first. There would be rows over whose hair had to be done first or who got their teeth brushed first.

Jake loved his baby brother but only if he deferred to him in everything. Jake wanted to be first, but Kaelem wanted whatever his big brother wanted, so he had to be first too.

"I'm going first!"

"You're not! He went first this morning, Mammy!"

"You went first yesterday."

"Did not, you did."

"You did!"

"I'm going first!"

"You're not! He went first this morning, Mammy."

I used to worry about the neighbours listening to the rows, day in, day out. I signed up for this, but those poor people didn't. The battles would go on in circles like this every day.

Despite the rivalries, the threat to move them into separate bedrooms terrified them.

"I'm telling the pair of you, Kaelem you're going back to your baby room and Jake you're sleeping on your own from now on. I'm not putting up with this nonsense anymore!"

"Ah, no Mammy!" Jake would plead. "We're going to be good; we're going to be real quiet. Aren't we going to be good, Kaelem?"

"Yes, Mammy. We will. Real good."

For the next five minutes, I'd hear: "Shhh! Shhh! Quiet Kaelem or you're going back to the baby room" before a full-scale row would erupt again.

Still, Jake loved having his little companion and a clone who wanted to do anything he wanted to do. He was still watching the children's TV that Kaelem loved, so they'd sit giggling together watching cartoons. They'd also build blocks or play house or read books.

Or sometimes they just killed each other.

We were conscious that Kaelem was taking a lot of the attention that we'd once devoted to his older brother. To make Jake feel that he wasn't left out, we held special 'Jakie days'.

Chris or I brought him off on his own, or we got a babysitter for Kaelem and went out as a threesome again. He loved 'Jakie' days.

But everything changed as Kaelem got older. Then, they couldn't be pulled apart. Kaelem would lose his life if he heard Jake was going anywhere without him.

Jake basked in the hero-worship of his little brother.

He sometimes complained, 'he's always copying me' but he enjoyed the influence he wielded over this smaller lad. He loved how Kaelem wanted to do everything he did.

He got a kick out of all the attention they got when we dressed them the same. It was like having his own mini-me. We have photos of Jake posing, giving the thumbs up, and you can see Kaelem mimicking his moves behind him.

They shared a love for music and dancing. We always knew when Jake was up because he started singing at the top of his voice in his cot. He sang garbled nonsense long before he could talk. As soon as he was toddling, he became Justin Bieber mad. 'Baby' was his theme song.

I can see him now, back before he even knew the words, giving it socks singing 'Baby, Baby, Baby, Ooh'.

Later, when Kaelem came along, the pair of them would perform it.

"When I was turteen, I had my first luff," Jake crooned, aged four, with the other fella behind him, wiggling in his nappy.

Jake loved fun and general silliness, and he taught me my lines in his favourite 'chocolate' sing-song rhyme.

Jake: "Okay, Mammy, you start."

Me: Whatcha doin'?

Jake: Eatin' choc'lit

Me: Where'd ya get it?

Jake: From the doggy.

Me: Where's the doggy?

Jake: In the corner, making more!

Then he'd shriek with laughter, his head thrown back as he staggered around in sheer delight.

Jake found his calling when he discovered Jesters. His cousin Kayla joined the local children's drama school so of course, Jake pestered us to let him go too.

We presumed that it was another passing interest and it would be over within a few weeks. Instead, it was a passion that lasted right up until the day he died. From the very start, Jake was in his element.

I should have known because he loved singing, dancing and acting the maggot from the time he was a tot. He adored this mini-stage school, and he loved Kevin who ran Jake's group. He was mad keen to attend every single class.

"Is it Jesters today, Mammy?" he'd keep asking. "What day is Jesters?"

He loved rehearsing the rhymes, music, songs and dances every week. At the end of the year, all the students get to perform in a big stage show in the Watergate Theatre in Kilkenny. Jake loved that above all else. He couldn't wait to get into a costume and get on stage and perform. He loved an audience.

He was so looking forward to the opening night of his second annual stage show in the Watergate. It breaks my heart that he never made it. He died only a couple of hours before the curtain went up.

I remember a few family occasions where the adults arranged a silly version of the X Factor for the kids.

Jake would have to get up and sing his party piece, Baby. We'd all shout 'G'wan Jakie Brennan!' just to see his eyes light up and the bashful smile on stage. His reaction made everyone laugh.

He'd come back, all shy, his brown eyes downcast, making little puffs as if out of breath from the exertion of singing.

But he could never hide the tell-tale smile and the dimples appearing on his face. He loved any chance to show off. We all laughed at those small huffs he used to do after his big performance.

It was as if he needed oxygen to steady himself after all the excitement.

He was a funny little kid because he liked being in the spotlight, and at the same time, he liked to pretend that he didn't want attention.

He let on that he only performed due to public demand; that he didn't like the limelight.

"Mammy, don't gel my hair cos everyone at school keeps touching it," he said one morning.

Jake was very particular about having his hair gelled every day, but I didn't argue.

"OK, I won't so."

His face dropped as I put away his tube of gel, but he didn't say anything.

The next morning, I made sure to remind Chris about the new hair situation.

"Remember, don't gel Jakie's hair, he doesn't like it anymore," I said, winking at his dad.

Jake was in a quandary. He didn't want to admit that he wanted the gel. But if he didn't admit it, his classmates might never have a reason to touch his hair again.

His need for attention won out.

"I do like gel, Mammy, I do," he muttered under his breath.

Jake also loved to dance. He was the first on the dance floor and the last off it.

He'd be a ball of sweat with a big red face from all the dancing, but he couldn't get enough of it. And he wanted nothing more than to have me dancing with him all night too.

I had no choice in the matter as soon as they played Naughty Boy's La La La or Maroon 5's Moves Like Jagger because they were 'our songs'. I used to play them in the car on the way to school, and he loved them.

Around the time he went to heaven, he was going through a phase of addressing me as 'woman'. His school pals were all copying reality TV star Paddy Doherty's catchphrase from shows like When Paddy Met Sally, Big Fat Gypsy Wedding and Celebrity Bainisteoir.

He rocked up to me one day during a First Holy Communion party and said: "Woman, let's go, they're playing our song."

I was talking to a friend, Yvonne Denieffe, at the time and she nearly choked on her drink with laughing.

My sister-in-law Kathleen remarked that he was never happier than when we were dancing together.

"I've never seen a young lad like him," she said. "He loves it, and he never takes his eyes off you the whole time."

It was true. It was like Jake wanted to stake a claim.

"This is MY mammy," he was announcing to the world. He wanted to be with me.

Once he got me out on that dance floor, I couldn't get back in again. He wouldn't let me go.

I've often thought if I could only get back out on a dance floor with you one more time, Jakie, I'd never come off it again.

5. PRINCE JAKE'S WEDDING

Chris and I finally made it up the aisle on my 28th birthday. We got married under the gothic arches of St. John the Evangelist Church in Kilkenny on a hot and sunny Wednesday afternoon, March 28, 2012.

Jakie Baby, you weren't even four-years-old, but you made sure you were centre stage on the altar.

And Kaelem, even as an 11-month-old baby, you were determined not to be outshone by your brother. We could hear your yells echoing under the vaulted church roof until one of my sisters took you outside.

When we first announced the wedding date, Jake wasn't at all interested. He looked at us blankly when we said we were getting married.

"What does 'getting married' mean?" he said.

He was aware that my surname was Hayes and that he and Daddy's second name was Brennan.

"Well, when Mammy and Daddy get married, I won't be a Hayes anymore, I'll be a Brennan like you and Daddy," I explained.

"Oh," he said and went back to his colouring book.

He only got interested when I revealed that the day involved dressing up.

"When we get married, Daddy wears a suit like a prince and Mammy wears a princess dress. You'll wear a suit like a prince too."

He looked up straightaway. This was far more interesting than Mammy changing her surname.

He remembered the princesses at Disneyland and his fairytale books were full of beautiful princesses. He and Kayla had royal costumes, and Jakie would wear the princess dress as often as he'd wear the prince outfit.

His uncle Robert used to tease him and threaten that he'd take a photo of him in a princess dress and show it to everyone in school. Jakie couldn't have cared less. He posed for the photo, wearing a frilly dress, high heels, lipstick and a big cheeky smile.

I had his undivided attention once he knew he was dressing up as a prince for the wedding. He thought about it for a moment.

"Am I going to marry you?" he asked, eyes agog.

"Well, you'll be wearing a prince suit like Daddy, and both of you will be my wonderful men forever, so, yes, I suppose I'll be marrying both of you."

From then on, he was more excited about the wedding than anyone else.

Jake would have been very disappointed if he'd known that I'd no interest in wearing a big meringue dress. I never had that little girl's dream of being a princess bride. If I had to wear a dress, I wanted something a bit different, a bit out there.

I looked in all the bridal shops for the kind of dress that I imagined myself wearing, but I was disappointed. The price tags on the dresses were outrageous, and nothing appealed to me.

"Samantha, I'm not feeling it," I said, after yet another failed shopping expedition. "I'm beginning to think there isn't a dress out there for me. Let's face it, I'm not the bride-y type."

After we ran out of bridal shops to see, we tried the charity store, Barnardos, in Carlow. They had a body-hugging gown with a long train. It was the closest I'd seen to a dress I liked; it also cost €200 rather than the €1,200 price tag of the bridal shops.

If it had been white, that would have been my wedding dress. But it was champagne, and the shade didn't appeal to me, so I moved on.

A friend referred me to a woman who sold new and second-hand wedding dresses from her home outside Castlecomer. We went to her house, and I flicked through her rails of dresses.

Nothing.

The woman pulled one frock out of her collection.

"Try this one on," she urged.

I held it up to me in front of the mirror. It had never been worn, but it was off-white rather than white and seemed to have a big skirt and ruffles. I hated it.

"The state of this!" I mouthed to Samantha.

I handed it back.

"No thanks, it's not my kind of thing," I said.

"Just try it on," the lady said. "You'll be amazed how good it looks off the hanger. It will suit you."

We were in her private home, and I felt I had to try it on to be polite. I rolled my eyes at Samantha as I went to fit it on.

The woman handed me a petticoat, which she said to wear as an underskirt. The ordeal was getting worse by the minute. I braced myself, stepped into the petticoat and slipped on the dress over it.

God, why was I doing this?

I felt I should have been honest with this woman and told her I wasn't interested.

Then I looked in the mirror, and suddenly I could see it. The dress was more traditional than I ever thought I wanted to wear.

The bodice was fitted, and the skirt was draped in ornate layers and scattered with white roses.

It was unusual, and the fabrics were beautiful. I loved it. I asked the woman for another petticoat, and when I looked in the mirror, I knew, without doubt, it was the dress for me.

I paid €250 for the dress. By the time I added in the petticoats, the veil, minor alterations by a dressmaker and the shoes, it all cost under €450. I couldn't have been happier.

I tried on the dress for the girls a few days later, and of course, Jake was up in the bedroom with us.

He gasped when I turned around in the dress and veil.

"Ah, Mammy!" he gasped, his brown eyes wide with awe.

"Mammy, you look like a princess!"

A girl couldn't get a greater compliment from Jake

He was even more excited when he discovered his mammy would arrive at the church in a limousine. He could hardly say the word, but he came to me one day with a plan all arranged in his little head.

"I've looked at the princesses, Mammy," he said. "And when the lim'seem comes, I open the door and hold your hand and do this."

He swept his arm across his middle and bowed as he'd seen it in the fairytales.

"Will I do that, Mammy? I'm a prince, so that's my job, right?"

"Yes, Jakie, that's your job. You'll help me out of the limousine."

Jake was dressed in a tiny replica of the suit that his dad wore for the wedding complete with a waistcoat and a rose corsage. He couldn't have been any prouder.

"I'm like a real prince now, amn't I Mammy?" he said gazing at himself in the mirror.

He stayed with his daddy and the groom's party the night before the wedding. He was a Mammy's boy until he thought it would be more fun to be with the boys, and then he'd decide he didn't like girls so much.

My bridesmaids all wore long, red gowns on the day and I carried a trailing bouquet of my late dad's favourite flowers, red roses. Keeping with the red theme, I bought red stiletto shoes and nylon stockings dotted with red love hearts.

I picked up my skirts and flashed the red shoes and red spotted stockings at my mother on the morning of the wedding. She groaned and shook her head.

"I knew you'd do something odd," she sighed.

I arrived at the church on schedule at 2.00pm to marry my Christopher. It was unseasonably hot and sunny for March. You wouldn't find a hotter day in August.

The first face I saw in the crowd was Jakie; he was waiting on the church steps for me as he promised.

He had a beaming smile on his face as he approached the car, but the limo driver was too quick for him. The driver sprung out of the car and opened the door before Jake made it down the church steps.

Jake was gutted. Tears welled in his eyes, and he looked ready to bawl. I knew he'd be inconsolable if his big 'Prince' moment was denied to him. But in the melee around the car, no one could understand me.

"Close it! Close the door!" I begged as people reached in and tried to help me from the car.

I tried to pull the door closed again.

"Pamela, tell them, tell them to let Jake do it!"

The confused limo driver finally realised his mistake and shut the door again. The crisis ended. Jakie opened the door, offered me his hand and bowed ceremoniously like a proper prince.

"Oh, thank you, handsome prince, Jakie," I said.

I remember him so well at that moment. He was beside himself with delight, all dimples, and tiny teeth and dancing brown eyes.

Jake was also our ring bearer on the day, and no one took a job as seriously as he did. He went up the aisle ahead of me with his cousin Kayla, who wore a little white dress. They were like a miniature bride and groom.

Afterwards, everyone teased: "We saw you going up the aisle with Kayla. Are you married to, Kayla, now, Jakie?"

Jake shook his head so hard his entire body twisted with it. He was adamant.

"No, I married me Mammy!" he said.

My two younger brothers, Darren and Jason, gave me away in place of my beloved dad who died when I was five-years-old.

They each agreed to escort me half the way up the aisle. When they couldn't decide on which one would bring me to the altar, they had to toss a coin. Darren lost the toss and walked me into the church while Jason gave me away to Chris.

Darren reckons he got the more important job that day because when I got to the church door, the emotion and the gravity of what was happening struck me. I felt light-headed. I placed a hand on my wildly beating heart and tried to catch my breath.

"What's wrong with me? I'm feeling really nervous," I said looking in shock at Darren. "That's Chris up there waiting for me, why am I so nervous?"

Darren recognised last minute jitters and took hold of my arm. I could see Jason already standing in the aisle looking back at me, waiting, smiling.

"Deep breaths. Come on Sis, you can do this, you're grand," said Darren.

And it took a minute or so, but I was.

I focussed on Chris, waiting for me at the altar. He was crying already, but I was smiling. I couldn't stop smiling.

Jake was on the altar at this stage too, loving every minute of it, enjoying being in the heart of this big occasion.

Maybe, it was stage fright, but I shook with nerves throughout the ceremony. Pamela was my maid of honour, and I remember whispering to her: "God, I can't stop shaking, what's wrong with me?"

Chris was in tears throughout; he can never hide his emotions. I never shed a tear which was great because I didn't want to wreck my make-up. I laughed and smiled instead.

I know most people get married first and then have kids, and I love and respect that tradition. But to me, seeing my little Jake on the altar, holding the rings, with a proud head on him and seeing Kaelem in the arms of my sister, made our vows even more special.

I felt like I had everything that I ever wanted that day. I was a mother of two beautiful children, and I was marrying their father who I loved with all my heart and who was crying because he loved us so much.

I felt like the luckiest person alive. That day I felt whole.

Loads of people said that it was one of the happiest weddings they ever attended. Looking back, it was wonderful. I was the most joyful bride in the world marrying Chris.

The reception for 125 adults and 50 children was held in the ballroom of the Langton House Hotel. I managed to get in to see the room before the guests which allayed any fears I had. The red theme continued as I wanted it, with the room filled with arrangements of red roses.

Afterwards, I collected all the flowers from the church, and the reception and I brought them all down, along with my bouquet, to my dad's grave.

The day was so hot that we spent most of it out the back and I greeted all the guests in my white gown and sunglasses.

Jake was hyperactive with excitement. When he saw the wedding photographer, he decided it wasn't enough to be the bridegroom, the prince and the ring bearer. He became the official cameraman too. In half of our wedding album, you'll see Jake with a phone up to his face, pretending to take photos.

We struggled to find a song for our first dance. We wanted a song from our favourite band, Snow Patrol, but the lyrics weren't suitable for a first dance.

We found our song, by accident, while having dinner with the kids in an Italian restaurant on John Street, Kilkenny.

As we were eating, Chris put down his cutlery and said: "Listen!"

I could hear this song on the radio.

"I wanna grow old with you; I wanna lie dying in your arms," the singer crooned.

I thought the lyrics were perfect. The girl in the restaurant turned up the radio and got the name of the track for us.

That's how Westlife's I Wanna Grow Old with You became our wedding song. I loved it even though Westlife are not what we'd have on our iPods.

Jake believed he was marrying me so of course, he demanded to be in the first dance at the wedding. From the time he was a baby in my arms, Jake was a possessive little man. If Christopher tried to lean in for a kiss, he'd push his father away.

"No Dadda!" he'd say.

When he grew older, and he saw us cuddling or kissing, he'd push his way between us.

"She's MY mammy," he'd say glaring at Chris.

Of course, Chris would start messing with him: 'No, she's MY mammy!'

Then the 'MY-mammy' wars would kick off. They were always at it. They'd have these mock fights over me all the time. It was 'a thing' between Chris and Jake.

So of course, when it came to our first dance, Jake was having none of it.

"She's MY mammy!" he told Christopher. "I married Mammy too, didn't I Mammy? So, it's MY dance too!"

In the wedding video, you can see him wedged between us on the dance floor. He wouldn't even let us talk to each other. Chris wasn't entitled to be there at all in Jake's head. It was HIS dance.

Then dozens of balloons dropped from the ceiling, and he forgot about us and ran off after them instead.

I remember that first dance so well. I look back and wonder how I could have been so happy once. Now when I hear the song and listen to the lyrics, I can barely stand it. It's like a whole other world.

The song, which meant so much to Chris and me, has taken on an entirely different meaning since Jake died in my arms.

It hurts so much that it's like someone has punched me in the gut when I hear it on the radio now.

Another day without your smile; another day just passes by.
But now I know how much it means for you to stay right here with me.
The time we spent apart will make our love grow stronger.
But it hurts so bad; I can't take it any longer.
I want to grow old with you; I want to die lying in your arms.
I want to grow old with you; I want to be looking in your eyes.
I want to be there for you, sharing everything you do.
I want to grow old with you.

Jakie loved our wedding day. We had to get him a copy of the wedding video so that he could watch it over and over again. But I haven't been able to look at it since he went to heaven. I don't know if I'll ever be able to watch it again.

The day after our wedding, we hired a DJ to play in the Brog Maker to have another more relaxed celebration for family and friends.

It was so hot that we had to tell the DJ to go home because everyone was out the back lapping up the afternoon sunshine.

Chris and I stayed until 9.00pm and then we walked home with the kids. Everyone offered to take the kids that night, but we refused. We wanted to go back together.

I wheeled Kaelem in the buggy, and Christopher carried Jake chattering non-stop on his shoulders. We were such a happy little family.

We laughed at the notion of being 'Mr and Mrs' and extended our hands to marvel at the new wedding rings glinting on our hands.

The rings were inscribed with: 'Christopher & Roseann' and our wedding date, March 28, 2012.

We could never have imagined that glorious sunny evening that those rings would soon be pressed into Jakie's little hands to go down with him in his coffin.

6. A SCHOLAR AND A GENTLEMAN

If ever there was a child who was ready for school, it was Jake.

His aunties stormed the schoolyard for his momentous first day at Presentation National School in September 2012.

In my mind's eye, I can still see everyone snapping photos and Jake standing in his new navy crested jumper and blue shirt with a beaming smile in the middle of the chaos.

Jake might have been ready for school, but I wasn't. I fussed around him and must have kissed him twenty times that morning. My little Jakie Baby was growing up.

Jake was such a social creature that he loved school from the start. The classroom was the ultimate playground for him. He delighted in having all these new and exciting little people around him.

He also soaked up everything at school. Before I had him strapped into the back seat of the car, he was chattering about all the wonderful, new things he'd learnt.

He loved learning to read, unlocking the mysteries of words on a page, and he threw himself into all the arts, crafts and activities of the school day.

More than anything though, he loved his teacher, Miss Millea. He was mad for Miss Millea and craved her undivided attention.

He learnt to get that attention by clinging to my leg and pretending he didn't want to go to into class. Then he'd look up at his teacher with doleful brown eyes, and she'd hold out her hand and say: "What's wrong, my Jakie Baby? Do you want to come in with me?"

Miss Millea's hand was an instant cure for all Jake's woes, and he'd hop and skip his way into the classroom without a problem.

Of course, when the other boys in the class heard the teacher calling him 'Jakie Baby', they started teasing him and calling him that too. But Miss Millea scolded the boys.

"He's MY Jakie Baby, not yours. You're not allowed to call him that."

Jake didn't care what the boys called him as long as Miss Millea held his hand and called him 'Jakie Baby'.

He loved attention from the older women in his life, and he got it because he had this very endearing way about him. I know every mother thinks that about her child, but so many women remarked upon his charm while he was still alive.

Before Jake started school, his playmates consisted of his cousins or the children of close friends like Samantha. We never corrected Jake when he referred to them as his cousins too because they were as close as family after all.

But when he went to school, he assumed all his twenty-something classmates were cousins too. He was confused to discover that cousins and friends are not the same things.

"No baby, he's not your cousin, he's your friend," I explained to him on countless occasions.

But he was quick to make friends, and he liked the company of girls, as much as boys. He invited his girl friends along with his boy friends to his birthday parties.

He loved joining in girls' imaginary games of role-playing and dressing up. In fact, he preferred that kind of play than computer games or football.

His brother Kaelem is the complete opposite; he scowls if you suggest playing with the girls.

Kaelem was only a toddler when Jake started school, but he missed not having him around. It was like his best friend disappeared for much of the day.

The only way to console him was to see Jake off in the schoolyard every morning. It became a sacred routine for Kaelem to go to school with Jake.

If he woke late and found that his brother had already gone to school, he turned the house into a war zone with a tantrum of epic proportions.

We soon realised that we were better off to wake him and use the school run as leverage to make him eat his breakfast.

"You can't go to school with Jakie and all the big boys unless you eat all your cereal," became a regular threat.

Jake brought Kaelem around the yard every morning, showing him off to his friends. He was so proud of his little brother. His friends would crouch, hands on their bended knees to talk to Kaelem like they were grown men instead of five-year-olds themselves.

I laughed every time I saw it.

"Hello, Jakie's little brother," is how they'd greet him and Kaelem would revel in all the attention from the 'big' boys.

Jake made so many plans. I listened to him explaining the school routine to Kaelem in the back of the car.

"When you come to my school right, now don't be upset because you won't be in my yard," he said. "But don't worry because I'll come over to you and see you in your yard. But you'll get moved in with me, just not the first year."

This year, Kaelem is in first class, and he should be playing in the same yard with Jake every day. Instead, I enrolled him in an entirely different school because it was too painful to return to Jake's old school every day.

Sorry, Jakie Baby, I couldn't face that schoolyard without you.

Jake's school had signs bearing the words 'Kind hands, kind feet, kind words', and they encouraged the kids to live by the motto. The 'kind feet' was meant to deter boys from practising 'karate' kicks in the schoolyard.

The words inspired Jake. He hated conflict, and he couldn't hold a grudge for five minutes. Apart from his sibling rivalry with Kaelem, he wasn't competitive either. He'd walk away when the boys' play became rough or abusive.

"I'm not playing with him today, Mammy because he's not kind," he'd tell me.

Still, he was excited when he got the chance to join a local kickboxing club. I was hesitant, but I let him go.

"I suppose if he enjoys it, and he gets a bit of exercise running around with other kids, it'll be okay," I said to Chris.

From early on, we saw that he wasn't interested in actual kickboxing. But he loved wearing the uniform, learning the kickboxing moves and hanging out with lots of other kids his age. But when it came to one-on-one sparring and fighting, he didn't take to it at all.

He didn't have that competitive streak and couldn't muster up the aggression he needed to get into the game.

After a couple of weeks, Jake announced he was taking part in an event for the kickboxing school. Chris and I and a few members of the family came along to support him.

I understood that Jake was to appear in an exhibition. I expected the kids to go up on stage do a display of sorts. When we got there, it turned that it was an actual kickboxing tournament.

I wasn't happy to see him going into the ring, but I didn't want to stop him as he had his heart set on it.

They put him in a big, padded red helmet and a huge protection vest, so I knew he couldn't come to any harm. But my heart sank when I learnt Jake was fighting a little fellow who was the son of a kick-boxing trainer.

Both were wearing so much padding that they couldn't hurt each other, but Jake had never been in a physical fight in his life. I had to fight the impulse to snatch him out of the ring and hug him.

"Well, at least this won't last for long," I said to Chris. "Jake won't fight, and he won't like getting hit."

Jake's little opponent came out with all the moves, side-kicks and jabs. Jake stood there and half-heartedly copied a few things that he saw the other fellow do.

I expected it to be all over in seconds. Instead, Jake threw more heart into it than punches, but he didn't quit the match.

My brother Eamon, known as Ninja, and his wife, Kathleen, were as shocked as the rest of us when Jake showed no sign of quitting. Eamon let a roar out of him: "G'wan Jakie Brennan!"

None of us could believe that was our Jakie in there. My sister Pamela, her husband, Robert, and their kids Sherice and Kayla started shouting too: "G'wan Jakie Brennan!"

We all roared for Jake. You can see him in our video of the event doing very little but shuffling around. At times, he forgot about his opponent altogether, and he stopped to smile at his cheering fans instead.

The other lad won with ease, but there was so much cheering for Jake, that anyone would have thought that our boy won.

Jake came out as proud as if he'd won a world series kickboxing event. He went back to lessons once or twice after that, but I knew he'd already lost interest. Jakie was a lover, not a fighter.

Meanwhile, his brother is the opposite and could be a prize fighter if we let him. He throws himself headlong into everything so even when he's playing soccer, I can only watch him through my fingers. Kaelem won't be doing combat sports if I can help it.

Jake had another brief flirtation with sport when he started playing hurling at the local O'Loughlin Gaels GAA club. They train kids from the age of four, and once Jake spotted other children playing, he decided hurling was the sport for him.

He was so enthusiastic that I bought the whole kit for him; he got the helmet to the shin guards and the hurling stick.

But it was the same thing all over again. He didn't get the point of the game. He loved wearing the gear and mixing with all the other kids, but he couldn't get worked up over chasing a ball.

"Get in there, Jake! Get in there!" the coach would roar.

But Jake would look bewildered. It was fun running around on the pitch, but he didn't have any desire to 'get in there'.

We insisted that he continue with it for six months before he stashed the kit at the back of the wardrobe and we forgot about hurling.

There was a single cloud that hung over Jake's days in school, and that was a medical problem. When he needed to use the loo, he needed it immediately. It only started impacting on his life when he went to school.

He was potty trained at two, but when it came to night time, he was always having accidents. The bedwetting continued no matter what we did.

As he got older, it seemed to get worse. We could be on a motorway, and if we couldn't pull in somewhere fast enough, he couldn't hold it.

When he started junior infants, it became a concern. I didn't say anything to the teachers at first but then one day I went to collect him, and Miss Millea called me in. Jake was still in the class with her.

"Everything's okay," she said. "But Jake had an accident."

Jake looked shamefaced.

"Mammy, I said I had to go, but she said I had to wait until we put on our jackets," he said.

I felt terrible then that I hadn't told the teacher.

"I'm sorry, but he is one of those kids who when he needs to go, he has to go," I said.

Still, I didn't think much about it. Jake was only four, and he'd grow out of it. But then it happened again and again, and it was getting embarrassing for him.

He was in senior infants when he had an accident in the playground of the homework club. He hid under the slide because he didn't want his friends to see his wet pants. That broke my heart.

That was when I said 'enough'. I figured there had to be something wrong.

I made enquiries and got a referral to an incontinence advisor in the Health Centre Clinic in James's Green in Kilkenny.

I met with them on my own first because I didn't want to make a big deal of the problem for Jake. I explained the situation and told them that I had cut back drinks at night and followed all the usual advice, but nothing worked.

The nurse assured me that it's not all that unusual. Up to 20% of five-year-olds have a problem with bed-wetting at night.

She told us to continue praising him when he woke at night and went to the bathroom.

"Focus on any improvements and not on wet nights," she said.

She also said we'd been doing the wrong thing to cut back on his drinks. She said we needed to give him more to drink and help to make his bladder bigger.

"It's about helping him to get used to greater amounts of liquid," she explained.

He loved the occasional blackcurrant juice, but that was off-limits because the colouring can send the bladder into spasm or something.

Cutting out fizzy drinks wasn't a problem because we never allowed them in the house and because he never got them, he didn't like them.

One time at a friend's birthday party in the Watershed Leisure Club in Kilkenny, he was running around, and I knew he needed something to drink.

The only drinks at the party were fizzy, and I couldn't buy mineral water in the club because I hadn't brought my handbag. But he took one sip of lemonade, grimaced and shook his head.

In the end, I had to hunt down one of the staff and persuade them to get a glass of tap water for him.

The clinic gave us a big chart to monitor Jake's intake of liquids.

We had to note the time of his last drink, whether he drank milk or water, the last check we did at night and when he woke by himself to go to the toilet.

There was also a column to note whether he stayed dry at night or whether the bedwetting was large, medium or small.

Jake was to drink six to eight 200ml beakers of liquid a day which we had to note on the chart. We also had to buy a special jug and measure his wee once a day at the same time.

The child was really under the microscope. I filled up every column in the chart every day for months.

It didn't take long to discover that his bladder only held 100ml compared to the average of 210ml to 250ml for a child his age. It was clear he had a problem.

They kept telling me to increase his liquid intake but no matter what we did, the contents of his bladder never went much over the 100mls.

They told me to keep working at it, and they would review the situation and take the next steps in a few months' time.

About two months after Jakie died, my phone rang. A woman said she was a health nurse from St James's Green. I assumed she was calling to make an appointment for our youngest, Savannah.

"No, I'm ringing about Jake. I see that he's due back to us this month," she said.

I got a lump in my throat, and my eyes filled with tears, but I managed to say: "I'm sorry, but Jake is in heaven."

There was a shocked silence, and then the woman couldn't apologise enough. She wasn't to know.

It still hurts me to this day that I'll never get to know what was wrong or what we could have done to help him. I never found out what the next steps would have been.

It upsets me to this day that we never got to the root of the problem, that I never got to help him, and now I never will.

7. LITTLE SISSY, SAVANNAH

Jake loved being around girls, and his favourite girl of all was his baby sister, Savannah. They only had four short months together, but he fretted about her, minded her and adored her.

I remember how he used to softly rub her plump right cheek with the back of his two forefingers like she was his good luck charm.

Chris and I first mentioned the idea of having another baby with the two boys in 2013. They decided they were okay with the idea, but Jake had one condition.

"As long as I get a sister. I have a brother already."

Jake looked up to his cousin Kayla who was three years older than him. She had a brother, Mason and a sister, Sherice. It was a case of keeping up with the Jones for Jake who wanted one brother and one sister too.

"If we have a girl, then I'd be the same as Kayla, Mammy. We want a girl."

"We don't get to pick, Jakie. Holy God decides if you get a brother or a sister."

Jake thought I was being difficult and decided to change tack.

"It would be much better for YOU if we got a girl, Mammy."

"Why? I don't mind if it's a boy or a girl."

"Because you're on your own, Mammy. There's Daddy, me and Kaelem and then there's only you. You're the only girl in the house. You need a girl baby, not another boy."

He had his heart set on a sister. When I was 24-weeks pregnant, I went for a 3-D scan. I wanted to know what we were having, and Chris had got over his need to be surprised in the labour ward.

We brought Jakie and Kaelem along for scan. You can see everything on a 3D scan as clearly as a photo, so we knew we'd find out the gender of the baby.

Kaelem was demanding a girl now too because he wanted everything that Jake wanted.

"Now look, boys," Chris warned. "Whether the baby is a boy or a girl, we're going to be happy, right?"

Jake and Kaelem didn't look convinced.

The woman who did the scan was great with the boys and spent loads of time explaining what was going on. The whole thing fascinated them.

"Look, you can see the baby and see all the lovely little fingers and toes?" she said showing them a clear image of the baby.

They oohed and aahed over the 3-D photo, as they waited for her to get to the point.

"Boys, it looks like you're having a baby sister!"

The two lads looked at each other and did a jubilant dance complete with fist pumps and high fives.

"Yes!" said Jake in triumph.

"Yes!" said Kaelem, copying him.

Later, Jake reminded me that the impending arrival of a girl was the best news for me too.

"It's good, Mammy because now you won't be on your own anymore."

Jake loved being around girls, but his attraction to older women was evident from the start.

Long before he fell in love with his teachers, he fell for my best friend, Samantha. He referred to her as his girlfriend as soon as he could talk.

He was smitten by her blonde hair, big brown eyes and her kind smile. He was devoted to her, and his great arch-enemy in life became her boyfriend, James Hurley.

Samantha was always around, especially when Jake was younger, so she was like his second mother. From the time he was a tot, he'd ask her to bring him to the bathroom which was a very special honour.

He was always careful not to hurt my feelings because he didn't want any bad feeling between Samantha and me. It was always clear that I was his Mammy, and Samantha was his girlfriend. We both had very separate but important roles in his life.

Jake was very territorial about everything he believed was his. He didn't want anyone in his bedroom in Nanny's house; he didn't like Daddy kissing his mammy, and he disliked James because he was a rival for Samantha's affections.

He revealed one of the reasons he joined kickboxing was so he could kick James out of her house. When Samantha had her son, Kyle, Jake believed that he was the father.

It was simple in Jake's head: he was Samantha's boyfriend, not James.

I tried talking to him, but he maintained this unshakeable belief that he was in a romantic relationship with Samantha.

One day he approached me with a question.

"My nanny's name is Nanny. Why do you call her Mammy?"

"Because she's my mammy, but she's your nanny. When you have little kids, they'll call me Nanny too."

Jake looked at me with impatience.

"But Mammy, I have a kid."

"No Jakie, you have to grow up first."

"Mammy I have a girlfriend," he sighed. "My girlfriend is Samantha. We have baby Kyle. You know that."

He was adamant. He was five-years-old and still convinced this was true. My sister Pamela used to crack up laughing listening to him.

"My God, Roseann, you know you'll have to break the news to him sometime?" she said.

It's fair to say that Jake wasn't always faithful to Samantha. He couldn't help falling for older women. He never harboured any romantic notions about his small girl friends at school.

But he had a thing for mature females. His affections were always returned because he had a smile that charmed all the ladies.

He showed a preference for blondes because he fancied my fair-haired sister-in-law, Ann Bolger too. He liked to taunt my brother, Michael, or Yapper as we call him, about Ann. Jake was so young that he couldn't even pronounce Yapper's name when he first tried to steal his girlfriend.

"Rapper, you know Ann is MY girlfriend, don't you?" he'd demand.

Jake basked in Ann's attention, and he loved it when she asked, "How's my little boyfriend?"

Of course, he was also smitten by his teacher, Miss Millea, another blonde who called him her 'Jakie Baby'.

We'd see him blush around one of the older girls, Jenny Brett, who used to help at his homework club. He'd glow with bashful delight when she paid him and his homework project extra attention.

Chris used to give him a terrible teasing about Jenny and Jake lived in terror that she'd hear what his dad was saying.

Jake's crushes on women were intense and passionate and very cute. I often thought he was an old soul in a little boy's body. I sometimes wonder if he was in a hurry to have a girlfriend and a child because, on some level, he knew he didn't have much time.

His romantic obsessions with Samantha, Ann, and Jenny continued to the end.

As my pregnancy with Savannah progressed, Jake got more and more excited at the prospect of his new sister's arrival. He liked to come into our bedroom and put his head on my belly and say, 'Hello, my little sissy. How's my little sissy?"

Of course, Kaelem followed, and the pair of them called her 'Little Sissy' from then on.

Savannah was the quickest and easiest birth of the three as she was also the smallest of the three, weighing in at 7lbs 6oz. She flew into the world thirty minutes into the morning of February 9, 2014.

With her shock of black hair and her sweet button nose, she was a replica of Jake and Kaelem when they were newborns, except that she was smaller, and she was dressed in pink.

I wasn't able to move in the bed because I suffered a haemorrhage after the birth. I clearly remember the two boys arriving all hyper to the hospital and ready to clamber all over Savannah and me.

They loved their drawing boards and chocolates from their new sister. In return, they wanted to hug both of us, but neither of us was able for their boisterous attentions.

The boys were no longer sure that a new sister was such a good idea.

Still, they danced and jumped with excitement when we arrived home from the hospital. Then they bawled when we went back again after she developed yellow jaundice.

When we got home for the second time, Jake was upset and sulky. He was fed up with an absent mother.

"You're not going away again to the hospital are you, Mammy?" he said, eyeing me with suspicion.

I was adamant.

"No baby, Mammy's done with hospitals and babies now. Definitely."

The two boys were really starting to enjoy Savannah by the start of the summer of 2014. She had finished with the 'boring' sleeping and feeding stage, and she was starting to notice them.

Her eyes would follow them around the room, and she'd reach out to them. When they paid her attention, she responded by laughing and kicking her legs wildly.

She laughed at anything, and then they couldn't get enough of her. After that, it was a competition to see who could make her laugh more.

Before he'd leave for school, or go anywhere, Jake made a habit of coming over to her, rubbing her on the cheek and saying 'Bye-bye, Little Sissy!'

Jake was a creature of habit. He liked to create lots of customs and rituals around every family event.

We'd hold a movie night or day at home on Fridays or Saturdays depending on Chris's schedule. Chris was working as a chef by now, so free weekend nights were scarce sometimes.

Jake could hardly wait until 7.00pm if it was a movie night and he would have the room arranged well in advance. He had lots of movie night rules which were all devised by him. The blinds had to be closed, the side light had to be on when we were eating, but then it had to go off.

We'd all have to wear our pyjamas, and Jake and Kaelem shared this one armchair. Jake would fix pillows on the chair to have it right and have his blankie ready for the pair of them.

He'd arrange his popcorn in a bowl and a few jellies in another. He had to have pizza like his dad but in his own small box from Dominos. These little ceremonial touches were an essential part of Jake's movie night.

The boys got to pick a movie each from the local video store. To stop the rows, I had to put the DVDs behind my back, and they'd pick a hand each to decide which movie was going on first.

Some movie nights were more successful than others. There was one occasion where they picked a movie called Ted with a cute teddy bear on the cover. I wasn't prepared for a foul-mouthed teddy bear.

Chris and I leapt for the television remote at the same time. Jake and Kaelem burst into tears and cried for Ted to be turned on again. Chris and I looked at one another in shock.

"No, Babies, we can't watch that because Ted's a bold bear, a really bold bear!"

The Home Alone movie series was their absolute favourite. We had to watch the series again and again. The two boys would giggle and wriggle in the chair together during the 'naughty' bits. It's awful, but I can't bear to turn on any of those movies for Kaelem anymore.

For a long time after Jake died, Kaelem sat on his own, on their special chair. He looked so lonely there. Now Savannah is starting to watch the movies too, so the two of them curl up together on the same seat.

We're also back to the days of hiding the DVDs behind my back to sort the row over whose movie goes on first.

It's painful at times. I feel a sense of guilt because things are moving on and it feels like Jake has been substituted with another child. At the same time, it's good to see the growing companionship between Kaelem and Savannah.

I see Savannah looking up to Kaelem now, the way he used to look up to Jake. And I'm hearing Kaelem trying to teach Savannah things like Jake once showed him.

"You do this Savannah, see? No, like this. You press this and hold it like that. Yes, that's how you do it…"

Kaelem was three years and one month old when we lost Jakie, but he talked about him again last night as I put him to bed.

"Mammy, I miss Jake."

"Remember, if you're upset, Kaelem, close your eyes and think of him, and he'll be with you, and he'll help you."

"But you said he'll be with Savannah too, how can he be with Savannah and me too?"

"Baby, he'll know which one needs him most on which night."

My heart ached when he replied, "But I need him every night."

It's on family occasions that I really feel Jake's loss. He loved nothing more than a family outing; he loved 'going on an adventure' as he called it.

Sometimes we waited till it was nearly dark and we went for a walk in the woodland at Castlecomer Discovery Park. For these outings, Jake liked us all to wear wellies and to carry a stick and torches.

We pretended that we were looking for the Gruffalo, a fierce creature from Jake's storybooks.

Chris would run off ahead and jump out on us, and we'd go running and screaming from the Gruffalo. I know the last time we did it, I was heavily pregnant with Savannah.

The other outing that he loved was fishing with his daddy in Castlecomer Discovery Park or at Wallslough Village. The actual fishing didn't interest him so much as just being with his dad, having a picnic and climbing trees.

The week before he died, we planned an outing with some of his cousins to Kilkenny Castle. Jake was very excited about visiting a castle. A castle to Jake was the home of princes and princesses and a place for us to have lots of adventures.

We set off that morning with a picnic packed to eat in the grounds of the castle. But we weren't far from home when the sunshine disappeared, the sky went dark, and the heavens opened.

Jake laughed and squealed with the other kids as we all ran back home in the pouring rain. The day was a washout, so we moved the picnic indoors, and we swapped Kilkenny Castle for a movie day.

Jake loved a movie day, but he was still anxious to see the castle, so I assured him that we would go again soon.

"Baby, we've got the whole summer ahead of us; we'll have loads of time to see Kilkenny Castle on your holidays. We'll pick a nice sunny day next time, we'll pack a big picnic again, and we'll see the castle then," I said.

It was one of many things that he never got to do.

He never asked for much. Happiness was simple for Jake. It was doing something together or being somewhere together. He revelled in every family gathering or outing. He beamed when he was surrounded by family.

Nothing made you happier than all of us being together, did it Jakie?

I look back now, and life seemed so carefree and easy then. I wish I had that old life back because nothing feels the same anymore.

8. BEST DAY EVER

Sunday, June 8, 2014

We've lots of family photos, but there's one taken at Dublin Zoo that's our most precious. You can see Chris holding on to Jake and Kaelem perched on the railings surrounding the World of Primates lagoon.

I'm standing on the other side of the boys with four-month-old Savannah dozing in my arms. It's a warm June day, and the backdrop is blue skies and the lush, green leaves of summer.

An instant earlier, I'd been giving out to Chris because he was wobbling the boys and pretending that he'd push them into the water behind them. I was always trying to get nice family photos.

"Stop messing Chris; I want them to smile for the camera!" I said.

In this one, Jake is leaning on my shoulder, holding his new lion mask and posing with a cheeky grin.

I can see now that he was starting to sprout in height; he was six-years-old but wearing clothes for eight to ten-year-olds. Kaelem is looking suspiciously at the camera, as he always does.

Chris appears to be saying something, probably: "Hurry up and take it, will you?" to his sister, Alison, who's the photographer.

It's a snapshot of a happy family and a reminder of a lovely day out together. How could we ever have guessed it would be our last ever family photo?

We planned the trip to Dublin Zoo with Alison, her husband Shervin (Sherry), and kids, Taylor-Rae and Nathan. Jake was very excited because we arranged to travel on the train.

But that morning, the weather forecast didn't look great, so we travelled in our cars instead. I regret it now because Jake was disappointed and apart from a rain shower or two, it turned out to be a lovely day.

Jake wanted a lion mask from the zoo shop, and of course, Kaelem had to have the same. They hid in the bushes wearing their masks, then jumped out and roared at us, and everyone had to pretend to be scared.

Chris discovered a life-sized model of a dairy cow that you can milk at the zoo's Family Farm. He called Jake over to show him the rubber udders underneath the cow and then squirted him in the face with the 'milk'.

Jake, of course, thought this was hilarious and had to copy his Dad.

"Aunty Alison, come down and look at this," he said, and he squealed with delight when he managed to squirt her in the face.

We brought a picnic with us, and both adults and kids had a great day.

As we were leaving the zoo, Savannah's eyes started to turn red, and she began sneezing. She was having a bit of an allergic reaction from the animals, their hay feed and the cut grass in the zoo.

All three kids have inherited the same allergies that Chris had as a child. But Jake peered into Savannah's buggy, with concern.

"Mammy, she's not well, she's not right."

"She's fine, she's a bit over-tired, and she might have hay fever, but that's all," I assured him.

He kept checking on her, bending into the buggy and rubbing her cheek.

We got the kids into the car, and all three fell asleep on the journey home. I looked back, and Jakie had nodded off with his finger still curled up on Savannah's cheek where he'd been stroking her.

"Chris, you have to look at this," I said. "They're so cute."

The picture of Jake sound asleep with his finger on Savannah's cheek is one that I'll cherish in my memory forever.

We all stopped at The Orchard House in Kilkenny to have dinner. Jake checked on Savannah again as I fed her.

"Mammy, you're right she's okay again."

"Didn't I tell you that, Jake? She's fine."

Jake and Kaelem joined a brother and sister in the play area outside the pub. The boy was Jake's age, and the girl was the same age as Kaelem. When it was time to pack up, Jake didn't want to go home

"I don't want to leave my new friend."

"Sure, we'll be back here again Jake; you'll see him another day."

"Can I meet you here again?" he asked the little boy.

I saw that brother and sister again after Jake died and my heart sank. I keep having these constant reminders of how much he lost; how much we all lost.

Dublin Zoo was our last family trip, and it's where we posed for our final family picture. I don't know if I'll ever face going to Dublin Zoo again. And the pain of knowing that we'll never get to take another family photo again, will stay with us forever.

At 6.30am, I went to the gym and then rushed back afterwards to help Chris get the kids ready for school.

I can never find the door key, so I knocked, and Jake, who could see me outside, pulled open the door. The instant I saw him, I stopped in my tracks and stared in absolute horror.

"Oh my God, Baby, what's wrong with you?" I screamed.

Jake's eyes were an inflamed mess of red, blue and purple, and they were swollen almost completely shut. He looked like someone punched him in the eyes. Yet, Chris, had him dressed and ready to go to school.

"Why didn't you get him to a hospital, Chris? Look at my poor child!" I shrieked.

I was so panicked that poor Jakie started to get upset. All I could think of was Jake losing his eyesight.

"Calm down, Rosie, I think it's just an allergy from the zoo yesterday," said Chris. "The doctor's surgery will be open soon, and I'll bring him then."

It never dawned on me that it could be an allergic reaction. I'd never seen anything like this happen before.

Dr Sweeney prescribed anti-histamines and other drugs to reduce the symptoms. We kept Jake home from school because they made him drowsy. All he wanted was cuddles from Mammy and Daddy, so we stayed on the couch and watched cartoons.

Within a few hours, the swelling around his eyes had disappeared, but he still felt sorry for himself. I remember us all sitting on the couch, Savannah napping and Kaelem watching cartoons. I had Jake wrapped in my arms all day.

I didn't know it then but looking back it was a perfect day at home. We were together as a family, lying in each other's arms. We'll never have a perfect day like that again.

Tuesday, June 10, 2014

Jake had three weeks left in senior infants until his summer holidays started. His teacher, Miss White, issued an open invitation to parents to join the class for a half hour of 'free play' every Tuesday and Thursday until the holidays.

She said it was an opportunity for fun in the final three weeks of the term. The more serious business of First Class would begin in September.

I volunteered to go for all six sessions, so we couldn't bring Kaelem in the car that Tuesday morning. He made a big fuss, but Chris distracted him by lifting him onto the kitchen sink so we could wave to him from the car.

Jake's group were at the water-play activity table, so he beamed with pride when his teacher put me in charge of that station.

The other children were curious.

"You Jake's Mammy?"

"Yes, I'm Jake's Mammy."

"My Mammy's name is Jean. Do you know her?"

"No, but I might know her to see."

"I know Jake's Mammy. I was at Jake's house, wasn't I, Jake's Mammy?"

"Yes, I remember you. You were at Jake's house."

The chat continued like this for the full half hour as we played with shapes and water. Jake couldn't have been prouder that his Mammy was in charge of his activity table.

You were such a funny little boy, Jakie, so happy, so easy to please.

Wednesday, June 11, 2014

After Jake finished school, I dropped him at the Watergate Theatre for a full-dress rehearsal of Jesters' end of year show.

I got back to discover that our lovely landlady, Ingrid, had dropped by and left a baby gift for Savannah and a bottle of wine for me.

It was one of those evenings where I felt exhausted and was too tired to put Kaelem and Savannah into the bath. Chris came to the rescue.

"Let's just get them to bed; I'll be up early in the morning, and I'll shower them."

Jake was later than usual getting home because of the dress rehearsals. He was all excited about the show the next night as he went upstairs to get ready for bed.

He came back downstairs in his boxer shorts. Jake always loved his pyjamas, but when he noticed that his Dad wore boxers at night, then he had to be the same.

"I'm not cold, this is what Daddy wears," he'd insist, back arched, obstinate arms folded across his chest.

I watched him from across the living room and realised in astonishment how much he had stretched. He was going to be tall like all my brothers who are over six foot in height.

People sometimes forgot how young Jake was, because of his height and because of his verbal skills. But he was still a six-year-old baby and could regress to baby mode in an instant.

"Get up off to bed, you little divil," I said. "What are you doing down here again?"

"Will you carry me up like a baby?" he asked, shyly.

Savannah was the new baby in the house, but both Jake and Kaelem were demanding their share of babying too. I felt wrecked, but I picked him up in my arms anyway and carried him up the stairs.

"Look at the size of you. Far from a baby you are now; I can hardly carry you!" I said.

But it never mattered what size you were, Jakie Baby, you always fitted perfectly in my arms.

Even after I got Jake into bed and gave him all his kisses, he begged me to stay a bit longer.

"Do my song, Mammy," he said. "I'll go to sleep then."

We had our own version of the lullaby, Hush Little Baby. Sometimes life was hectic, and I didn't get to sing it to him every night.

Between that and his fifty kisses, it was a long bedtime routine especially when you've two other kids as well. But when I had those few minutes to wind down with him, it meant a lot to him.

Hush Little Jakie, Don't You Cry.
Mammy's going to buy you a lullaby,
And if that lullaby don't sing,
Mammy's gonna buy you a diamond ring
If that diamond ring don't shine.
Mammy's going to buy you whatever you want.
Hush little Jakie, you're Mammy's Little Man
Hush little Jakie, you're Mammy's Little Man
Hush hush Jakie go to sleep.
Hush hush Jakie go to sleep.

As with everything to do with Jake, the song came with its own ritual. I had to sing the words first; then I had to hum the entire tune while stroking my palm down Jake's face, pulling his eye-lids closed on the way.

Then he'd pretend to sleep, while I crept out of the room and hummed the lullaby all the way down the stairs.

At the bottom of the stairs, I'd usually hear him yell: 'Thanks, Mammy!"

So, I sang the lullaby to him the night before he died. I didn't finish the whole song because I was so tired. Of course, that's another thing that I regret now. I wish I'd made the extra effort to do it all for him.

But he was happy. As I said, it never took much to make Jake happy.

I hope it still makes him happy because I sing that song to him all the time.

Don't I, Jakie Baby?

Thursday, June 12, 2014.

Returning from the gym early in the morning, I tapped on the door, and Jakie let me in as usual. He was already washed and dressed, and Christopher was busy towelling off Kaelem.

I always loved Jake's hair when we washed it. Nine out of ten times he gelled his hair, but when it was newly washed it was so dark and glossy, it set off his sparkling brown eyes.

"Look at you, you're looking all shiny," I said ruffling his damp hair.

He gave me his little smile.

"I'm running upstairs to get dressed," I told him. "I'll be ready to go in a few minutes."

He was happy watching his cartoons on his portable TV in the kitchen. He also knew that I was going to school with him that day to take part in the second of his play mornings. Kaelem wasn't impressed that he was being left at home again.

"No Kaelem, you can't go this morning. Mammy has to help the teacher," I tried to tell him.

Christopher tried to humour him as we got into the car and drove off.

It was Jakie and me in the car together again. I hadn't checked his reading the night before because he'd been at the dress rehearsal. So, he practised his reading in the car with me as we crawled in traffic.

It turned out that I was the only parent who volunteered that morning. Some parents had full-time jobs, and others had to mind younger children. But I was glad that I had the time to be with Jake before the baby in him disappeared altogether.

Miss White asked if I'd oversee the role-play station where we played 'doctor's surgery'. The children took on roles as the doctor, nurse or patients.

But Jake was at the hand-eye coordination table threading beads and making chains. He wasn't happy that I was playing with other children. He had this very sulky head on him even when I asked him to make me a special chain.

Still, he could never brood for long, and I caught sight of him giggling at something said by one of his friends.

"What a little cutie, he is," I thought, watching him. "He's getting bigger, but he's still a baby behind it all."

He looked over at me at another stage, and I gave him a big wink. He flashed his smile and winked back at me. Then playtime was over, and I had to leave.

He started clinging to me, so I asked Miss White if I could take him out for a minute. I got down to his eye level once we were outside the classroom.

"Why are you getting upset, Jakie? Mammy's got four more mornings in the classroom, so we'll get to play the doctor's surgery again, okay?"

He nodded, but he was still morose.

"I'm going to pick you up from school today, and if you're a good boy, I'll bring you a Push Pop."

He loved these awful Push Pop lollies that are stocked in some of the local shops. It was a rare treat for him to get one, so it was the ultimate bribe.

"You have to be good for teacher though," I warned. "We'll do that doctor's surgery together I promise. But teacher won't let me come back if you're a bold boy."

"I'll be good, Mammy," he said, and he gave me a hug and a kiss and went back in.

As soon as I got back to the house, I put Kaelem and Savannah into the buggy and went off to town with my sister, Catherine.

It was a lovely sunny day, and we went shopping for things that we didn't need. I was also looking for a few things for Savannah's christening which was coming up in ten days' time.

We lost track of time, and I realised that I was going to be late to collect Jake. I rang my sister Angela, who was picking up her boy and asked her to tell Jake that I was almost there.

"Ange, tell him I'm coming through the car park, and I'll be there in a minute."

I'd promised him that I'd be there and after what happened earlier, he wouldn't be happy if he thought I'd forgotten about him.

Angela found Jake waiting in the line for me.

"Your Mammy's after ringing me and said she's on her way, do you want to walk out with me?"

He looked at her and scowled.

"No, my Mammy promised to pick me up!"

"She's coming through the car park so walk out with me, and we'll meet her."

He huffed about it, but he followed Angela.

I made it onto the school property as he arrived out with her. I could see he had a little puss on him.

"Sorry Baby, I'm late, but I'm here!" I laughed.

He could never hold a grudge, and he smiled back.

"So were you good at school?

"Yep!"

No crying after I left?"

"Nope"

I presented him with his Push Pop, and because the day was still lovely, Catherine and I and the three kids headed back into town.

I still needed a waistcoat for Chris to wear to Savannah's christening and grey canvas shoes for Kaelem.

We made our way to MacDonagh Junction Shopping Centre where we took the elevator. Jake was nervous around elevators. Someone must have told him a scary story about lifts. As soon as we got in, the lift jerked and stalled for a second.

Catherine teased him: "Oh no, Jakie, I think we're stuck!"

Jake's face was a picture.

The instant that lift door opened, he snatched the front of the buggy and ran out dragging us with him. He wasn't spending a second longer on that lift, but he wasn't leaving his mammy or his siblings behind him.

We laughed at his panic-stricken face. He saw the funny side himself but only when we were far away from the elevator.

As soon as we got into TK Maxx, Jake spotted a tub of plastic animals that he wouldn't put down.

Jake loved animals. We had a Labrador Retriever dog who was perfectly named Rover because, no matter what we did, he escaped out the front door or the side-gate or over the wall.

Chris built an enclosed run for him out the back, but he'd get out of that too and run helter-skelter out of the estate. It was only a matter of time before a car hit him on the main road.

He got away from us one final time, and someone handed him into Dogs Trust. We took their advice and let them re-home him in the country.

These days we have a yappy Jack Russell-cross called Betsy. She skitters around our floors on two-inch legs, guards the house and thinks she's a pit bull.

Back in TK Maxx, Jake clung to a box of plastic animals as if he'd found the Holy Grail.

"No Jake, you have loads of animals at home already."

"Mammy, they're not like these, these are zoo animals. I've no zoo animals."

Our visit to the zoo on Sunday was still fresh in his mind. He looked so hopeful and anxious that I didn't have the heart to say no, so I bought them for him.

I ran upstairs to see if they had a waistcoat for Chris and left the buggy and the kids with Catherine. She let him open his new toy while they were waiting. When I got back, Jake was ecstatic after discovering the box contained two of every animal.

"This is brilliant!" he beamed. "Me and Kaelem can have a set each now!"

We sat in the play area in the shopping centre afterwards and treated Jake and Kaelem to ice-creams. Jakie, of course, tried to chance his arm and get three toppings instead of two as agreed.

Afterwards, we continued shopping, but Jake began to get bored and started his new habit of mimicking Paddy Doherty.

"Woman, would ya come on, would ya?" he yelled.

"Don't be cheeky, Jake, you call me Mammy!"

Jake turned to Kaelem in the buggy.

"Kaelem tell Mammy: "Come on, Woman!""

Kaelem always did what Jake said.

"Wan Woman!" he shouted from the buggy.

Catherine and I couldn't stop ourselves laughing, and Jake was delighted.

Then making our way home, we passed an empty block of office buildings. Jake couldn't resist pressing a button on an intercom panel.

"Oh my God, Jake, did I just see you press that button?" I said, feigning horror.

He nodded, his eyes widening.

"On no, Jake! You're after knick-knacking!"

Catherine and I tore off down the road with the buggy killing ourselves laughing. He ran after us terrified. He didn't know what 'knick-knacking' was but presumed it was something awful. It took him a while to realise we were joking with him.

Then Catherine's shopping bag handle snapped, and the contents spilt on the path just as we were crossing at pedestrian lights.

Jake's face registered horror before he dived on everything and stuffed all of Catherine's purchases back in her bag. I think he was afraid that the lights would change, and Catherine might be left behind.

It was like the fuss he made earlier getting everyone off the shopping centre lift. In hindsight, he might have been like my late dad who saw danger lurking around every corner. My brother, Michael, known as Yapper, is similar and is known as the official worrier in the family.

On the road home, we could hear him rehearsing his songs for the Jester's show in the Watergate that night. It was an Irish themed show, and he was singing cheerily to himself:

Oh, Molly, my Irish Molly, My sweet a cushla dear;
I'm fairly off my trolley, My Irish Molly when you are near.

Usually, he'd complain that he was tired, and he'd demand to climb on the buggy but not that day. He was always a sweet-natured child, but this day he was even happier than usual.

Catherine and I had to wait for him to catch up at one stage; he was trailing behind in his own little world.

"Come on Jakie, keep up," I said to him.

He beamed up at me.

"This is the best day of my life!" he announced.

Catherine and I laughed.

"Oh, just because you got a Push Pop and an ice cream in one day?"

But Jake was right; it was a great day. On other days, Kaelem could be like a bag of cats and Savannah might be teething, but there was none of that. There were no tot-sized tantrums and everything about the day had been easy.

We did silly things, we laughed a lot, the sun shone, and we had all the time in the world. We were all happy.

Still, Catherine and I thought that Jake's remark was funny.

"Did you ever hear the likes of it from a six-year-old?" I laughed. "'This is the best day of my life!'"

Oh, Jakie, my little Jakie Baby, how could you, or I, ever have known? That wonderful sunny day was not just the best, but the last day of your life, and the beginning of the darkest days of mine.

9. THE PREMONITION

From the time I knew I was pregnant with Jake, I had this deep-seated fear that something would happen to him.

This feeling overwhelmed me at times, but it was so irrational that I only ever shared my fears with my sister, Pamela.

During the pregnancy, I had this secret dread that he wouldn't survive the birth. I had trouble with my other pregnancies, but I never felt this scared. There was a darkness there; I couldn't see myself with a baby in my arms.

When Jake was born, the anxiety didn't go. I felt I wouldn't see Jake talking or walking. I felt like I'd never get to keep him. When he was talking and walking, I had this fear that he'd never make it to his first day at school.

It was a black cloud that was always there, sometimes it lay at the back of my mind, other times, it would wash over me in a wave of panic.

I put it down to being a neurotic new mother or to the return of my childhood obsession with death.

"Would you ever stop obsessing about Jake dying?" Pamela said on many occasions. "He's grand. This is all in your head. It's just like when you were a kid all over again."

As a child, I was consumed by a terror that everyone I loved was about to die. It began after the man I knew as my father died when I was five years old.

My natural mother Ann, who had me when she was 19, struggled as a single mother. When she moved to Wales, I became part of her mother and father's large family.

They were my grandparents, but I copied the other kids and called Ann's parents, Mammy and Daddy. Her siblings became my sisters and brothers.

Mammy and Daddy knew that they were going to have to tell me the truth sometime, but they didn't see any point in correcting a little child.

Anyway, they always treated me as one of their own. I never felt any different from any of their natural children.

To this day, Joan and Michael Hayes are my parents, and their children are my brothers and sisters.

My dad, Michael, was an army man through and through. He tried to impose discipline on a large family household by giving everyone a chore list and doing regular checks in the house.

According to my older brothers and sisters, he was short of getting out a white glove and checking for dust. But to me, he was always this great, big teddy bear. I adored him.

He looked fit and strong, but from a young age he suffered from congenital heart problems. He had to retire in his 40s after suffering heart attacks, and he didn't have enough years served to collect a pension, so money was tight.

His lifestyle didn't help his heart condition. Doctors warned him not to smoke or drink whiskey, but we lived across from the army barracks, and he loved to meet the men in the local pub.

He was also a stressed man who worried a lot about us. He saw danger lurking around every corner for us kids. We brought home one of those orange space hoppers one time, but he punctured it because we'd "fall and crack our skulls".

He'd see peril in every little thing even a lollipop.

"For God's sake Joan, take that lollipop off Rosie. It'll come off the stick and choke her!"

I remember one time, the doctors tried to admit my sister Pamela into hospital, but he didn't even trust them to keep her overnight.

"Better for me to sit with her at home and keep an eye on her," he told them.

We'd see a more relaxed side of him sometimes after the pub closed. He'd come back to the house to have a singsong with some of his army friends.

I'd jump out of bed, make my way down to sit in the middle of them, and Dad would say, "Rosie, sing your funny rhyme about diarrhoea!"

Daddy used to think it was the funniest thing ever. One of my brothers taught it to me, and I loved it how all the men would fall around laughing when I recited it. They probably laughed at the tiny voice rather than the rhyme, but I loved performing for the grown-ups and making my dad laugh:

Walkin' down the street,
Got a funny pain
Dye-yo-ree-ya
Dye-yo-ree-ya
I ate some cheese
It ran down my knees
Dye-yo-ree-ya
Dye-yo-ree-ya.

When getting up the stairs got too much for Daddy, he moved into the downstairs room. He would sometimes go to the pub, but once he was at home, he was in the bed.

When I was three or four, Mammy and I used to sit with Daddy in his room to watch the telly together. Mammy sat in the chair beside him, and I'd lie on the bed or the floor.

Mammy slept upstairs to keep an eye on the children, and he used to bang a brush on the ceiling when he needed her.

It was near dawn on May 10, 1989, when we heard the bang on the ceiling. Mammy and I came downstairs. Daddy said he wasn't feeling well. She sent me for a glass of water as she got a tablet that he had to place under his tongue. Then she closed his bedroom door and wouldn't allow me back in there with her and Dad again.

Afterwards, I remember the hustle and bustle with neighbours and family coming and going in and out of his room. I remember someone screaming 'Get up, Daddy!" but I don't know who it was.

My next memory is standing on a wooden chair eating an apple and looking at everyone around me crying. I was taking it all in.

I thought 'everyone is crying, so I'd better do it too' so I scrunched my face and tried to whinge. But I still didn't know what was going on.

Then an ambulance came. I learnt much later that Daddy was already dead. He had a massive heart attack and died in the bedroom. He was just 50-years-old. They sent the children upstairs, so we didn't see him leave the house

Ann came home from Wales for the funeral. She and Maggie brought me into town, but they stopped outside the undertakers. They wanted to check how Daddy was laid out. I remember the conversation.

"We can't bring Rosie in."

"We can if she wants to come in. Do you want to come in and see Daddy, Rosie?"

Of course, I wanted to see Daddy.

I can see still see him in his coffin, in a dark corner to the left of the room. He wasn't in the centre of the mortuary for some reason. He looked so still, and his face looked bigger or stretched.

I didn't understand why he looked like that. I wasn't at the funeral because they didn't bring kids in those days.

But from then on, I had a massive fear of death. All I knew is that I had a daddy one day, and then he was gone, and his room was empty, and no one talked about him again. At least, they didn't talk about him in front of the kids in case they upset us or whatever.

I worried about everyone, especially Mammy. One night, Mammy went to my sister Maggie's, but it was getting late, and there was no sign of her. I was inconsolable.

"Mammy should be home by now. Where's Mammy?"

There were hardly any phones, never mind mobile phones then. Catherine had to go down to the local pub to ring Maggie who had a landline. Mammy came on the phone and explained that the car wouldn't start.

Catherine came back, and I heard her say to my sister, Mary: "I ate Mammy! She knows what Rosie's like. I told her she should have rung and got a message to us."

I had Mammy dead in my mind a million times over. If she went to the shops, I'd get anxious.

At night, I'd sometimes call out to her 'Mammy, goodnight!"

I needed the reassurance that she wasn't dead.

If she didn't answer, my heart would start racing.

"MAMMY!'

"What? What, Rosie?"

I'd woken her up.

"Night, night Mammy."

"Night, night Pet."

I developed obsessive behaviour about lines on the pavement for example.

"If I don't walk on the lines, my mammy won't die tonight," I'd think.

If I made a mistake and walked on the line, I wouldn't sleep for fear that I'd let her die.

Was it those old childhood fears that made me worry about losing Jake? Or was I just an over-anxious first-time mother? Sometimes I wonder if I had this sixth sense, a premonition from the beginning, that I would lose him.

Whatever the reason for it, I always felt this black cloud of dread about Jake. But as the years rolled on and Jake grew up and went to school, that sense of unease began to fade away.

I calmed myself; persuaded myself that I was being ridiculous and started to believe that Jake was going to be okay.

It was then that all my darkest fears came true.

The sunny afternoon that Jake announced was the 'best day' of his life, we got back to the house sometime after 4.00pm.

Jake had skipped alongside me, rehearsing his songs for the show that night, all the way home. He asked if he and Kaelem could play with the new box of animals in the front garden. They wanted to use the driveway to line up their toys.

There was plenty of space because Christopher was gone off with the car. A friend's child, Siofra, was with them for a while. I let them play together, watching from the kitchen sink as I got their dinner.

Jake got busy sharing the toy animals between himself and Kaelem, so they'd both have one of each.

Christopher had prepared a dinner of pork chops, mash and vegetables that I could reheat in the microwave. In the fridge, I saw the bottle of wine that Ingrid had dropped over the day before.

"I might have a glass of wine in a minute," I thought and placed an empty wine glass on the kitchen counter.

Jake came in and asked if they could play out the back garden because they wanted to use the trampoline. There were sliding aluminium blinds in front of the back doors, but they jammed on me.

"I can't get them open Jake, but it's time for your dinner anyway."

"Can we have our dinner out the front then?"

We had a small children's table and chairs which I placed outside the front door in the driveway. I brought out their dinner, cut up Kaelem's food and went back into the kitchen, carrying Savannah. I started to clean up.

First, Jake was singing and rehearsing his songs for Jester's show that night. Then I heard him teasing Kaelem over something.

"Nah-nah-nah-nah-nah!"

"Cut it out Jake, be nice to your brother!"

"Nah-nah-nah-nah-nah!"

"He's teasing me, Mammy!"

Fighting was a great distraction from eating their vegetables.

"Stop it, Jake, now!"

This time he started to imitate me nagging him.

That was new; he never gave me any cheek, so I called him into the kitchen.

"That's not a nice thing to do, Jake."

"I didn't say a bad word."

"I know, but it's still not a nice thing to do to your mammy."

He gave a big sigh and raised his arms in exasperation and hit his funny bone on the kitchen counter.

"See? Maybe Holy God didn't like you jeering your mammy like that," I said.

That drove him mad altogether, and he stormed outside in a temper rubbing his arm. Usually, I gave his arm a magic rub and kissed it better, but when I went out, I discovered that they had hardly touched their food. I forgot about his magic rub and fed them each with one arm while trying to hold Savannah in the other.

Then about 5.30pm, Chris pulled in. Jake started telling him the story about the fright he had in the lift and about his mammy and his aunty running away on him.

Chris had eaten earlier, so he kept an eye on the kids while I ate my dinner. Our front door was beside the kitchen, and I talked to Chris about the waistcoat I'd bought him for the christening. The empty wine glass was still sitting on the counter.

"I'll have that glass of wine when I go upstairs to get ready for Jake's show," I thought. Pamela was bringing her car, so I didn't have to drive.

I'm so glad I never had that glass of wine in the light of the horror that was about to unfold. It's easy to be unfairly judged or accused if you have the faintest smell of alcohol on your breath.

We didn't know if Chris was going to the Jesters' show yet. We could bring Kaelem, but we needed someone to watch Savannah. It was all up in the air. Chris said he didn't mind; he could go to the show the next night instead.

The children asked to play on the small green across the road. They liked to collect stones, rocks, leaves, twigs and things. I was always emptying the boys' pockets of the rocks and muck they brought home.

Trees and nature fascinated Jake, and he'd play and rummage for hours in any green space.

The estate was still and silent as usual; there weren't even many cars parked in the driveways apart from our car. I let them cross over.

Chris and I stood in the garden talking about what we were going to do that evening about Jake's show. I still hadn't rung my niece to ask her to babysit.

"I'm going to settle Savannah and get ready to go," I said. "Make up your mind if you're going tonight because I need to ask Donna to sit with her."

We still hadn't a plan when my brother-in-law, Patrick O'Hara, who we call Pakie, pulled in. He parked on the road just past our driveway.

He came to return Chris's lawnmower which was in the back of his Renault Grand Scenic. The boys wanted to cross back from the green to see their Uncle Pakie. I looked to the right, towards the entrance of the cul-de-sac, and beckoned for them to cross.

I was always wary of a car belting in around the corner and speeding down our cul-de-sac. But there was good visibility as it was a wide, straight road and the corner was a good 100 metres away from our house. There was little or no traffic anyway.

The only cars that passed our home belonged to the handful of neighbours that lived in the dead end of the cul-de-sac.

We lived at number 15 of 23 houses on the road so only there were just eight houses beyond us.

We had a couple of problems with neighbours who lived in one house down there. There were times when they raced down the street past us, so I always looked to the corner to watch out for anything speeding towards this end of the cul-de-sac.

I should also add that our two boys were small, but they were streetwise. Jake knew he wasn't allowed put a foot near a road with moving cars unless he was holding my hand.

We had read all the pre-school road safety books like 'Simon's Surprise' and 'Josie's Picnic', or 'Charlie Goes to a Party'.

We had the full pack of books, and I read them as bedtime stories, so they were both aware of road safety. The books focus on holding hands, stopping, looking and listening and feature scenarios such as a ball rolling out on the road.

"Oh no, Jake, the ball is out on the road, what does Simon do now?"

"Simon has to leave the ball and ask an adult to get it for him."

"Good boy, Jakie!"

Weeks before he died, Jake was awarded his 'Safety Licence' after completing road safety activities course from the Road Safety Authority. He was so proud of that licence.

Outside our house, Pakie lifted out the mower, and the boys clambered straight into his boot.

In the front passenger seat was a guy called Karl Gleeson, who was about 17, then. He and Pakie were on their way to pick up my nephew Paddy to play football. The kids played in the car, and they peppered Karl with a hundred questions.

I went into the kitchen to put fix a bottle for Savannah, and I could hear Pakie winding up Chris outside. Chris is very precious about his lawnmower and his garden tools.

"Chris, you're not going to be happy with me."

"What did you do, Pakie?" Chris asked resignedly.

"I think I broke your lawnmower."

Chris rushed to start up the lawnmower, and I could hear Pakie laughing to himself.

He turned to go and get Jake and Kaelem out of his car.

"Out you get, lads, I have to get going."

I moved outside the door, rocking Savannah in my arms, leaving her bottle to heat. She was out of sorts because it was already after 6.00pm and she was due to be fed and put down. She was grizzling to herself and half-asleep.

I was saying goodbye to Pakie; Kaelem was beside me and Jake was in front of me looking for my attention.

"Mammy, can I cross over? Mammy, can I cross over to the green just for a few minutes?"

He must have asked two or three times, but I was talking to Pakie, so I didn't answer him.

Chris was the one who answered.

"No Jake, you have to get ready to go to the show."

But I knew that Savannah had to be fed, changed and put to bed first. It had been a lovely day but a busy day, and I wanted to wind down for a few minutes upstairs. I looked at my watch. It was almost 6.25pm.

I thought, if I fed Savannah and got her down, then I'd have ten minutes to myself to get ready, freshen up and even have a glass of wine. Then I could get Jake into his costume and be ready for Pamela who was calling for us around 7.00pm.

"Give him a few minutes Chris, because I have to get Savannah down and get myself ready. You're going to be here anyway, so you can keep an eye on them."

Jake was looking up at me, waiting for me to tell him he could cross the road as Chris traded insults and laughs with Pakie.

He waited for permission. That's the thing; he never darted out on that road. My kids listened to me, and they still do.

I looked to the right, to the corner where cars entered and drove down the road.

I didn't look towards the left, the dead end of the cul-de-sac. There was a blind spot at our front door because the two terraced houses to our left jutted out from our row of houses.

The dead end of the cul-de-sac was so short that I never worried about it anyway. People would pull out of their driveways and hardly get into second gear by the time they reached our house.

I didn't think that you could build up any speed from that distance. Also, the road was wide enough for a driver to see a child and for the children to see a car approach.

The road was clear. The only thing stirring was a slight breeze in the evening sunshine. Everything was quiet apart from the loud banter going on between Chris and Pakie.

I looked down at Jake and smiled.

"Go on, Baby, you can go on over for five more minutes, and I'll get you ready then."

Savannah was starting to cry; Pakie was retreating down the drive to his car and shouting, "Bye, bye, see you later. Bye Kaelem, bye Jakie."

I realised the sun was bothering Savannah; it was right in her eyes, so I stepped under the shade of the small porch at the front door.

It was then that I caught the glint of a car. It came from nowhere, in an instant, a nanosecond. Two tons of moving steel smashed into our lives.

There was the roar of the engine and then the loudest bang. This wasn't the thud of hard metal colliding with soft flesh. This was a bang; the boom of a sledgehammer on metal; a deafening, explosive bang.

The sound sent me reeling back through our front door. As I stumbled back, I squeezed my eyes shut, gripped the door jamb with one hand and screamed Jake's name into the blackness.

I didn't need to look; couldn't bear to see; I knew straight away that I'd heard the sound of our lives being shattered, forever.

10. MAMMY, I DON'T WANT TO DIE

Everything becomes confused and surreal. Voices sound muted, and people seem like a distant blur. In my memory, everything moves in slow motion.

In parts, my recollections are shadowy at best and at other times, I have memories that haunt me in cinematic detail. When I try to tell the story of the horror, I feel like I'm back there; it seems like it's happening all over again.

I have a vivid memory of opening my eyes and seeing a shadow; something falling from the sky. It's so fleeting that I can't be sure of the height, but I know it's Jakie.

There's no mistaking the sound that follows: a thunk, thunk, thunk, the noise of something being churned by car wheels. It's the sound of my baby being tumbled under that car like a rag-doll in the drum of a washing machine.

I have no memory of running through a garden strewn with toys or running past the parked car in the drive. I can only explain that it's like I open my eyes again, and Jake is there.

I'm outside our neighbour's house to our right and Jake is on the road. He's standing, swaying. We're facing each other.

And he comes to me. He's limping, with a strange, twisted gait; a wounded pup. I can see his snow-white pallor even as I run to him.

His legs fold as I reach him; he collapses into me, and I fall to my knees supporting him.

"I'm sorry, Mammy," he says.

He thinks he's in trouble because he's been hit by the car.

"Baby, you're okay; that wasn't your fault. You did nothing wrong; you did nothing wrong."

I'm in a soundproof bubble with Jake. The world around is muffled, and it's just my baby and me inside.

Outside, I catch a glimpse of Christopher. He's running and running towards the end of the street. He's banging on the windows of a moving car with his fists.

"Why didn't you stop?" he screams from very far away. "Why didn't you f**king stop?"

It's all background noise because Jakie and I are in our bubble. I hold him to me; my body is quaking with terror and wracked by sobs.

"You're okay Baby; you're okay; relax Baby, I have you."

My mind is spinning, trying to absorb what's happening; trying to work out what happened.

Jake was on his feet. He must be okay; he stood up. I must be wrong. That couldn't have been Jake in the sky; that rumble from under the car had to be something else.

I talk and try to reassure him; try to be soothing.

"You're okay Baby; you're okay; relax Baby, I have you."

But he can feel me shake and hear me hyperventilate. There's a ball of fear lodged in my throat, threatening to choke me.

Then he says the words that make the blood in my veins run cold.

"Mammy, I don't want to die."

I want to squeeze him to me and never let him go, but I don't know where he's injured; how to hold him.

"Jakie, you're not going to die; Listen to Mammy, I have you now. You're not going to die. You're okay Baby; Mammy has you."

My heart is hammering so fast, and I'm crying so hard that I can't breathe. At least Pakie is beside me now.

"Roseann, he's grand. Calm down; he's grand."

"He's white; he's so white."

There's another man beside me, a neighbour I know to see.

"Take it easy; take it easy; he's in shock, but you're panicking him," he says.

"Mammy?... Mammy?... Mammy?" He's fighting to get up, and he's reaching for me.

"Yes, Jakie, yes Baby, I'm here…he's white, he's so white, please tell me that he's okay."

Faceless people pull me to my feet and pull me away from him.

"You're panicking him; Jake's okay, and he's going to be fine, but you're panicking him."

My legs feel like liquid, and I can't catch my breath. I have to pull myself together. I stagger in circles on the road. I'm trembling, choking with sobs and wheezing with breathlessness.

The wife of the man who is with Jake is in front of me. I know both to see, but I've never talked to them before. She's holding her arms out towards me

"Can I take the baby?" she says.

I look at where she's reaching and realise that I'm still carrying Savannah. She's cradled in my right arm, wide-eyed with the commotion and limbs jerking in protest. She must have been there all along. I hand her our baby.

I pace, back and forward, round and round. I quiver, weep and wring useless hands. I try not to glance at that knot of people, crouching or kneeling on the road, all surrounding Jake. If I can't see it, maybe it's not happening.

There's an older neighbour here now. He says he saw everything through his living room window. He lives on the row of houses that run perpendicular to our road. His living room faces down our cul-de-sac.

He doesn't know my name, but he grips my shoulder, tries to make me focus, tries to make me see what I don't want to see.

"Mammy, it's not good," he says. "Mammy, I don't want to upset you more, but that car went over your little boy. She rolled over your little boy; you need to be with him."

Pakie yells at me: "Rosie, he's looking for you!"

I recognise the fear in Pakie's eyes now, but I compose my face and go to Jake. Breathe Rosie, breathe; don't frighten the child.

"Baby, Mammy's here; Mammy's here."

He's half sitting, half lying, and his brown eyes are like big, dark pools in a grey-white face

My heart shatters into a million shards as he pleads again, "Mammy I don't want to die."

I smile through my tears as if he's being silly.

"You're not going to die Baby; you're not going to die."

His T-shirt has lifted a little, and I'm sickened at the sight. There's a black rubber tyre mark across his grey belly. I can see the pain etched on his face. The stench of faeces reaches my nostrils now too. My poor child is destroyed.

He reaches for me, tries to pull himself into my arms; he wants to be cradled, to be rocked. But strangers' voices are instructing me: "Put him in the recovery position! Put him in the recovery position!"

I want to hold him, grab him to me but maybe I can save him. Maybe I should protect his crushed belly.

"Baby, please lie down; Mammy's here; please lie down for Mammy like a good boy."

He's weak. He lies back, and I lean over him, my weight on one arm on the road, the other cradling his head which had been resting on a rolled-up jacket.

But now I see blood spurting from his mouth; I turn his head to the side, and I look to Pakie in rising terror.

"There's blood; there's blood coming up."

Pakie tries to calm me: "It's alright Roseann, it's his tongue; he's probably bitten his tongue, or hit his teeth."

"No, no, no, it's coming up his throat."

"Mmmy...Mmmy."

Jake's voice is different now; he's struggling to get the words out. It's like his jaw has locked and he's trying to get words through clenched teeth.

"Mammy's here, Mammy's here, Jakie."

I lie in as close to him as I can without putting any weight on him. I'm looking into his eyes; we're almost nose to nose, breath to breath.

"Mammy's here, Baby, you're alright."

But he's not; every breath is laboured; he gazes into my eyes with those big brown eyes.

"I love you, Baby, I love you. The men are coming to fix you; the men are coming. Don't worry Baby; you're going to be okay."

I have no idea why I'm saying, "the men are coming to fix you."

His voice comes in gasps now, and I can just make out what he's saying.

"Daddy?"

I look up and can see Christopher holding onto Kaelem. He has the phone up to his face, which is a picture of crumpled desperation.

"Daddy's right here, Baby; he's with Kaelem, but he's on the phone to the men who are coming to fix you."

Jakie gasps, "I love Daddy."

I'm close to shrieking, but if I start, I'll never stop. I have to hold it together.

"I know you do Baby, and he loves you too," I sob. "He's on the phone to the men coming to fix you."

The Driver, who I could not name even if I wanted to, is hovering.

"I was not speeding," she says.

The Driver, who struck and crushed my baby and kept driving, says it over and over.

"I was not speeding; I was not speeding."

I hear her even in this strange, faraway world where I lie on the road with Jake.

"I was not speeding; I was not speeding."

The older man from the end of the road shouts at her: "You were speeding, and you're always f***ing speeding!"

She's in my ear now, trying to get in our bubble.

"I was not speeding; I was not speeding."

"Go away! GO AWAY!" I scream at her.

She never once asks about my baby. He's lying beneath me, skin translucent white, a crimson stream trickling from his mouth.

I tell Jakie that I love him and that he's going to be okay, over and over and over again. I stroke his cold face and plant tender kisses on his brow.

His gasps are fewer and growing farther apart; his breathing is fading. I place my hand softly on his icy chest and belly, and they're not moving anymore.

Jakie's eyes are open, looking up at me but the light in them is fading.

"Pakie, I don't think he's breathing; he's not breathing," I sob. I'm trying to stifle the screams that are about to explode from deep inside me.

"Baby? Baby? Mammy loves you."

I stare into his eyes, willing life into him with all my being, but even as I stare, his eyes cloud over.

"He's going, Pakie; he's going!"

My face is right up to his. I see his life force drain away, and I see the colour of his eyes fade from dark brown to grey. It happens in seconds.

And then I know. My baby is gone.

I hear the ambulance siren, but I know it's too late. Jakie's face is soaked in a river of tears as I tell him I love him and beg for a sign of life.

"Come back to me Baby; please Baby come back!"

But I know. I know. I saw the life leave those eyes and saw his brown eyes turn to grey.

The paramedic looks so capable, so confident as he swings down from the ambulance cab.

Blind terror grips me, but there's a split second where I dare to hope. This man has a reassuring face. He knows what he's doing.

His face says, 'business as usual', and his business is saving people.

"Jakie's gone, he's gone on me," I weep. "Please, Jakie come back. Here's the man; here's the man who's going to fix you."

Then he looks at Jake for the first time, and I see the shadow pass over his face. His whole bearing changes, the assurance is gone, and his mouth becomes a grim line. I'll never forget that man's face and his expression as long as I live.

My last hope is dashed.

He calls to the other paramedic for this thing and that. He phones for a resuscitation team to be on standby at the Emergency Department of St Luke's.

A man from our road starts doing CPR on Jake as they cut open his clothes. They slice through his navy school tracksuit bottoms and his blue T-shirt with the Presentation school crest.

His socks, grubby from running around the play area in McDonagh Junction just a short time ago, are on the road along with his black and blue runners.

They're working furiously, frantically, but I know. I know it's useless. I saw Jakie's eyes. I saw the paramedic's face.

I get to my feet. I can't watch this anymore. I'm not able to watch. I make it as far as our garden, drop to my knees and clasp my hands and beg. I beg for Jakie's life even though I know he is gone.

"Please don't take him! Please don't take him!"

I pray loudly and with an urgency born of anguish and desperation I've never experienced in my life before:

Hail Mary, full of grace.
The Lord is with thee.
Blessed art thou amongst women,
And blessed is the fruit of thy womb, Jesus.
Holy Mary, Mother of God,
Pray for us sinners,
Now and at the hour of our death.
Amen.

"Please God, don't take my baby; please Daddy, please Daddy, I can't live without him. Please, Daddy, give him back to me. I beg you, Daddy. Please, please, don't do this to me, I can't live without Jakie."

I beg for divine intercession, but all I hear is a jeering voice in my head; a cold and evil voice that's taunting me.

He's gone, you stupid, f**king woman. You saw your own child's eyes; you know he's f**king gone; you've seen him go.

I know it's true, Jakie's gone, but I can't believe any of this is really happening. It can't be happening.

An eerie calm comes over me, and the tears stop. Everything is just fine because this is not happening.

I get to my feet and walk into my kitchen. My eye settles on the pointed blade of the bread knife lying the kitchen counter.

It's all like a strange dream. My mind tells me that I can't feel more pain anyway. I can end it all in an instant with that knife. I'm drawn to the blade, hypnotised by it. The knife offers an escape...

"I'm sorry; I'm coming to see if you're okay...?"

The voice startles me; the trance is broken.

It belongs to a woman who lives two doors down; another kind stranger who I've only waved to in the past.

In a split second, the calmness disappears. Terror rises to the surface, and I break down again.

"He's dead, isn't he? He's dead!" I weep.

"No, no, he's not, they're working on him now!" she says.

And I'm back on my knees again, begging God, begging Daddy, begging the universe. How can they hear me begging and see Jake and yet choose to do nothing?

"Daddy, don't do this to me again; I can't take this, I can't take this."

Cries of anguish reach us from the road outside. Scrambling to my feet, I run out and see my sisters and family have arrived on the scene.

"What's wrong?" I cry, looking around like a fool. "What's wrong?"

Like I don't know what's wrong. Like I don't know that my child is lying dead on the street.

Someone says they have a pulse. There's activity now, and the tight knot of people around Jake starts to unwind.

They're taking him to the hospital. People line the street and speak in hushed voices like they're afraid they'll wake our baby. The paramedics bear his lifeless form into the cavernous space in the back of the ambulance.

I pace forward and back, forward and back. I can't get in there with him. Christopher is in the ambulance by his side, holding Jakie's hand, talking to him, tending to him, doing everything I know I should be doing but I'm not able anymore.

I can't bear to see my lifeless baby. I don't know why, but I can't. My heart can't take it. I can't take it anymore. There's a wild animal clawing my stomach, chest and throat. I feel I'll black out from the pain.

Faceless people help me into the front seat beside the ambulance driver. Sirens wailing, we leave the estate.

A garda motorcycle outrider clears the way ahead. I draw my trembling legs to me, wrap my arms around them, and I rock. I rock and rock and rock myself in the seat.

I mumble into my knees: "My poor baby's dead, my poor baby's dead, my poor baby's dead."

"It's not looking good," the ambulance driver says.

I don't respond. I know my baby is dead. No one is listening to me, but I saw my baby die. I can hear Chris crying and pleading in the back of the ambulance.

"Come on, Daddy's little man. Come on Daddy's little man. Come on my Jakie."

That evil voice is back in my head again. It threatens to come out through my mouth.

Jakie's f**king dead; for f**k's sake I saw him f**king die. Why the f**k doesn't anyone listen to me?

But I don't let the evil voice speak out loud. I saw Jake die. Chris didn't. Chris needs to realise himself that Jake is dead. I can't tell him.

With a garda outrider, we must be moving at speed towards St Luke's Hospital. In my mind, the world is still moving in slow motion.

We pass the entrance of Newpark Close where many of my family live. I look, and I see everyone standing there. I remember each of their faces frozen in worry; captured forever like in a flash photo.

It feels like I've detached from myself. My mind has removed itself from that body that can't take any more. I survey all around me including myself rocking, rocking, rocking.

We pull into the ambulance bay, and Jake is whisked away in a flurry of white coats. Our baby disappears behind locked doors, and nurses steer Chris and me into the family room. People pour into the room within minutes.

I don't feel detached anymore. I need to get sick. The dinner I'd eaten a lifetime ago is choking me. I'm heaving, but I can't get sick.

I repeat a mad mantra.

"I need to get sick. I need to get sick. My baby's dead. My baby's dead."

Well-meaning people with soothing voices try to tell me Jake's not dead.

"You don't know that he's dead; the doctors are working on him."

"I F**KING KNOW MY BABY'S DEAD!"

Now the evil voice in my head is coming out of my mouth.

"I saw my baby die! I saw the life go out of his eyes; my baby's dead! Why won't anyone f**king listen to me?"

Anger rages in me.

Why would God do this to a baby? Why isn't Daddy helping to save him?

"F**k you all up there. What did I do? What did my baby do? What did I do in this stupid world to deserve this? F**k you all up there. You f**king let him die, and you did nothing to help him!"

People are staring at me in my madness, but I'm beyond caring.

"F**K YOU ALL!" I shriek.

More and more people arrive. There are too many in the room, and I need air. I go outside; pacing up and down. People try to hug me, hold me, but I want no one near. I push them off me. I walk up and down, up and down, head racing, heart breaking.

Christopher's mother and father arrive. My brother is here now. More tears, more wails. I look around, and I see grown men falling to their knees.

This is real. This is f**king real!

Anxious faces say that the doctors are looking to speak to Chris and me. We're brought to meet the doctors in the resuscitation area.

I'm resigned. I know what they are going to say. I don't need to see the grave expressions, the solemn shakes of the head, the sympathetic looks.

I look beyond them where I see my baby lying. He's laid out cold and naked. Medical staff are still moving around him, but he has no blanket, no boxer shorts. Jakie would hate that. I'm standing there staring at my dead baby with no clothes on.

"So sorry to have to tell you this… we tried… adrenaline…severe internal injuries… nothing we can do…"

Chris cries torrents of tears, but I am stony-faced. I want to scream at them.

How dare you leave my baby lying there naked?

I walk out instead.

When I return, Jakie has a sheet pulled over him, and only his perfect, six-year-old alabaster face and shoulders are exposed.

"Where's Samantha?" I ask, addressing no one and everyone.

I've seen Pamela, Angela, Mary and Catherine…I've seen everyone except Samantha.

"Did anyone tell her? Samantha has to know."

Hands shaking, I take a phone and call her.

"Samantha?"

My voice breaks. She's still living in that lovely, normal world where we lived an hour ago. A world where Jakie is alive.

"What's wrong, Rosie?"

"Samantha, Jakie's dead on us… Jakie's dead on us."

"Rosie, no, no! What are you saying?"

It feels too real to say it aloud. Jakie's dead. Jakie's dead on us. I haven't the strength to say more. I pass the phone to someone else.

I can't take it; I have to leave again. The pain is so intense, so agonising that I could die myself. I want to die to end this torment. I can't stand it anymore.

I return when they move Jake into the family room. The hospital says that Chris and I need some time alone with him, and they try to clear the space, but I stop them. Jakie loved his big, mad, extended family. He'd want everyone here.

Chris's sister Alison arrives wild-eyed and not believing what she's heard. She sees Jakie laid out in front of her and she passes out.

I take one of Jakie's hands in mine and notice that his nails look dirty. Odd things float through my head. They were clean this morning. I wonder if the dirt in his nails is standing out because his hands are so white now.

Then I wonder if I am the worst mother ever. He has dirty nails, and he is lying dead in front of me. What have I done? I was meant to look after him and look at him; he's lying dead in front of me.

"I'm so sorry Baby; so, so, sorry," I tell him. "I love you Jakie. I shouldn't have let you cross that road. What did I do to you, Baby? What did I do?"

A nurse wraps her arms around me, and I bury my wet face in her.

"You did nothing," she says. "That child was well loved and well cared for. Look at all the people who are here for him. They all love him. You did nothing wrong."

It makes no sense to me. If I did nothing wrong, why was he taken? I did everything right. I tried to do everything right. Nothing makes sense anymore.

I have no idea of time. But the hospital says it's time to move our baby. They explain slowly and carefully that Jake will have to have a post-mortem or autopsy. They say it's necessary in all cases where there is sudden death.

They say they will take Jakie to the mortuary in this hospital first, and then to University Hospital Waterford for the autopsy. Christopher objects. He doesn't want them to take him away. He doesn't want to leave him. I become the logical one.

"Chris, love, they have to take him," I say. "We don't need to leave him yet. We'll follow him to the mortuary."

I walk so calmly out of St Luke's with Chris. It astounds me that I can be so calm. We could be going out for a stroll on a lovely summer's evening instead of following our baby's body to a morgue.

We walk the long, winding path down to the hospital mortuary and they bring us to Jake again. I see a garda waiting; writing in his notebook. Chris is asked to formally identify Jake.

Chris has Jake's little socks in his hands; he picked them up off the road at some stage, and we each hold one. I sing Jake's song to him over and over, over and over, and stroke his face the way he likes it.

Hush Little Jakie, Don't You Cry.
Mammy's going to buy you a lullaby,
And if that lullaby don't sing,
Mammy's gonna buy you a diamond ring
If that diamond ring don't shine.
Mammy's going to buy you whatever you want.
Hush little Jakie, you're Mammy's Little Man
Hush little Jakie, you're Mammy's Little Man
Hush hush Jakie go to sleep.
Hush hush Jakie go to sleep.

The undertakers arrive. They tell us quietly that they're here to bring our little Jakie to Waterford.

I tremble with the horror if it. I can't bear to think of our baby spending a night alone in a cold morgue or think of them slicing open his little body.

Chris and I are asked to wait outside. We mutely watch as they emerge carrying an adult-sized brown coffin, one that they have stored in the morgue, and slide it into the hearse.

Then we gaze at that hearse as it slowly winds its way from the hospital carrying away our first-born child.

How can this be possible?

A few hours ago, our baby laughed and danced and sang and said this day was the best day of his life. Now he's lying in a brown coffin.

A few hours ago, we were a normal, happy couple. Now we're ghosts with red-rimmed eyes staring at strangers who are carrying away our dead child.

We stand in silence, watching until we can no longer see the hearse. We hardly know what's happening except that our baby is gone, and that life as we know it, is gone forever too.

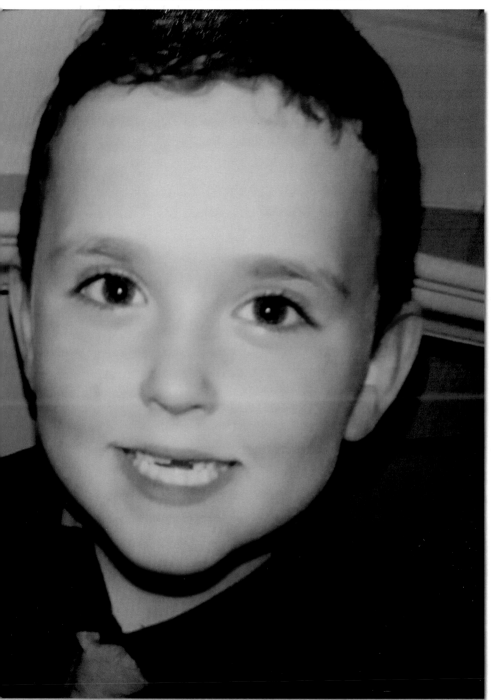

Jake at a family communion just a month before he died.

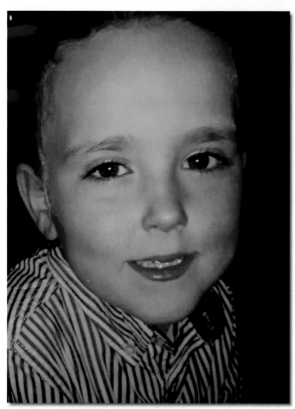

Jake at his 6th birthday – the last that he celebrated with us.

Jake rehearsing for a role in a show and Kaelem copying him in 2014.

BROTHERLY LOVE

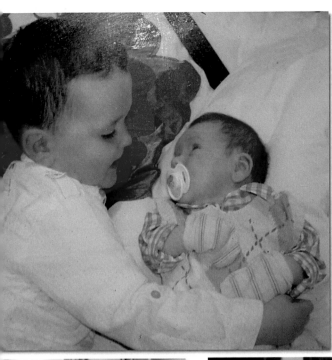

Jake dotes on his new-born brother, and Kaelem gazes back in adoration.

Jake & Kaelem loving their matching outfits for a family confirmation in 2014.

Christmas 2013: The boys on their couch, under their blankie, for the Late Late Toy Show.

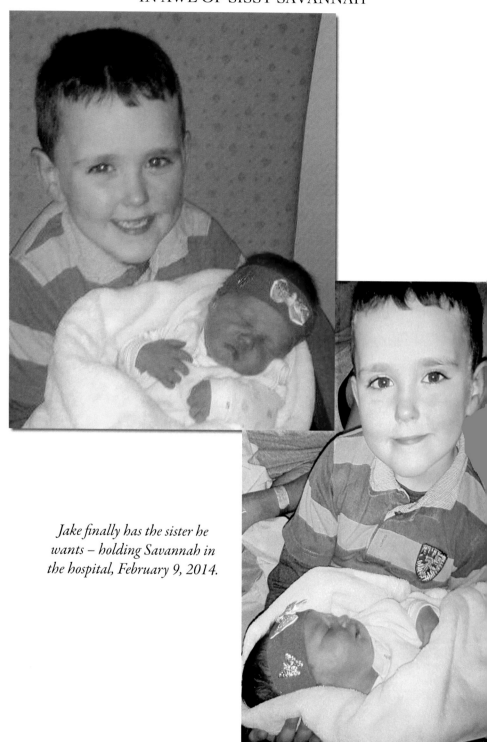

Jake finally has the sister he wants – holding Savannah in the hospital, February 9, 2014.

Jake mesmerised by Savannah on my knee.

Jake so proud after Savannah falls asleep in his arms.

BABY JAKIE

Jake adorable in vintage style – taken at a photographer's studio.

Jake in his christening gown.

Jake busy going places and crawling at three months.

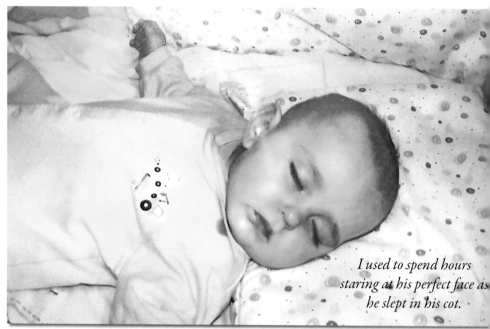

I used to spend hours staring at his perfect face as he slept in his cot.

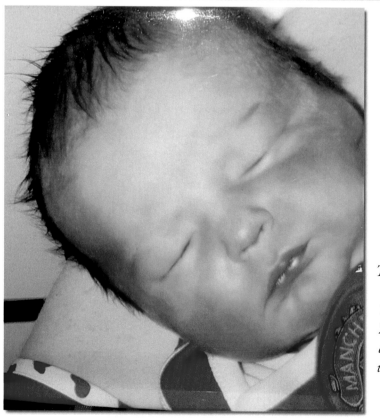

Taken the morning after Jake's birth, Thursday, April 3 2008, wearing his dad's team colours with a Manchester United babygro.

JAKE THE PERFORMER

Jake poses in his costume for his Jester's stage show in 2013.

TOP: Jake loves it as he's carried by his Aunty Mary (Hayes), cousin Donna (Doyle), Mammy & Aunty Maggie (Dempsey).

ABOVE: Jake and Kaelem strut their stuff on the dance floor at a family night in The Brog Maker.

*Jake on his
'adventures': ready
for a bear hunt in
The Discovery Park
in Castlecomer.*

*Jake in his last St Patrick's
Day Parade in Kilkenny
marching with Newpark
Resource Centre.*

JAKE'S FAMILY

I loved how Jake lay into me for a cuddle at every opportunity – in our kitchen in Lintown before a day out in 2014.

Christmas 2013: Chris, Jake, Kaelem and me while expecting Savannah at Santa's grotto in Rancho Reilly in Carlow.

TOP: Proud dad, Chris, with Jake, Kaelem and newborn Savannah in our Lintown home.

BOTTOM: Perfect three: Jake with Kaelem & little sissy Savannah – one of the few photos that we have of all our three children together.

Our last ever family photo: Dublin Zoo June 8, 2014.
Jake died four days later.

Jakie and I share a cuddle and a smile before I leave for my mam's birthday in June 2013.

All dressed up for a niece's confirmation, March 2014: Jakie and the women in his life - Mammy and Savannah.

*All we have left now - Savannah at Jakie's grave beside
Easter roses from Jakie's Crew.*

11. DENIAL AND FURY

The light was fading when we arrived back at Lintown Grove, and the gardaí had taped off much of the road to carry out forensics.

We spotted Jakie's blue and green little runners, the ones he'd been dancing around in hours earlier, carefully placed on our kitchen windowsill.

I recall going up to Jakie's bedroom, putting my head on his pillow, looking around.

This isn't true; this can't be true; this can't be happening.

I looked in disbelief at the Manchester United flag on his wall, his books, his toys, his little white teddy Ruby. It felt like the horror of the last few hours must have happened to somebody else.

I lay on my child's bed in cold shock. It was too outlandish, too horrific, too impossible to be true. Then it hit me.

Jakie's dead; it did happen. This is real. This is f**king real. Jakie's gone, and I can never hold him again.

I was like a wild animal then. I roared and screamed, shrieked and cried.

"Why me? What the f**k did I do wrong? Why Jakie? What the f**k did that perfect baby ever do to anyone?"

I screamed this over and over until I was exhausted. After, I sat there staring at a point in the distance in numb shock.

Then it was like everything began to build up again. My energy, my tear ducts and my rage levels filled to bursting point. My heart started beating faster, as it came to me that I would never hold him again. I roared and screamed and shrieked, and the cycle began all over again.

Different people came into his room to us, and I pleaded with them to tell me it wasn't true; to tell me that he was coming back. Everyone looked at me with bloodshot eyes, but no one could say the words I wanted to hear.

I didn't know what pain was before this. This was intense, crushing and sickening physical agony. We both drowned in that ocean of pain for months and months afterwards.

Even years later, it can still hit at any time - a wave of grief that can send me to my knees. The longing to hold Jakie yet knowing that I can never have him in my arms again is an agony that never seems to fade.

I was confused, very confused at times. Even though I'm doing my best to describe things as I remember them, my recollection of every detail may not always be accurate.

Even in the black fog of that evening, I remember the gardaí arriving to ask for Jake's socks, of all things. Christopher got so upset about that. The little white sock with a navy stripe was the only thing he had from Jake of that day.

Christopher was: "No, no, no they're not getting them."

I handed over the one that I'd been holding on to and persuaded him to let go of his. What difference did it make anymore?

I took out Jakie's zip-up school jacket for Chris while I clutched Ruby, Jake's favourite teddy.

The scruffy white teddy was Jakie's favourite possession. A Christmas present from our friend and neighbour, Emma Flood, this bear with its floppy Santa hat, went to bed with Jake every night.

Jake also slept with a blankie that had a teddy head called Bella. To us, Bella looked like a girl bear with her little blankie hanging from her like a dress. But Jake was adamant that Bella was a boy.

His white teddy was chunky and manly like a boy, but Jake insisted it was a girl and called her Ruby. Bella and Ruby got 'married' around the time of our wedding. But Jake was most indignant when we got the sexes mixed up and referred to Bella as 'she' or Ruby as 'he'.

Remember how mad you'd get every time we got it wrong, Jakie?

The house was full of people. Both our families were there, but I can still see my nephew Bocky, who's in heaven now, in the kitchen that night. He was our rock at Jake's funeral, and he was the first to volunteer when we started campaigning.

Yet, he died only two years after Jakie and just eight months after being diagnosed with cancer. He was 26 years-old, and his three small children lost their adoring dad.

At one stage that night I sat at the kitchen table, staring out the back garden at the trampoline and Jake's toys. I was exhausted, cried out but still shaking. I never knew you could shake so much.

The tortuous, endless cycle of 'if only' swirled through my mind.

If only I'd been able to open that door…if only Jake was in the back garden…if only I hadn't let him cross the road…if only…

In the beginning, my mood veered from denying that Jakie was dead to raging because he was dead.

I remember ranting about the back door of the house that night.

"What the f**k's wrong with it? It wouldn't open for me. It wouldn't open! I would have just let them out the back! Jake would still be alive, but that f**king door wouldn't open."

Anytime I went quiet, well-meaning people would ask the question: "Are you okay?"

*Am I okay? How the f**k can they ask me that? How could anything be okay ever again?*

A red mist built up inside me until one person too many asked me if I was okay. I picked up a vase on our table, and I hurled it across the kitchen at the wall. It hit the wall and bounced back, chipped the table and then shattered in every direction.

"How the f**k could I be okay?" I screamed.

I was raging. I was furious with God, with the house, with the road, with The Driver whose car smashed my child, but mostly with myself.

*This f**king stupid house. I picked this house. I did it. I killed Jakie.*

I wanted to smash the whole house. I could have gone on smashing all night. I hated that house, the house that I'd brought Jakie to. They had to hold me to stop me breaking up everything around me.

I wanted to smash and smash. But everyone was breaking down in pieces around me, and I was terrifying people with my fury. I had to stop.

I kept thinking how I had let him cross that road. I could have made him come in. I could have put him out the back garden. Guilt ate away at me, relentlessly torturing me.

I thought about him lying out there on the road. I thought about when I'd left him; when they told me that Jake was only in shock; when they said that I was making him worse.

I left him.

I felt guilty for stepping away. I was tortured because I hadn't cradled him in my arms; that I made him lie down; that I hadn't held him the way he wanted to be held when he was dying. By not holding him in my arms, I denied him the last little thing he ever wanted.

I agonised over all the things I should have, could have, would have done if I had the time all over again.

During the following days, and weeks and months, Kaelem and Savannah were the only reasons to get up in the morning, the only reasons to keep living.

The daily routines and the demands of caring for the kids stopped me going completely insane in the months after Jakie died. In the immediate days after Jakie went to heaven though, there was chaos, and all family routine disappeared.

Kaelem still didn't know anything in the first few days except that Jakie had gone to hospital. Darren and Pamela took him to their house for a 'sleepover' with their child, Rhys.

It was difficult to think straight, but I reassured myself: "Kaelem is with Rhys, he's okay."

I remember asking the sea of faces in our kitchen: "Where's Savannah?" They assured me she was safe in the arms and in the home of other relatives.

"No, no, Savannah has to come back here," I insisted. "No one knows her ways. She wakes during the night, she gets upset, and you have to carry her a certain way. Bring Savannah back."

I had to have Savannah in the house with us. With the help of my cousin and good friend, Edel Bolger, Savannah stayed at home during the days after Jakie's death. Samantha, Pamela, Catherine and I put her into her own bed at night.

All through that first terrible night, I rocked, screamed and cried. My sisters Catherine and Pamela, my friends Nicola Dunne and Samantha McCullagh, her partner James Hurley, and Chris's brother Eddie all camped with Chris and me in the sitting room the night Jake died.

We didn't know it then, but it was to become the first night of many, many black nights that we all spent there.

Our bedroom faced out on the road where Jakie died, and after dark, I couldn't face going in there. I couldn't face going upstairs at all at night.

I couldn't sleep, and I couldn't be on my own. All I could think of was our Jakie, lying alone in that cold, dark mortuary many miles away. Sometimes I'd doze with exhaustion, but then I'd wake with a jolt and scream his name.

My heart pounded, and my stomach twisted as the horrors of the day replayed over and over again in my head.

Mammy, I don't want to die...

Mick Kavanagh, one of the paramedics who had tended to Jake, was among the constant stream of callers to the house the next day.

I asked him that day, and I asked him again at the inquest if he believed that there was ever any hope for my child. He said he thought Jakie was gone by the time they arrived.

We have to do our jobs and get a pulse. We managed to get a faint pulse going, and we brought him to the hospital.

Jake's teachers, Miss White and Miss Millea, and his school principal, Miss Kelly came to the house that day. Jake always referred to them as 'Miss' though I don't think they were. I hadn't slept or eaten, and my behaviour was manic and erratic. I could see it in people's eyes; they were afraid for me.

Miss Kelly explained that it was a big school but by coincidence, Jake had grabbed her attention a few hours before he died. She explained that the infant classes had a lesson on musical instruments on his last day at school.

The teachers noticed Jake because he was mesmerised by the trumpet playing. Lost in the music, he closed his eyes and started playing his own imaginary trumpet.

"We all nudged each other and watched him wrapped up in his own world," she said.

She knew instantly who Jake was when Miss White and Miss Millea told her he was "the little lad, who played the trumpet." Jake never mentioned a word of his trumpet-playing antics to me that day.

Jake's distraught drama teacher, Kevin, from Jesters, called to us that Friday too. He said they were near the end of the show the night when he heard about Jake's death. They held the show in his memory the next night and held a minute's silence to mark his passing.

We got so much help and support from our neighbours on Lintown Grove and from people all over Kilkenny during those awful days. People delivered a constant supply of hot meals and sandwiches to the house, and everyone held their arms out to mind the kids.

Chris and I were all over the place, so Pamela and Catherine liaised with the local undertakers from Johnston's Funeral home. They told us that Jakie's body would come home that Friday night.

The funeral director Sammy Johnston organised the notices for the papers and local radio. We wanted Jakie buried with Daddy in St Kieran's Cemetery.

I wandered outside the house at times trying to make sense of what was happening. It still didn't feel real. It felt like I was trapped in some nightmare and that if I could only wake up, it would all be over.

The sun was still shining, the birds were singing, and the traffic was still moving on Johnswell Road. These things couldn't be happening if Jakie was dead.

More and more flowers were left outside the house. Kind people pulled up in cars, and kids stopped on bikes to leave floral tributes, cards and notes of condolence.

At one stage, I spotted a press photographer taking photos through the railings between our cul-de-sac and the busy Johnswell Road. The man was already backing away as I approached him. I think he thought I was going to attack him about photographing the house.

The truth was I could only think about Jakie, and I appreciated any interest in him.

"I'd like to be able to tell Jake's story and say what happened," I said to him.

"I only take photos," he explained. "But if you give me a number, I'll get a reporter to speak to you."

The next thing my phone started ringing. I started talking about Jake and how he died less than 15 metres from his front door with his daddy, his uncle and me standing there.

I said we let him cross a quiet cul-de-sac and now he was dead. If it could happen here, it could happen anywhere. I minded my child, and yet he was dead. I was just thinking out loud to the newspapers.

I had full conversations with members of the media in the run-up to the funeral, but I had no memory of it afterwards. I wanted to talk to anyone who wanted to talk about Jake.

I couldn't bear to eat anything. I had diarrhoea from a sick stomach, and even a sip of water made me retch and heave. My senses were heightened especially my sense of smell. Even the slight smell of perfume made my stomach churn.

People were hugging me, and I could barely stand it. Poor Christopher was getting sick too and couldn't hold down anything.

People kept advising me to take pills to calm me or to make me sleep. But I didn't want to take anything because I wanted to try and remember everything about Jakie's final days with us.

At the same time, everyone was trying to grasp what had happened outside our house. I couldn't tell people. I didn't see Jake being hit; I only saw his form falling in the sky.

The first thing Christopher knew about the accident was the sound of my scream. He saw Jakie in the air, and he saw him coming out under the back of the car. Pakie only heard the bang and my scream. He saw me run towards Jakie standing on the road.

The gardaí arrived at Pakie's door for a statement within a few hours of Jakie's death. He and my sister, Angela, were exhausted and still in shock.

"You do know the child is my nephew, don't you?" he asked them.

The gardaí turned up at our door the next day to interview Chris and me. They took me into one of the rooms to give my statement and took Chris into the kitchen.

We learnt they made an appointment to interview The Driver who crushed our child. She gave her statement 24 hours after she drove her car into our baby with her solicitor beside her.

I couldn't tell you The Driver's real name. I don't know it. It's a Polish language name, and I've never learnt it. I don't want to know it. I think I've mentally blocked that name from my mind.

We only knew her to see before she smashed her way into our family on June 12, 2014.

Most people on Lintown Grove acknowledged each other with a smile and a wave even if we didn't know each other. But we had never waved or exchanged a greeting with The Driver.

She got in and out of her car, a 2000 Opel Zafira, and drove up and down the road without a wave or a smile.

We had an insignificant encounter shortly after we moved into the estate. I had to flag her, wave at her to warn her that the children were trying out new skateboards on the path. I was afraid she'd turn in suddenly to her driveway and hit one of them.

I smiled at her. She glowered in response.

She lived five doors down from us. Numerically she lived seven doors down, but the two houses next to us were duplex homes. She lived only a few metres past us in the dead end of our cul-de-sac.

I don't know anything about her because we never, ever spoke with her before or after that day.

Complete strangers sent us Mass cards and flowers. The Driver, who drove the car that killed our baby never sent so much as a condolence card. She never contacted us at all, ever.

12. BABY'S FINAL REST

It sounds strange, but I felt happy that Jakie was coming home even if it was in a coffin. I was a much older, frailer woman than the woman I'd been the day before, but my heart lifted when I heard he was on his way back to us, where he should be.

I got a brief burst of energy and told everyone that we had to get the living room organised for him. I got out the brush to scrub the mat and to get the room clean.

I got Savannah ready for bed and even cut her nails in the hour before Jakie came home. I was coming in and out of reality at that stage; both Chris and I were still in complete shock.

My sisters used Jake's imminent return as an excuse to persuade me to wash and freshen up. By now, I couldn't be on my own for an instant, and they had to come into the bathroom with me while I was in the shower.

My weight was a constant 9 stone 13 lbs, but they weighed me that evening, and I'd already shed 8 lbs from the stress of the previous 24 hours.

I remember the women sobbing, and the men standing in stony silence as the undertakers carried the little white coffin into the house. They set Jakie up in the living room and called us in when they were ready.

I stared at his ghostly face and thought he looked older. Ice-cold and older. He didn't look like our baby-faced, sweet little Jakie anymore.

He wore the outfit that he was meant to wear for Savannah's christening. It looked like a smart, black blazer and white shirt but was a one-piece which he wore over black short trousers.

He looked so cold and lonely in that coffin that I got his 'blankie' for him. It was a blue blanket that Chris's mother gave him for his christening, and I tucked it up to his cheek, the way he always liked it.

He brought his blankie to bed with him every night, and he took it down with him for his eternal rest.

I was torn over his teddies, Ruby and Bella. I knew it was our baby's final sleep, but they both reminded me of him, and both even smelled of him so that I couldn't bear to part with them.

I held on to Ruby, and I kept Bella for Kaelem to have someday. Kaelem had an identical blankie which he called Bella too, so that went down in Jake's coffin instead.

They started reciting the rosary soon after Jakie arrived home. I stood by the coffin, but more and more people crowded into the room.

It felt like the voices around me were getting louder and louder and that people were closing in on me. I thought I was smothering. I never experienced a panic attack in my life before, so I didn't know what was happening at the time.

My sisters said my eyes suddenly rolled into the back of my head and I passed out, falling into the couch behind me.

Chris and I sat with our baby all that night and the next day, Saturday. We didn't let children in the room, so the adults came in to put their photos, drawings, letters and mementoes into the coffin.

Children were an integral part of the funeral, but I wanted his friends and his cousins to remember Jakie as he was - all dimples and smiles.

In the hours before the funeral, Chris took off his wedding ring and placed it on his baby's wedding finger. It wasn't something that we talked about or planned.

"You've made me so happy, Little Man. I'm so proud to be able to call you mine," he told him between the tears. "You brought Mammy and me together, and I promise that we'll stay together. But you better take this ring with you because you're married to your Mammy too."

Chris even caved in and let Jakie win their lifelong 'MY Mammy' fight.

"Okay, Little Man, you were right. She's your Mammy, not mine," he conceded.

It almost made us laugh.

I took off my ring too and put it into Jakie's hand.

"You're only holding on to this ring until we're together again, Jakie, and then you have to give it back to me," I told him.

Chris used to say that Jake was the rock who kept us together. When Chris and I fought, we really fought. But Jake always brought us back as a couple because our baby was never happier than when we were all together.

Jake had a way of bringing our focus back to the most precious thing in our lives, family.

People remarked how close Chris and I were during those early days. We clung to each other throughout, and I felt so safe when he was there beside me. Once I had a grip of his arm, I didn't shake so much, and my legs didn't wobble so badly.

We needed each other so much then. So, it was all the more shocking when we found our marriage falling apart in the weeks after.

Our parish priest Fr. Frank Purcell, who married us and christened Jake, was to be the chief celebrant at Jakie's funeral. He led the rosary on Saturday night, the night before the funeral. I vowed, for Jake's sake, that I was going to be mindful and present for this rosary.

Carrying a photo of Jakie in my hands, I stared into his lovely brown eyes. Christopher was beside me the whole time, his arm around me.

Afterwards, Fr. Purcell took hold of my hands to talk about Jakie's funeral. The Mass of the Angels was to take place in St John the Evangelist Church at 2.00pm the next day.

"Remember, while you're in that church tomorrow, it's your chance to give your child the send-off he deserves," he advised. "Whatever you want to be said about your little boy, tomorrow is the time to say it. I know this is very hard but do your crying afterwards. Do your little boy proud tomorrow."

It was the best advice I could have got. I was drifting and confused until then. For the first time in days, I started to focus and get organised. Rosie the planner emerged.

That night and the morning of the funeral, I came to life. Everyone was happy to row in behind me once they saw this new light in me.

"The priest said we only get one chance to get this right, so we're going to get this right," I said. "Pamela, Angela, you'll get up and talk about Jakie. You'll be well able, won't you? We have to make Jakie proud."

They agreed to write a eulogy, and they went outside on the patio to write it up.

I started organising who was carrying the coffin during each stage of Jakie's final journey. I compiled a list of pallbearers and arranged substitutes to take over from Chris in case he wasn't able.

We sat down to select music for the church and the graveyard. Fr Purcell appreciated that it was a child's funeral so rather than traditional hymns, he let us choose songs that Jakie loved.

Someone gave me a recording of the song, Dancing in the Sky by Dani and Lizzy. I broke down when I heard the lyrics. I tortured myself listening to them over and over again:

> *Tell me, what does it look like in heaven?*
> *Is it peaceful? Is it free like they say?*
> *Does the sun shine bright forever?*
> *Have your fears and your pain gone away?*
> *Cause on earth it feels like everything good is missing since you left*
> *And here on earth everything's different; there's an emptiness*
> *I hope you're dancing in the sky*
> *I hope you're singing in the angel's choir*
> *I hope the angels know what they have*
> *I'll bet it's so nice up in heaven since you arrived.*

As the Newpark Family Resource Centre was a big part of Jakie's life, I asked the manager, Sheila Donnelly, to arrange a guard of honour.

Jakie loved the place. He attended preschool there from the time he was two-years-old before joining the homework club which he enjoyed until he died.

I decided I wanted an army presence at the funeral in memory of Daddy. Two members of the Irish army requested permission to lead the cortege from the house in their service dress uniforms. One of them was my friend Yvonne's partner, Adrian, who recruited one of his friends and colleagues.

On the morning of the funeral, I remembered how Jake loved the bagpipes at our wedding. I sent people running off in all directions looking for someone to play them at his funeral.

A kind soldier at the barracks promised that when we got to the church gate that there would be bagpipes there.

At the last minute, I also decided I wanted balloons, red and blue ones, for the grave.

When Jake was about three, he asked: "Mammy, what's my favourite colour?"

"I'd say it's either red or blue."

He couldn't decide.

"Mammy, I think it's red AND blue."

"Okay, there's nothing wrong with having two favourite colours."

"What are your favourite colours, Mammy?"

"You know what, I think they're red AND blue too!"

From then on, red and blue became 'our' favourite colours.

"I don't care where we get balloons from; I'll pay anything!" I said.

The man who delivered the balloons in Woodies was off on Sunday, but he came in especially that day.

Everything at the funeral had some special meaning for us. After his teachers told me about Jake playing the trumpet the day he died, I wanted trumpets too.

Everyone was phoning everywhere to find someone who could play.

The principal of Jake's school, Marie Kelly, found two young girl musicians who played the trumpet. When they asked what I'd like them to play, I replied: When the Saints Go Marching In.

It was a total coincidence, but they also played Daddy's favourite song Down by the Salley Gardens that day, and it made me cry even more.

That Sunday morning, I also had everyone ringing around looking for two doves. The doves we released outside the church on our wedding day enchanted Jakie, and I wanted to have them again for him.

No one could seem to find doves on short notice. My brother Michael, known as Yapper, explained: "Roseann, they're not really doves. They're always white pigeons which fly home again after they're released."

He managed to collect two from a fancier that morning. He got pretty baskets to carry the birds to the church, and he even decorated the baskets in red and blue ribbons.

I made sure to give Pamela money to pay everyone, but I know that many people were very kind and insisted on providing their time or services for nothing.

The cortege left Lintown Grove in plenty of time to get to the 2.00pm mass at St John the Evangelist Church.

The two members of the Irish Army led the cortege with the trumpet players following. Around 14 people from the Homework Club formed the guard of honour on each side of the hearse. We all assembled behind, and we walked the one-kilometre distance to the church.

Gardaí closed the route to traffic, and the crowds got bigger and bigger as the procession made its way.

I concentrated on Jake's coffin, on holding on to Chris and keeping myself together.

Chris was almost bent over with the weight of his grief. The devastation of Jake's loss was written across his face, and he cried a torrent of tears that day. Burying his firstborn child broke his heart and the fact that Jakie's funeral took place on Father's Day made it even more emotional for him.

When we got to Mammy's house, two army men who were friends of Dad stood outside and saluted as the coffin went past. That really stood out to me. I was so proud for Jakie's sake.

Look Jakie, look at all these people and what they're doing for you. Even the Irish army is saluting you!

It was so hot and sunny that day. As the girls played the air of When the Saints Come Marching In, onlookers might have thought it was a festival rather than a funeral.

I couldn't stop thinking how Jake would have loved walking alongside us on this glorious sunshine day. And I thought of all the plans Jake and I made for his summer holidays.

Angela was due to take maternity leave shortly, and she and her kids were to go out with us all summer. We'd planned all these 'Funday Fridays' together, and Kilkenny Castle was one of the first outings on the agenda.

I couldn't understand how all our plans and our dreams could be gone forever.

Two of my girlfriends, Adriana Cahill and Kristen Campion, took turns wheeling Kaelem to the church in his buggy. He didn't understand what was going on, but I wanted him to be part of the day.

He'll remember parts of it, and I want to explain it all to him in time. He sometimes mentions "the big party" when he's talking about Jake. That's what it must have seemed like for him with the music, the balloons and the sunshine.

And that's fine. I don't want Kaelem to have the same hang-ups that I had after my dad died. I don't want Jake to disappear like my dad, so we talk about him all the time. He knows that Jake's gone to heaven but that he's still an integral part of our family.

My friend, Nicola Dunne, helped organise the music, so Jake entered the church to the sound of one of 'our songs', Moves Like Jagger.

Fr. Purcell reminded the congregation that Jakie had been baptised in the same church on September 6, 2008, at 5.00pm. He said Chris and I had sat in the very same seat in which we were sitting that day.

I loved how during the homily, he compared Jakie to our baby's favourite flower, a rose.

"In the most beautiful gardens, there is an occasional rose that buds but never opens," he said.

"In the same way, a child born beautiful, precious and unique but fails to come into its rightful growth and blossom. That child is gathered back into God's heavenly garden where all is made perfect and all mysteries explained."

He admitted that even if we had all the answers to all the questions, there would still be no adequate explanation for Jake's loss.

"It is so tragic, so painful," he said. "There is not a lot we can say to help you, Rosie and Chris."

He said Jakie's death was so tragic and devastating that some people might say the wrong things - such as "It was God's will."

"That's nonsense, don't ever believe it," he said.

However, he said that people who said this were "well-meaning" and just did not know what to say.

We felt that it was important to remember that it was a child's funeral, so we encouraged any of the children who wanted to recite poems or sing songs on the altar.

The Presentation School Choir from Jake's school performed throughout. People were so good, and everyone wanted to help.

During the offertory procession, many of Jakie's most precious possessions were brought to the altar. Kevin from Jesters brought up the costume that Jake was meant to wear on stage the night he died.

Granddad Brennan brought up golf balls because from a baby Jakie would go in under his stairs, take out a bucket of golf balls, spill them out and collect them all up again.

"They're my golf balls aren't they, granddad?" he'd say.

I brought up Ruby the bear and Pamela, who narrated the procession, said the teddy had been with Jakie "since the start". She told the congregation that I was under strict orders to pack Ruby for all family holidays and sleep-overs.

Also, in the offertory procession, was Jake's senior infants' reader. Pamela told the church that Jake admitted that he was afraid to go into first class "because the sums are too hard."

"His mammy reassured him that he would be well able," she said.

Christopher brought up the PlayStation joypad that he and Jakie used to play. Pamela told everyone about Jakie's fierce competitive streak with Chris.

She recalled Jake's triumphant cry: "Ha-ha! You lose!" whenever he got the better of his dad.

Jakie's teachers, aunties, uncles, cousins and family friends all rose to describe the impact Jake had had on their lives in his brief six years.

Jakie's teacher Susanne White got up to read a piece that she wrote about Jake. She recalled the stories he'd written in school about his parents and his sister and brother. She said she'd witnessed at first hand the close bond between Jake and me.

Pamela got up to read the eulogy that she and Angela wrote about Jakie.

"You've had two girlfriends on the go for many years and even had a son Kyle with one of them," she said, which may have confused a few people in the church. "You also had a new, recent crush that made our Jakie blush.

"Jakie, you're such a charmer. Your big beautiful smile has been in all our pictures, but nothing compared to the love and awe in your eyes when you looked at your mammy. She was the one, and the only woman you could ever love like that and all the family could never understand the special bond you had together.

"Please Baby dance in heaven and send the moves to Mammy because she needs them."

She also spoke about Jake's sense of fun and mischief.

"You never cease to amaze us with that big open personality willing to do anything to make people laugh like joining in with all the girls to dress up as a princess and model for the photos. That's our Jakie. He could walk better in heels than a lot of us. You truly are your mammy's son."

At one stage during the funeral, I could hear my friend Yvonne Power's child, Siofra, getting upset. I was used to her on playdates with the boys and recognised the cries. I took off down the church to carry her even though I must have known she was with her mother.

She was three at the time and she came instantly to me when I held out my arms. I gave her the photo of Jakie that I had in my hand, and she calmed down.

I must have been like a zombie that day. I turned to sneak back up the church and realised that everything had stopped, and everyone was staring back at me.

Fr. Purcell had held up his finger and indicated everyone should wait when he saw me going down the aisle to Siofra.

"Is everything okay Roseann?" he asked from the altar. I nodded in bewilderment and returned to the front of the church to let the mass proceed.

For the duration of Jakie's funeral mass, I wept and choked with tears, but I managed to control the raging torrent of emotions inside.

I concentrated on the single white candle flickering on the top of his coffin and held the fury and the terror deep within me.

When we were leaving the church, everyone smiled through their tears as they played Jakie's favourite song, Baby Baby.

The entire congregation joined in the chorus as we filed out of the church.

Jakie, you must have been proud of them!

I walked behind the coffin never taking my hand off it as we left the church. I don't remember the crowd in the church, but my sisters said it was standing room only. When we came blinking into the sunlight outside, I remember the churchyard was full too.

I had managed to keep my wilder emotions in check until we reached the church steps where they released the doves. As soon as I saw those birds soar away into the blue sky, the raw grief resurfaced, and I lost control.

"I love you Jakie! I want Jakie! I want my baby back!" I raged at the heavens.

My legs barely carried me as we walked behind Jakie's coffin from the graveyard gates to Daddy's plot at the very back of St. Kieran's Cemetery.

Arriving at the graveside was another harrowing experience. Facing the fresh mounds of earth by Daddy's grave, the reality hit that Jake wasn't coming back.

I'm not going to wake up. This is really happening.

As they lowered his coffin into the ground, I had a complete mental and physical collapse. The song Dancing in the Sky played as he went down but it didn't disguise the hollow thud of the sod of clay landing on our baby's coffin.

I fell on my hands and knees at the grave-edge. People held me back as red roses were tossed down over him, and my mother begged me not to jump. It was never my intention. I was just trying to stay close to my baby in his coffin. I still kept hoping this nightmare would end.

This isn't real. That can't be my baby they're lowering into the ground. Jakie come back, come back to me!

The crowds eventually melted away afterwards leaving Chris and me, standing shocked and trembling at Jake's graveside. I remember gazing numbly at the carpet of red roses that covered the coffin.

When I was very young, I got a red rose tattoo on my shoulder with 'Mam & Dad' on it. My sisters always said that Daddy's favourite flower was a red rose.

I recalled how Jakie used to ask: "Why have you a flower on your shoulder?"

"It's a red rose which is my daddy's favourite flower, Jakie."

"I love that flower, Mammy. It's beautiful. Will you put my name on that picture too?"

So of course, roses became Jake's favourite flower too.

And here he was, lying under a weight of red scented petals that were already wilting in the hot sun. Jakie and his roses were about to be interred into the ground forever.

Nothing made sense in the world anymore, and Chris and I clung to each other like the last survivors of a catastrophe.

Eventually, we noticed the gravediggers, waiting respectfully in the distance on that hot summer day. They were waiting to finish the job they started.

How are we supposed to walk away and leave our baby all alone down in a dark, dank grave?

Somehow, we tore ourselves from Jakie's graveside and made our way to the funeral reception in the Brog Maker, where I had worked for years. At very least, we needed to thank the owners Breda and Bobby Quinn.

They brought trays and trays of sandwiches to the house throughout the days and then put on a massive spread for all the mourners. Afterwards, they wouldn't let us put our hands in our pockets. They couldn't have done enough for us, and we'll never forget their generosity and kindness.

Pamela was already in the Brog Maker when we arrived. Her eyes were red, sore and crusted from all the emotion of the previous days.

She's very thin anyway and had nothing on the table in front of her. She swore that she wouldn't eat unless I did. She's stubborn and was sticking to her threat.

"I told you, if you're not going to eat, I'm not going to," she said.

She looked awful, so I felt I had to force food into me to make her eat. It was the first time I ate anything in the three days since

156

Jakie died. The food stuck in my throat. But someone brought me tea filled with sugar that went down easier.

People were talking and laughing and doing what they normally do when they're together. I've done it myself at funerals. But that day, and for a long time afterwards, I couldn't understand how people could ever laugh again.

I glanced over at Chris who was with his family, and he knew straight away that I needed to go. I couldn't bear the sound of laughter. It was the sound of people getting back to normal life.

We collected the kids, said our goodbyes and left. It was a beautiful sunny evening, and I could feel sunburn tingling on my head and arms from the day already.

Savannah was wearing the floral summer dress and matching hairband that I'd bought the last day we'd gone shopping with Jake. Kaelem was wearing the same dressy outfit that Jake wore in his coffin. They were meant to be worn at Savannah's christening which should have taken place six days later.

Chris had Kaelem upon his shoulders while I wheeled Savannah in her buggy as we walked home in the warm, evening sunshine.

All I could think of was the wedding party we'd held in the Brog Maker two years earlier. It was another sunny evening like this when we'd walked home the day after we married.

Back then, I had Kaelem in the buggy, and Chris had Jake upon his shoulders. What a different night that was. That evening, we laughed and talked and admired our new wedding rings while Jake chattered non-stop.

Now tears rolled down my cheeks as Chris and I trudged in silence. The children felt our solemn mood and fell quiet. Our wedding rings were gone forever, along with Jakie's excited chattering.

With every step we took, it seemed we were walking further away from that old happy world we once knew.

It seemed strange that the sun was bright and shining and yet our new world felt so empty, cold and dark.

13. OUR ANGEL JAKIE

My first instinct was to flee the house on Lintown Road and get as far away from it as possible, but Kaelem's child psychologist advised against it.

She said after the loss of his brother, he needed time to adjust, and a move might be traumatic for him.

So, we stayed living in what seemed like the bowels of hell to me. The house was so grey and bleak now that Jakie was gone. His memory haunted every corner of the house.

A mere glimpse of the road outside triggered flashbacks that could tear the legs from out under me and send me into weeping spasms for hours. I pulled the front curtains, and they stayed closed for years.

It sounds bizarre, but Chris and I and a handful of close friends and family camped in the living room every night for the first six weeks after the funeral.

Pamela, Samantha and Catherine stayed with Chris and me most of those weeks. Pamela and Samantha stayed all night with Pamela leaving for work in the mornings and Samantha getting back to her baby.

Catherine couldn't stand being in the house at night after a while because she thought she was hearing and seeing Jakie all the time. She would come over first thing in the morning instead.

My heavily pregnant sister Angela and my other sister Mary, along with friends, Nicola, Mary, and Yvonne, stayed up with us until after midnight most nights.

People were doing shifts and staying with us all the time.

I was barely alive in those early days. My stomach felt hollow, and my chest and throat felt so tight, I could hardly breathe never mind eat. I was nauseous, listless, breathless and confused.

People would have to repeat themselves several times to make me understand anything.

My nerves rattled. I leapt at the slightest noise. A door slamming left me cowering with fright. My whole body felt like it was twisted in a knot of indescribable pain.

Pamela admitted afterwards that she found it very hard seeing how distressed we were during those early days. She used to put her kids to bed and come over to us at 7.00pm. She said Chris would cry in his sleep and my screams at night would terrify her.

I screamed while I slept from nightmares, and I screamed when I woke to our living nightmare. Sleep was impossible. I only dozed, and I became terrified at night.

I reverted to the small child I was when Daddy died.

I still couldn't even have a shower without my sisters in the bathroom with me. I was shaky, trembling, scared. I didn't know my body or understand the voice in my head. Nothing made sense anymore.

Since then counselling has taught me I was suffering from post-traumatic stress, but I don't think I'd even heard of the term back then. All I knew was that physically and mentally, I was falling apart.

It was the same cycle all the time. I'd scream and cry until I'd exhausted myself. Then I'd sit rocking and rocking until my energy built back up and the explosion of grief, fury and loss started all over again.

We worried about the impact of Jake's death on Kaelem because we don't know how much he heard or he saw the day Jake died.

Chris picked him up afterwards and placed him in Pakie's car with the passenger, Karl Gleeson. Darren and Pamela took him away as soon as they arrived.

He didn't see the paramedics cutting Jake's clothes open or doing CPR, but he heard the panic and the screaming. All we knew for sure was that he saw and heard too much for a little boy.

For the first day or so, we let him think that Jake was still in hospital. He was still enjoying his 'sleepover' with Rhys, but Darren brought him home the day after Jake died telling him Mammy had to talk with him.

He was only three, but he was mad about his big brother.

I didn't know how to explain to him that Jake wasn't coming back. But I was worried that some other child would say it to him, and I wanted it to come from us.

I always remembered the shock I got when I was six-years-old, and a neighbour's child claimed that the woman I loved as my mammy wasn't my mother at all.

"Sure, your mammy's not your mammy, stupid. Your mammy lives in Carlow," she taunted.

I came running into the house and straight into the arms of my brother, Ninja.

"Is it true what she's sayin', Ninja?" I bawled.

Mammy found me crying on the stairs and sat me down and tried to explain it to me.

"It's only a little bit true," she said. "Your mammy is your sister but I'm your mammy too, and I'll always be your mammy."

I didn't want Kaelem to hear something life-changing like I did from another child. I wanted him to hear it from us.

"Kaelem, I want to tell you about Jakie, that he's gone to heaven."

"Yeah?"

"And that Jakie can't come back from heaven."

"Can I have that bun?"

"In a minute, Kaelem. I want you to understand that Jakie can't be here anymore."

"Okay."

I knew he didn't understand. I didn't want someone to tell him he was stupid, the way they told me.

"You know the way you have movie nights, and you sit on your chair with Jakie?"

"Yeah?"

"Well, Baby, that's what I'm trying to say. Jakie won't be able to do that with you anymore. Jakie won't be living with us anymore."

His bottom lip wobbled.

"I want Jakie!"

"I know, Kaelem, we all do, but Jakie got hurt by a car, and they couldn't fix him so Holy God took him so that he wouldn't be in pain. Jakie's gone to live with Granddad now."

He looked at me doubtfully, but he took his bun anyway.

After that, we let him ask questions as and when he wanted, and we tried to answer as best we could.

Sometimes those questions broke my heart. When we talked about writing a letter to Santa months later, he wanted to know if he could ask Santy to bring Jakie back for Christmas.

Jake's school principal, Marie Kelly, helped us to get him to a child psychologist straight away. I knew that I didn't want Kaelem to be like I was as a child. I spent most of my childhood living in terror of losing my Mammy and all my loved ones.

Straight away, Kaelem decided he wanted to move into Jakie's bed. He never went back to his own bed again, but it bothered me that for a long time he kept calling it 'Jakie's bed'.

I told him: "No, Kaelem, that's your bed. Jakie left that bed for you. Granddad's after getting another bed for Jakie in heaven."

I never wanted him to grow up thinking he was living in Jakie's world - in his bed and his bedroom.

It took several sessions, but it was a relief when the psychologist said she didn't need to see him again. She said he was a chatty, well-adjusted child and that she was satisfied that he had a close bond with his mammy and daddy.

Her earlier advice stood. She said we still shouldn't make any major changes in Kaelem's life for a while. Leaving the house on Lintown Grove, even though I wanted nothing more, was not an option.

We did our best to keep the children's routines as stable as possible. Kaelem came home after the funeral, and he and Savannah still went to bed at their usual times.

I'd tuck them in and read them their stories. It was still summer, and the evenings were long so that I could put them to bed, but I couldn't go up the stairs after dark. As soon as night came, and it got dark upstairs, I didn't want to go up again.

Someone gave me a Xanax after the funeral, but it only let me sleep for an hour. I refused medication in the beginning because I didn't want to get dependent on any drugs, but in the end, I had to accept more help. I couldn't fall asleep, and when I did, I couldn't stay asleep.

The doctor prescribed Dalmane, which treats symptoms of insomnia, but I knew I needed more than pills. I reached out for any support available.

After sorting out a child psychiatrist for Kaelem, I rang Kilkenny Bereavement Support. They put me on to First Light who help anyone affected by the sudden death of a child.

Ger O'Brien, who runs the organisation, drove straight down from Dublin to see me. She was wonderful. Ger, a woman who lost two sons, encouraged me to call her at any time. She's still on my phone under 'Talk'.

She assured me that what I was feeling was normal; I needed that reassurance. There were times I thought that I was going mad.

"You will never stop loving your little boy, you'll never stop missing him, but life does get easier," she told me. "You won't feel like this forever, but you will love him and miss him forever."

It made more sense to me than the empty and hurtful platitudes like "time's a healer" and "you're lucky that you have the other two".

Ger got me into counselling with a woman in Kilkenny, and later she got Chris and me into group counselling with other bereaved couples.

The support she and First Light provide for bereaved parents is incredible.

She gave me a sense of hope for the first time. I saw how she had survived and was helping other people despite her own terrible losses.

She's still here and has lost two of her children. She's still fighting so maybe I can do this.

We postponed Savannah's christening as it fell six days after Jake's funeral. We decided to hold it on July 12 instead, the day of Jake's month's mind. We never planned it, but the date was also the day we renewed our wedding vows.

By the time July 12 approached, I hadn't been outside the house except to visit Jakie's grave. I found it difficult to do anything and only agreed to go ahead with the christening because Jake would be part of it.

I hadn't the ability or the heart to organise anything for the christening, but I'd already made a lot of the arrangements before Jake died.

I'd bought new outfits for Chris and me, and I had Savannah's dress ready to go. We'd already asked Chris's sister Alison and my brother-in-law Pakie to be godparents.

Samantha and Nicola stepped in to organise an after-party at Ossory Park Community Centre for us. They made Jake an integral part of the celebration for Savannah.

They ordered a cake from Jake to mark her christening and his bear Ruby sat at the top table along with his photo.

Savannah's godmother Alison brought her a present of a white christening blanket. She had it embroidered with Savannah's name and the date and on the other side are the words: "Her Big Brother Jakie is now her Angel."

I still felt angry that Chris and I were only going through the motions with Savannah's christening. Instead of enjoying what should have been a special day, we were just trying to get through it.

I hated life. I hated pretending to be a regular, functioning person when I wanted to give up and tell the world to go away and leave me alone.

But the day was only the first of many happy family occasions that were robbed from us, wasn't it Jakie Baby?

Chris and I asked the priest to bless our new wedding rings at Jakie's month's mind and Savannah's christening.

We bought our original rings in Nolan's Jewellers in Kilkenny, but when we tried to order new rings, they wanted us to come into the shop to measure our fingers. I wouldn't have agreed to new rings at all if I realised that. I didn't want to go anywhere; I didn't want to meet anyone.

I looked like a dead person walking at this stage. I wasn't sleeping or eating, and I was suffering from depression and anxiety.

I couldn't even bear to drive for five months after Jakie died. I couldn't get behind the wheel of a motor after seeing what a car did to our baby.

My close friend Mary Conroy drove me, Chris and Pamela to the store in Market Cross. I dreaded the thought of being in the town again.

I remembered a friend whose aunt believes in angels and who used to say that there are angels for everything. She said that even when her aunt is looking for a parking space, she asks the parking angels to help her.

I didn't want to face walking through the town. I remember pleading with the angels.

Come on parking angels; please find us a parking space right outside.

There's never a spot outside Market Cross, but I'm not joking, we found a parking place right outside the door. Keeping my head down, I ran down to the shop. They sized my finger, and I walked out again. Pamela did all the talking for me.

But as soon as I tried to leave Market Cross, the mother of one of Jake's school friends stopped me. I didn't even know if I could speak like a normal person anymore. We exchanged a few words, but I couldn't continue and blurted: "I'm sorry, but I have to go now."

We asked for our new rings to be engraved with the words 'Our angel Jakie' along with our wedding date, March 28, 2012.

I expected Fr Purcell to give our new rings a quick blessing after the mass. Instead, Chris and I looked at each other in shock when during the mass he announced: "Can I get Roseann and Chris up here?"

He explained to everyone how Chris and I had given our wedding rings to Jakie.

"Now Roseann and Chris have new rings, and they are going to renew their marriage vows today," he announced.

We weren't expecting that, but it was like I had set it up because I was wearing a full-length white dress that day. I'd bought it before Jake's passing which was lucky because I wasn't in any condition to go shopping afterwards.

I also bought the dress without even trying it on because I mistakenly thought it was my size. I'd lost over a stone and a few pounds in the month since, and it only barely fitted me.

I didn't think I wanted it at the time, but Fr. Purcell turned the renewal of our vows into a very personal and lovely service. We didn't know it then, but repeating those vows became another thread that kept us bound together when we found our marriage unravelling.

Chris and I and our small party of friends continued to live like refugees in the living room every night. But after the month's mind, I realised we couldn't stay like this indefinitely.

I told Pamela and Samantha to go home, but they said they wouldn't go until I moved back upstairs. They insisted that I had to be able to stay in my own room.

Chris and I went back upstairs. I dreaded the move, but the girls stayed with me at night until the sleeping tablets kicked in. I'd still have to have the TV on in the room to fall asleep.

Even four years later, we have good days and bad days. Back then, all our days were bad ones, but they became especially bad once Chris and I were left on our own.

14. MARRIAGE ON THE ROCKS

We clung desperately to each other for the first few weeks. There's a saying that grief shared is grief halved, but it didn't work like that for us.

I soon realised that Chris couldn't carry the pain of Jakie's loss for me, and I couldn't do it for him. Nor could we shield each other from the pain we felt.

Soon we stopped turning to each other, and we turned away from each other instead.

We never acknowledged or even realised that we'd both grieve differently and at different times. I cried so much and felt the grief so intensely that I couldn't think straight. Chris would hear me crying, but he stopped coming to comfort me.

Then at times when I was drained and had nothing left to give, I'd hear him crying, and I'd leave him alone. I'd just been where he was. I couldn't let him bring me down again when I'd just clawed my way out of that pit of despair.

So, I let him cry while I went through my numb and empty phase. He didn't have enough strength to comfort me and deal with his own loss either.

We were both in so much pain from losing Jake that we no longer had room for the other person's grief. Maintaining a distance from one another was self-preservation.

I see now that we started drifting apart quite early on, but the brain isn't functioning properly especially in that first year after the death of a child.

We started living apart more and more.

At first, he knew I was scared to be upstairs, and he'd come to bed with me. But then he stopped and started sleeping downstairs on the couch. In the beginning, I felt hurt, but it wasn't long before I didn't care.

We were only two years married when we lost Jake. We were young. Chris was 27, and I had just turned 30, and our lives felt like they were robbed along with Jake's.

It wasn't long before I preferred the bedroom to myself and didn't want him with me at all. Sex or any intimacy became the last thing I wanted, and that made Chris feel even more alone.

Within about two months of Jakie's death, we were living separate lives.

I wanted to stay in all the time; he needed to get out of the house. I wanted to talk all the time about Jakie and wanted to go to counselling; he didn't want to talk at all.

As we grew apart, I threw all my energies into being the best mother I could be. I felt a failure as a mother to Jakie. I needed to get my confidence back, so I'd get up early each morning to scrub the house.

As soon as the children were awake, I turned my attention on them. I tried to be the happy, smiling Mammy that I was before Jake went to heaven but even more so.

In reality, I was smothering the kids and exhausting myself. But it was all I had. I wasn't working; I wasn't capable of working.

My original plan was to wait until Savannah was 6-months-old and try to get employment in childcare.

After what happened to Jake, I decided I'd never work in childcare again. I was supposed to protect my child, and yet I failed.

All I could think was that I cherished my child, I looked after him, and he still died. I felt how could I ever take on the responsibility of someone else's child when I wasn't fit to mind my own?

I didn't trust myself around my own children. It took a long time to build up my confidence and learn to be the mother I once was.

Meanwhile, work on the building sites had completely dried up for Chris at that stage. Even if there was work, he was in no condition to work anyway. He was at home with very little to distract him.

I started Jake's Legacy on Facebook within a month of Jake's death, and it took off a lot faster than I ever expected. I found it a great release for my anger.

Chris always encouraged me, but we still didn't talk about our growing problems. We moved around each other and co-parented but didn't communicate with each other.

We focussed on the kids and going to Jakie's grave, but there was no connection between us at all.

I didn't want the kids to hear me cry anymore, so I learnt to hide it. I functioned during the day as Mammy.

But once I put the kids to bed, I locked my bedroom door, sat on the floor and rocked, and watched videos of Jake, and cried for hours.

I felt like I didn't want Chris anymore, but the last thing I wanted was more anger in the house. I didn't want to expose the children to more disturbance. We concentrated on the kids and ignored the growing resentments between us.

I spent a lot of time at the grave. I decided that we were going to spend three hours at Jake's grave every day.

If something came up and I had to leave ten minutes earlier than the three-hour deadline, I'd make sure to get back to the graveyard for ten more minutes later.

I'd say to Chris: "If we can't give Jakie three hours a day, what kind of parents are we? If he was here, he'd take up more time in our day."

As the winter closed in and the weather got worse, I was still determined to stand three hours in the cold and the rain. Everyone tried to convince me to stop.

"Come on Ro; you can't keep doing this. You can't do this to yourself. It's doing no one any good."

Christopher would do the three-hour vigil with me in the beginning at least. I had this big rain jacket and two seats, and he would sit there to keep me happy.

The obsessive routines and patterns that developed after Daddy died started coming back.

Before leaving the grave, I'd have to say: "Love you, Jake, love you, Daddy" five times in a row and then "Love you, Jakie" five times and then "Love you, Daddy" five times.

Then there had to be a final three sets of "Love you, my Jakie, love you, Daddy." I wouldn't feel comfortable until I recited them all.

Everything was in sets of threes and fives. Three stood for my three children, and five stood for our family of five. I was obsessed with those numbers.

If someone sent me a message and signed off with two kisses, I'd secretly rage. To me, it was a message that they believed I had two children, not three.

Even today, I hate the numbers two and four. To me, they stand for everything that's wrong in my life: having two children and four in our family.

I still bring three flowers to the grave, every Thursday, the day that Jakie went to heaven. I carry a red rose for Dad, and two white roses for Jakie: it must be three altogether.

I've learnt that obsessive behaviours are a kind of coping strategy and they're common with people who are grieving. It's a way of controlling a world where death is random and doesn't make any sense.

Anger is a big part of grieving, and often the anger is directed at the person closest to you. Things that I might have tolerated before Jake died became real irritants afterwards. I fumed over little things that Chris did that wouldn't have fazed me normally.

We were both angry and in self-destructive mode.

Chris stopped coming with me to Jakie's grave in the mornings and started going on his own at night instead. He's not a morning person anyway, and now that he was depressed, he found it even harder to get up.

But I began to hate him and resent him more and more as time went on.

He was resentful too and hated me just as much for nagging him. At night, he got the dinner and put the kids to bed and went to the grave. But I didn't see that.

As far as I was concerned, he refused to help me with the kids and refused to go to the grave. I felt exhausted all the time, and still, he slept all morning.

At night I didn't want to do anything except go upstairs, lock the door and grieve.

I was angry when I saw him watching his soccer and TV shows and all the usual stuff he watched. I was furious when he went out.

I couldn't understand how he could do that. I couldn't be bothered with watching TV the way that I used to. I didn't want to socialise like I used to. The normal things in life felt so meaningless to me now.

I didn't just push Chris away; I pushed everyone away and became more and more solitary and isolated.

I'm mindful that I'm always talking about Jake and me, but Chris just loved him just as much. He's still lost without his 'Little Man'.

I remember how he loved bringing Jake off for a haircut. They'd go into the Authentic Turkish Barbers on Kieran Street in town and he'd get Jake's hair cut the same way as his - all spikes.

Then Kaelem came along, and Chris loved going out with his two little boys.

The barber guys were great with the two boys, and everyone in the shop admired them. Jake and Kaelem came away thinking they were great with their hair cut just like their dad. It was Chris and his two boys.

I saw how he put off getting a haircut after Jake died. He and Kaelem badly needed to go to the barbers, but he couldn't face it.

When he finally mustered up the strength to do it, he said his heart broke going without Jake. It still hurts him even years later.

He feels he should have a boy on each side of him, and now he has one empty hand.

Chris doesn't cry like me and doesn't talk like me, so he doesn't express it in words, but he can't hide it in his eyes. I see him going out to work when he kisses or touches the photo of Jake just inside the door and says "see you later, Daddy's Little Man."

Christopher has always been the proudest father. Even though we were young, and he was such a young man when we had Jake, he was a brilliant father

We had hiccups and near break-ups in the early days of our relationship too. We were young; we hardly knew each other in the early days when Jake arrived.

But no matter what happened between us, he would never have left Jake. He was the best Daddy to Jake; he still is a great father to Kaelem and Savannah despite his pain.

The kids' homework and school are critical to him. He wants all his kids to have a future, to go to college, so they don't have to be a labourer or work in low paid jobs like he has had to.

He was always very proud of how well Jake did at school. He admired his handwriting, and if Jake was flagging with his homework, he'd encourage him. "Come on Jake; Daddy knows you can do this better."

Kaelem and Savannah are what keep us going now. Chris keeps up with Kaelem's homework, and he'll be the same when Savannah starts school. He concentrates on the kids and their future.

He was determined that Jake was going have an excellent education and he was going to go to college. He's equally determined for the other two. We want them to have a good education and a good career.

Back in the first year after Jake died, I kept life as normal as possible for the kids with a lot of help from my sisters and friends. In days when I'd struggle to make a sandwich, Pamela cooked and blended all of Savannah's baby food.

My sisters were great at bringing over home-cooked dinners. I found it difficult to swallow food in the year after Jakie's death. The doctor prescribed nutritional drinks as the weight continued to fall off me. But Kaelem always had a home-cooked dinner at night.

The summer that Jake died, I recruited my teenage niece, Donna, to bring Kaelem to all the places kids want to go. I wanted him to do all the summer things that kids do, but I wasn't fit to do them with him.

Recently, I saw photos of Kaelem from that summer on my friend Mary's Facebook Memories. I could see he was at Jellietots Playcentre in Kilkenny, so I looked closer to see who had brought him there.

I was shocked when I recognised my hand and my rings in one of the photos. The pictures were taken two months after Jakie died, but I must have wiped the day from my memory.

I should have remembered it because it must have been painful to go there. Jake loved Jellietots, and we held three of his birthday parties there. He and Kaelem had a joint party there in April before he died.

Things were bad then, and dates are all a bit hazy. Everything about those first years is shrouded in the fog of grief.

All I know is that within a few months of Jake's death, I unravelled to the extent that I was admitted to a psychiatric unit for the first time in my life.

15. JAKE'S LEGACY

In the days after Jake's death, I constantly searched for answers to the question, 'why'?

Why was he taken so young? Why did this happen to me? Why did I let him cross that road? Why did God allow this to happen? Why is life so unfair? Why did he die? Why did this happen? Why? Why? Why?

The evening that Jakie was brought home after the post-mortem, these questions were tumbling over and over in my head.

I was a complete mess. My sisters forced me into a shower to get me cleaned up before Jakie arrived.

It all came to me while standing under that shower; it was like the water washed away a black fog for a few minutes.

In a moment of clarity, I realised that Jakie's death had to be for a reason. I heard the words as clearly as if someone spoke to me:

You're meant to do something in Jakie's name.

The words were so vivid and clear that I said it to my sisters when I got out of the shower. I still had no idea what I was supposed to do in his name, but I knew I was meant to do something.

"What does it mean?" I asked them. "What am I supposed to do?"

The message ran through my head for the next few days. But still, I hadn't a clue what I was supposed to do. My thinking was woolly, and my mind was all over the place. I was barely clinging to my sanity.

My sister Catherine knew a psychic on our estate called Joanne Doran who asked to see me in the days after Jakie died. I'm a bit of a sceptic about these things, but she told me things about my son that only he and I would have known.

But more than that, she ignited the first flicker of a fire in me after Jakie died. I never felt weaker or sicker in my life, but she said I had a powerful aura since Jakie's death.

"I'm telling you, Roseann, you have great power now. People will listen to you. I can feel an energy burning within you, and you need to do something with it."

Joanne's words inspired me. It was another sign after hearing that voice in my head.

Andrew McGuinness had just become the Mayor of Kilkenny. People told me he was young, energetic and wanted to make a difference.

Something got into my head, and I rang him saying: "Andrew, I don't know why I'm ringing you or how you can help me, but I was told that you will help."

Andrew closed his office and came straight to our house. He joined Chris and I who were staring, ashen-faced, at a photograph of Jake surrounded by candles.

We spoke about everything from speed ramps and speed limits to depression, loss, and what could be done to make a positive difference in Jake's name. I didn't know what I wanted to do. All I knew was that I had to do something, and the germ of an idea started forming.

One of the many things that stood out about Jakie was his love of children. People used to remark how Jake was always mesmerised by children and babies.

Most boys his age wouldn't pay attention to babies, but in any room full of people, Jakie was drawn to the smallest and youngest. He had to go over, peer into a cot or buggy, talk to them and stroke their cheeks.

One day, not too long before he died, he asked: "Mammy, could we have more kids?"

"Why would we want more kids?" I asked. "I have three of you, sure that's plenty. How many more kids do you want anyway?"

"A hundred," he said without hesitation.

"A hundred?" I laughed. "Holy God, I'd pull the hair out of my head. All I'd be doing all day is feeding and changing nappies."

"Mammy," he said, looking up at me with his earnest brown eyes. "I'll help you."

Every time I asked what he wanted to be when he got bigger, he replied: "I want to mind kids like you, Mammy."

After he died, so many people said to me that Jakie must be meeting and greeting all the small children who go to heaven.

I thought of Jakie and his love of children, and I knew that he would want to protect them from what happened to him.

In the days after Jakie's death, I was shocked to discover that the speed limit in housing estates was 50km/h. I never thought about the speed limit before. I just presumed it was slower. Everyone was talking about it at the funeral.

I'm part of a big family of twelve, and none of us knew 50km/h was the speed limit in an estate. The problem wasn't just in the Lintown estate. It was all over the country.

It made me very angry to learn shortly afterwards that the County Councils had the authority to reduce the speed limit to 30km/h since 2004.

For ten years, children had been needlessly dying in housing estates all over Ireland. It felt like Jakie was just another road death statistic.

I realised that reducing the speed limit was something I could do to stop other children dying the way Jakie died.

Above all, I knew that Jakie would be the first to get behind a campaign to save the lives of other children. If we could save just one other child's life, it meant that Jakie's death would have some meaning. There was something I could do in his name.

I teamed up with friends, family and neighbours to form a small committee. My sister Pamela, psychic Joanne and Lisamarie Manuel, another mother on the Lintown estate, agreed to join me as the voices and faces of the campaign.

Chris worked behind the scenes, attending every meeting along with my sisters Catherine, Mary and Angela and my friends, Mary, Samantha and Nicola. When we needed a bigger crew for campaigning, we had more family and friends who volunteered.

We started examining road accidents and the statistics behind speeding. Common sense told us that a speed limit of 50km/h in a housing estate was crazy. We soon learnt that 5 in 10 adults will die if hit by a car at 50km/h while 1 in 10 will die if hit at 30km/h.

When someone exceeds the limit and drives at 60km/h, 9 out of 10 adults will die in a collision.

We knew the local councils had the power to reduce the speed limit in residential zones to 30km/h. We felt that was still too high when it came to children's safety.

We decided on three objectives for our campaign. Firstly, we wanted speed reduced to 20km/h in housing estates all around Ireland. Secondly, we wanted the installation of speed bumps in these areas.

Thirdly, we demanded an education programme for adult drivers rather than children. We felt that schools, parents and safety organisations were always teaching our kids about road safety.

In the weeks before he died, Jake had achieved his 'Safety Licence' – an RSA-backed initiative involving road safety for children.

It wasn't much use when adults didn't know how to drive in a residential area where there were vulnerable road users.

"It shouldn't be left to kids to worry about road safety," I said. "Kids get lost in play. Adults need to learn that it's their responsibility too."

We sat around and brainstormed how to start this campaign. We hadn't a clue, but we agreed we needed a name.

"It has to have Jake's name in it; it has to be about Jake," was my only condition.

I can't remember who suggested Jake's Legacy, but everyone agreed that it was the perfect name.

Then we needed a platform to launch our campaign, and Joanne said her partner could set up a Facebook page for us.

On July 6, just over three weeks after my baby's death, our first post, a school photo of Jakie, went up on our Facebook page. The campaign, Jake's Legacy, was born.

The campaign gave me a direction, a focus for my anger and a reason to get up in the morning even when I didn't want to face the day. I had a fire in my belly and a new-found purpose.

I was determined that Jake's name and spirit would live on, and his death would mean something.

We adopted the slogan 'Is Jake's life not enough?' for our campaign T-shirts and our hash-tag on social media. We took to the streets of Kilkenny with our T-shirts and leaflets to raise awareness.

The Mayor, Andrew McGuinness, was behind us from the start. He met with us in person or was at the end of a phone anytime we needed him. He was endlessly supportive and dedicated his term as mayor to the campaign.

Andrew invited us to the chamber for his first council meeting as Mayor. He drafted a proposal to reduce speed limits in housing estates and read out a letter from me appealing to members to support his motion.

I couldn't see how anyone could object to the proposal, so I saw red when I heard the debate and launched a blistering attack on those opposing the motion.

In the end, I stormed out of the chamber with everyone in the campaign following me, and we continued with a noisy protest in the foyer of City Hall. Andrew even joined us in the protest before returning to finish the Council meeting.

Days later he arranged for us to meet with city engineers to discuss reducing speed limits and creating traffic calming in housing estates.

He finally managed to get unanimous support from the council for traffic calming measures in Kilkenny housing estates on behalf of Jake's Legacy and our family.

We were very moved when he also unveiled a bench in Lintown in Jake's memory during his term as mayor.

Meanwhile, some friends made a call to the Kilkenny hurling team boss, Brian Cody, and he also backed our campaign.

Everyone knows Brian as the greatest manager in the game of all time, but he was also the principal of St. Patrick's De La Salle national school in Kilkenny at the time. Brian related to our campaign to save other school children by reducing speed in residential areas.

Through him, GAA heroes like Henry Shefflin and the rest of the Kilkenny team offered their support, signed jerseys and helped to promote the campaign.

Because of great local support like this, Jake's Legacy took off a lot faster than any of us expected. Within a week or two we had over 5,000 followers, and numbers were rising fast.

The public support gave me great comfort. I knew we had to be doing something right when complete strangers from all around the country started backing us.

Our media campaign kicked off within days too when I was invited to speak on Carlow and Kilkenny radio station, KCLR.

My mind was still a complete mess, and the girls tried hard to drum statistics and information into me, but I couldn't focus.

I had never done any public speaking before, and I never wanted to be in the public eye. The old Rosie wouldn't even dare to answer a question in school. I was painfully shy when it came to public speaking.

On one occasion I was asked to say something in praise of our principal, Cathy McSorley in Kilkenny City Vocational School. I really admired her and thought she did great work in the school, and I wanted to express that. I had just two lines to say but I bottled it, and Pamela had to stand up and say the lines for me.

I was far too shy to do a radio interview.

I was petrified with nerves the day we went to KCLR. I brought Pamela with me as my back-up because I didn't think I'd be able to do it. I felt I'd never remember all the facts and figures that we'd assembled. I also thought I was going to puke I was so nervous.

"You'll talk for Jakie and me, won't you?" I begged her.

I went into the radio studio with my heart pounding out of my chest in case they addressed a question to me. I hoped that I could leave it all to Pamela.

Just as we were about to begin, I said to myself: "Come on now, Jakie and the Angels; help me get through this."

The red light went on in the studio to show we were live on air. Suddenly, I swear to God, the person that I used to be disappeared, and someone else took her place.

I started spouting the statistics and information that I didn't even know that I had taken in. I told them Jakie's story and said that if this campaign saved even one other child's life, then we would regard it as a success.

I knew then that Jakie was there, pushing me, encouraging his mammy to get out there and talk for him and other children like him. Everyone else was as surprised as I was. This was a new Rosie.

The people at KCLR were the first to interview me, and they have continued to be a great support down through the years. After that interview, more and more media contacted me, and I kept telling my story, and the campaign snowballed very fast.

A few days later, Joanne Doran and I met with local Carlow-Kilkenny representative and the Minister for the Environment, Phil Hogan. We hoped he'd be the first of many politicians to support our cause and help bring about new legislation to reduce speed in residential estates.

Instead, he oozed with sympathy over my loss and then tried to pat us on the head and usher us out the door. He wasn't alone. He was representative of many politicians we were to meet over the coming years.

I told Phil, as I've told a lot of other TDs, that I wasn't meeting them as a grieving mother.

"The grieving mother is outside the door now," I said. "I'm here as a concerned citizen and to represent road victims and children."

I mentioned that I met Tony Cullen, the father of Clodagh Cullen, another child who had lost her life on an estate in Kilkenny.

"Does there have to be a child killed in every housing estate in this country for the Government to open their ears and hear people's cries?" I asked.

I said the council only acted when they had blood on their hands. I asked the Minister to commit to supporting Jake's Legacy and to contact the Taoiseach's Office to arrange a meeting for me with Enda Kenny.

He vowed to do that and to make representations to the Road Safety Authority, and the Kilkenny County Manager. He also said he'd pass on the details of the campaign to the incoming Minister, Alan Kelly and that he'd keep in touch with us.

All his promises came to nothing. He went off to Europe the following week, and we never heard from him again.

We were naive. We were to learn that promises from politicians run as freely as water from a tap.

Earlier that year, on St Patrick's weekend, Taoiseach Enda Kenny told a gathering of Americans: "My number is a public number, you can call me anytime."

I checked his entire website, the phone book, everywhere and couldn't find that number. However, I got the number from a journalist, and I called him, but his phone rang out. I kept calling.

Then as I was fixing the kids' lunch a day or so later, my phone rang.

"Well, how's it going?" said the caller.

"Well, who's this?" I replied.

"You rang me," said the mysterious caller.

"I'm sorry, but I'm after ringing a lot of numbers all morning. I don't know who you are."

"Who are you anyway?" he asked.

"My name's Roseann Brennan."

"Oh well…" he sounded like he was about to say it must be a wrong number or something when it dawned on me.

"Is that you, Enda Kenny?"

"It is."

"Enda Kenny, how's it going? I've been trying to get my hands on you."

On July 24, I got my meeting with Enda in Government Buildings.

By then we'd learnt that one of the conditions of planning permission granted for our estate in May 2000 was the provision of speed ramps by the developers.

By 2009, there was still no sign of these ramps, and the residents had petitioned the council to build them instead. The residents spent their own money to erect traffic-calming signage.

Kilkenny County Council issued an enforcement notice in 2010, giving the developer three months to build ramps. The notice warned that the developer might be guilty of an offence if outstanding works were not completed.

We tried to find out why the County Council didn't issue proceedings or implement the works itself but met a brick wall.

Enda promised to investigate why speed ramps weren't installed in our housing estate. He even told the media afterwards: "I have undertaken to contact the county manager about that matter."

He added: "My hope is the loss of little Jake will not have been in vain."

He also said he'd arrange for me to meet with Transport Minister Paschal Donohoe and Environment Minister Alan Kelly.

The campaign received more national coverage when I made my first TV appearance on TV3's Ireland AM breakfast show in early August.

A few days later I was also invited on to the Ray D'Arcy radio show. Maybe because he has young children himself, he became a great supporter of the campaign and invited me on the show several times.

But it was all so nerve-wracking and exhausting. I dreaded doing these interviews. I remember a teenage girl in our area coming up to me around that time and breathlessly saying: "I saw you on the telly!"

She seemed to think that it was so glamorous and exciting to be on TV. Nothing could have been further from the truth. I wanted to lie in the dark all day then. It took a lot out of me to get out of bed, drive to Dublin and build myself up with false energy so that I could do these shows. I used to implore the heavens for help to get through it.

Come on now Jakie and the Angels, help me do this!

Then afterwards, there was a sense of collapse; a sickening feeling of futility in the car on the way home. It happened every single time. I was slapped with the reality that no matter what I did, Jakie wasn't coming back.

Then I'd see the photo of Jakie on the TV afterwards or on the news, or in the newspapers. It was so surreal to see him there.

That's our baby, and he's dead.

I didn't want to be on TV or in the newspapers; I just wanted my baby back. Some days, it felt so pointless that I didn't want to go on.

But then Pamela would remind me: "This is for Jake, Roseann. He's helping you get through every interview; he wants to make the roads safer for kids. He wants to save kids' lives, and you're the only one who can do it for him."

Her encouragement would get me going again, wouldn't it Jakie?

We got into the first of several meetings with Transport Minister Paschal Donohoe in August that year.

We were happy when the Minister agreed to a nationwide survey of local authorities. The survey sought to discover how many councils had used the 2004 bylaws to lower speed limits. The study also asked how many estates had speed ramps.

The results of the survey were released the following month, and they were shocking. The 30km/h speed limit hadn't been applied to a single housing estate in 30 out of 31 local authority areas.

Cork City Council was the only local authority in Ireland to reduce speed to 30km/h in some residential areas. They implemented 30km/h speed limits in 135 of their 550 housing estates.

The survey also revealed that only 14% of the country's housing estates had speed ramps in them and the cost per speed ramp was €3,200.

It was clear that it could no longer be left to the local councils to decide on speed limits in estates. We said that the Government would have to make the 30km/h bylaw mandatory or things would never change.

We also learnt that the County Councils had no authority to impose speed limits on private estates. Our housing estate, Lintown, was one of the thousands of so-called 'privately-owned' estates. These are estates that haven't been 'taken in charge' by the local authority.

In 2016, there were over 5,600 completed housing developments around the country that had not been taken in charge by local authorities.

They were a hangover from the crash when developers disappeared or went bust before a proper handover to the local authority was agreed.

The only way to impose a lower speed limit in these estates is for the Government to legislate for a new mandatory nationwide speed limit.

We made endless telephone calls, wrote hundreds of emails, and made countless requests for information. We spent months meeting with Government ministers, department officials, local authority staff, and the Taoiseach.

By now, Jake's Legacy campaign had received national media coverage, and the Facebook page had over 14,000 likes and hundreds more every day. We were working on the campaign all day at times, and then I'd spend lonely nights at Jakie's grave.

I had a mantra: "If we can even save one child's life because of something we achieve, won't it be worth it?"

Every politician I met, I asked: "Do you think it's okay to be able to legally drive at 50km/h in a residential estate?"

None of them hesitated.

"No, I don't," they'd reply.

"Well, what are you going to do about it?" was always my next question.

By November that year, we had the Environment Minister, Alan Kelly calling on local authorities to reduce speed limits in housing estates. Kelly said that "as a parent of young children" he was "very taken and impressed" by the campaign.

He asked that road safety audits and speed reduction measures be part of the planning application process in new housing developments.

We continued to push Paschal Donohoe for mandatory nationwide speed limits, but he kept pushing back. He insisted it should be left to each County Council to decide on where to reduce their speed limits.

We argued that thousands of other estates in private hands all over the country, including our own, were exempt from council guidelines. The speed limits had to be mandatory.

At the end of the year, we won an honour at the Road Safety Association's Leading Lights awards for our contribution to road safety.

The ceremony at Farmleigh House in the Phoenix Park in December raised more awareness of our campaign. I accepted the Community Education award that night on behalf of Jake's Legacy campaign.

But behind the scenes, I was fed up with the lip service rather than action that we were getting from politicians.

By then we'd learnt that the number of children who died on Irish roads had more than doubled between 2013 and 2014. There were seven fatalities among the under 15s age group in 2013, and that was bad enough. But in 2014, Jakie was one of 15 children who died in road accidents.

A new year was about to start in 2015, and yet nothing had been done to stop more children dying.

Transport Minister Paschal had sent out a circular calling on all local authorities to review speed limits in residential areas in October. But apart from that, he had done nothing to push ahead and reduce speed.

We went to Dublin for yet another meeting with Paschal. I wanted the speed limit lowered from 50km/h to 20km/h, but I was willing to compromise and accept a 30km/h limit if it was made mandatory in residential areas nationwide.

Paschal hummed and hawed and came up with excuses why it couldn't be done. I believe it only requires political will to save more children from road deaths. However, Paschal came up with a list of obstacles to imposing a mandatory national speed limit of 30km/h in residential areas. I'm still hearing excuses.

After the meeting, I went to the media and publicly questioned his courage and his commitment to reduce speeds and protect children.

"I have just had a meeting with Minister Donohoe, and he talks as though it will be a massive thing to get this introduced and we don't know whether he has the courage to do it," I said. "We are not accepting it anymore. What I saw on my baby's face, I will never let happen again.

"If I can help protect other children with a lower speed limit on housing estates, I will know that my baby died for a reason. I never want this to happen to another child."

Shortly after, Paschal invited us to another meeting in Government Buildings. Pakie drove me up from Kilkenny to attend it. Minutes into the meeting, I realised that we were being fobbed off with another load of waffle.

He was patronising, insulting our intelligence and, he was wasting our time. I was furious.

It was a struggle just to get up and get dressed those days. The only reason I kept coming all the way to Dublin was that I thought I could achieve something worthwhile in Jake's name.

But here we were sitting in Paschal's office yet again, and it was a wasted exercise.

"Did you really bring us all the way up here to spin us more crap and repeat what you already said to us in an email last week?" I asked.

He was mid-sentence with more condescension when I interrupted him again.

"You think you're something special, don't you Paschal?" I asked my fury building.

"What do you mean?" he blustered.

I was too far gone to stop now.

"You don't seem to realise that you come from the same place as the rest of us, Paschal," I yelled. "From your mother's bloody fanny!"

He said something like there was no call for that kind of language, but I didn't care anymore.

"We're here to try and make a difference, and you're dragging us up and down to Dublin wasting our time. I'm tired of you waffling and offering your condolences for our loss. You didn't know our child, and it looks like you don't care about him or any other child. You're giving us the run-around and using us for photo ops, and we're bloody tired of it!"

Pakie and I stormed out of his office. We were raging and very disheartened about it all. We were hitting our heads off a brick wall with the Minister for Transport.

We rang home to update everyone on our latest pointless meeting. It was my sister Angela who suggested that as we were in Dublin, we should call to see Sinn Fein's deputy leader, Mary Lou McDonald.

"I've heard that she's very straight," she said. "She's not a bullshitter, and if she can help you, she will, and if she can't, at least she won't mess you around."

We were never a political family anyway. But maybe it was because Daddy was a soldier in the Irish army that we never had any dealings with Sinn Fein before.

But from the very start, we said this campaign was beyond party politics. We felt what we were doing should be above politics because it was about the safety of all our kids.

I was adamant: "If Mary Lou McDonald can help us, then we want her on board."

We turned up at her office, but it was closed. Someone said that she might be at the GAA club in her constituency, but she wasn't there either.

Then someone else told us that he knew where she lived, and he gave us an address and described the house.

Pakie and I turned up outside the house. By now it was dinnertime, and it was dark.

"I don't know Pakie; I hate landing on her door like this without an appointment or anything."

"Look we've come all this way up here and got nowhere today. Let's give this a go."

"You knock on the door then."

"No, you do it."

"No, you."

Finally, one of us plucked up the courage to knock on her door. I braced myself for rejection, but Mary Lou herself answered the front door.

She didn't look at all bothered by the interruption even though she had a tea towel in her hand and I could see she was in the middle of making dinner.

As soon as I introduced myself, she said: "I know who you are and what you're doing, come in Roseann, you're very welcome."

She introduced me to her teenage son and told him all about me.

"I think you're wonderful and what you're trying to do is terrific."

She even invited us to sit down with her family for dinner, but we declined and instead we talked. She was very clear that she supported the aims of our campaign and that she would be proud to back us.

"I promise that I'm going to help you," she said.

After the crushing disappointment of a wasted meeting with Paschal Donohoe, we returned to Kilkenny on a high. I came away for the first time after meeting a politician believing that this one meant her promises.

I was also a bit embarrassed thinking about our home intrusion afterwards. We should never have turned up on her doorstep, but in our defence, it had been a very bad day.

Still, Mary Lou was as good as her word, and when she was in Kilkenny, she arranged to meet me again.

She drafted a bill, which was dubbed Jake's Law, to amend road traffic legislation and introduce a 20km/h speed limit in residential areas. She said she and Sinn Fein hoped to get cross-party support and have it passed in the Dáil.

In the following weeks, we met her and her officials. I even got a big, warm, bear hug from Gerry Adams.

Every person we met in Sinn Fein was approachable, decent and a pleasure to deal with. After the condescension and stonewalling of Fine Gael and some of their stuck-up assistants, the Sinn Fein people were a breath of fresh air to us.

We had a new sense of hope in the campaign at last.

We knew that even with the help of Mary Lou, we had to raise the stakes if we were to force the Government to take our campaign seriously.

We needed to show them that we meant business. We announced that we would sleep outside the Dáil as part of our campaign to have residential speed issues addressed.

We decided to stage a three-night, four-day protest on Kildare Street in the middle of February.

"This is about shaming the Government into action. For six months now, I've been dragged up to Dublin to be given pleasantries by a Minister who has shown he doesn't really care about this issue," I told the media.

We decided to hold our vigil from 1.00pm on Sunday, February 15 until Wednesday 18 at 6.25pm - the time of day when Jakie died.

"This is about showing them we mean business – that we are no longer willing to be lied to," I said. "I've asked Paschal to his face if he thinks that the councils are doing their job in controlling speed limits on housing estates, and he refused to answer me."

"His own studies show that the numbers of kids killed on our roads last year doubled, and most of those were in housing estates. This all comes down to money – money the Government isn't willing to spend to protect children. They are basically telling us that our kids aren't worth saving."

Chris and I set up camp outside the Dáil with a small core of supporters. My siblings, Catherine, Jason and Pamela, and her husband, Robert, camped out with us. Brother-in-law Pakie, close friends, Emma and Samantha, and my niece, Donna, were there throughout too.

A campaign supporter, Noel Quigley, who came to Dublin to back us on the first day, never went home for three days either.

The eleven of us slept out in torrential rain and gusts of wind the first night. We had only the shelter of umbrellas and leaking sleeping bags. It was the worst start possible.

The second night was bitterly cold too, but at least it stayed dry. The worst of the weather was behind us by then.

People said we must have got a real sense of what the homeless go through, but that's not true at all. It's far, far worse for the homeless.

At least, we had access to a bathroom as Sinn Fein funded a room for us in the Kildare Street Hotel down the end of the road.

It meant we had a clean toilet and could have a shower every morning and I could also put on a bit of makeup before I had to face the cameras.

We had the kind support of local restaurants and cafes who sent us pizza and sandwiches, so we had no shortage of food.

Also, throughout the three nights and four days, we were never alone. We had so many supporters, friends and family calling that there was a constant festive feeling about our vigil.

Jakie's story has touched the heart of many people including a musician called Alan Gannon from Donegal. He was inspired to write a beautiful song called Misty Morning Fog in his honour.

Alan said he might drop in on our demonstration and I asked, if he did, to bring his guitar. He got on the bus and came all the way from Donegal to join us outside the Dáil.

It was a beautiful afternoon for a sing-song, and I recall Paschal's name was mentioned in some of our lyrics.

The brilliant people behind the Love 30 Campaign, who also fight for lower speed limits in our towns and cities, came out with us in a show of solidarity one day.

Even little old ladies came by to tell us that they thought we were doing marvellous work, so our spirits remained high. A group of Dublin women who called themselves the Pink Ladies also came by several times to join us and raise our numbers and morale.

The media gave us a lot of support with their coverage, and they documented our vigil outside Leinster House gates every day.

We were outside Leinster House to make a statement, to show the Government that we were serious and to let them know that we were going nowhere.

I told the media that Paschal and Enda had personally told me that they backed Jake's Law. I urged the two of them to put their money where their mouth was and to put our kids before profit.

"Speed kills, and you don't just take a child's life, you ruin a whole family," I said. "Who wants to live with regret in their lives due to a small mistake that could have easily have been avoided?"

Some people thought we were mad demonstrating on the street, but I didn't care. I was doing something for my baby. I felt like I was there for Jake and that it might make a difference to other children, including my own.

At the same time, I missed being with the kids, and I missed going to Jake's grave. But I hoped that by being outside the Dáil, we could make the Government pay attention and help make sure that more parents didn't suffer the tragedy that we did.

On the second day outside Leinster House, the Dáil started debating the Sinn Féin private member's Road Traffic (Amendment) Bill, dubbed Jake's Law which called for the introduction of a 20km/h speed limit in residential areas.

I met with Fianna Fáil's Micheál Martin and John McGuinness outside Leinster House. They were supportive of the campaign, and Micheál assured us that all of Fianna Fail would back the bill.

John was very sincere in his support and gave a powerful speech on Jake's Law in the Dáil debate.

He thanked deputies Mary Lou McDonald and Dessie Ellis for bringing the bill forward. He said he attended Jake's funeral and he said it was "the greatest outpouring of grief and sadness that I have ever witnessed."

He added: "Roseann Brennan, her family and her supporters have done this state a great service and remember it is out of trauma and sadness and the death of their child that they are doing this, and I would say that Jake's death should be the end. We should give a really positive response in funding and everything else to empower the councils to deliver, not just for that family, but for all families."

Mattie McGrath TD also backed the campaign by getting in under our sleeping bags for a photo opportunity.

That evening as the debate went on, the RTE Six One News cameras arrived down to the Dáil gates to interview us.

I told RTE that we'd met with lots of supportive TDs from Fianna Fail; that the Sinn Fein party had sent us out coffees and that Mary Lou had been up and down to see us every day.

But I told them our Government ministers including Paschal were noticeable by their absence.

"I haven't seen Paschal whose office is just across the road and who I've had five meetings with," I said on the Six One News. "I've met with the Taoiseach and the Minister for the Environment too, but they haven't been out to me. They said they backed Jake's Legacy. So, I hope when they're in the chamber that they are men of their word, and they stick by what they said and pass Jake's Law."

RTE asked me again about support from Fine Gael and the Minister for Transport.

"No, they haven't come out, and I haven't seen Paschal at all, and I thought that we had a good working relationship," I said. "But he hasn't taken time out to say 'hi' or anything like that or even given me a call."

The first thing the next morning, Paschal scuttled over to our small demonstration like he was our best friend in the world. He had a few photographers in tow to capture the magic moment for the media.

He said that Fine Gael wouldn't be opposing the bill, so it was expected to pass.

Speaking in the Dáil that night, Enda Kenny said that he had met with me, discussed our "sad case" and said I'd brought the campaign "to national attention".

Then Paschal said he accepted the principal of a Sinn Féin proposal for a 20km/h limit but shot down any attempts to make the speed limit mandatory.

He insisted that imposing blanket speed limits was 'problematic'. He said those best able to define a residential area were the local authorities and councillors.

The Government said that the measures raised in the Sinn Féin bill would be addressed in their own Road Traffic Bill 2015 which would be published in the summer. But there was no clear timetable for implementation of speed limits.

The whole thing was a joke. We felt betrayed and let down again by the Fine Gael Government.

"I want times. When is this all going to be put on paper? That's saying we're just going to put you off for another year or two," I said. "While the minister accepts there needs to be speed limits in housing estates he is still leaving it to county councils to exercise discretion in the matter. He is not going to impose Jake's Law.

"It all comes down to money. If the Government makes it mandatory, they will have to spend money on implementing the new speed limits, and they don't want to do that."

I also posted a video on Jake's Legacy saying that Paschal had lied to my family and that Fine Gael trampled on my Jakie's memory.

"They let people believe that they were passing Jake's Law and it was a load of lies," I said.

We knew that Paschal was washing his hands of responsibility and passing the buck to local authorities again.

The following month, he unveiled new guidelines for 'slow zones' across the country in urban areas. It allowed local authorities implement a 30km/h speed limit in residential areas if deemed necessary.

He also provided a paltry €2 million for all 31 local authorities in the country to help introduce 30km/h speed limit. Kilkenny County Council alone estimated they needed a budget of €240,000 for the new signage and road ramps.

I accused the minister of reneging on his commitments again.

"I feel Paschal Donohoe trampled on my baby's legacy," I said. "The way I see it, Paschal Donohoe and the Fine Gael party did not want the bad publicity when I was sleeping out in the cold and rain."

I also rubbished the funding they made available for signage to make speed limit changes a reality.

A few weeks later, Dublin's Fingal County Council backed a motion calling for speed limits in housing estates to be reduced to 20km/h. They also sent a letter to Paschal outlining their support for the reduced speed limit.

Sinn Fein Councillor, Natalie Treacy, called on Paschal to pass Jake's Law as part of the Road Traffic Amendment Bill 2015. But, the only reply they got was from Paschal's private secretary saying that the contents of the council's letter were 'brought to the attention' of the Minister.

The jury at Jakie's inquest in March 2016 also made a special recommendation in their verdict that 30km/h speed limits be introduced in housing estates. The coroner Dr Brendan Doyle wrote to the Department of Transport outlining the jury's recommendation.

We continued to be a thorn in Paschal's side at every opportunity, but in May 2016, Shane Ross became the new Minister for Transport.

We were relieved to see the back of Paschal, but things didn't get any better when Shane Ross took over.

I rang and rang the new Minister's office and left endless voicemails for his private secretary. When I finally spoke to a human being, they claimed they never received any of the emails that I'd sent.

I kept copies of everything, and I could see that my emails had been sent, but the Minister's office insisted they'd received nothing. They needed me to email them again.

"Hang on I've seven sisters and a mother, and I think two of them between them all can send an email," I said. "So, if you can't email, you can't get a response from the Minister for Transport's office?"

I called and called again and again and not once did Shane Ross pick up the phone to return my call. There were so many times when I felt like giving up. I never wanted to have to do this, and it took a lot out of me to speak to so many people.

But every time I felt like walking away, I could feel Jake inside me. I felt like I was doing this for him, to ensure no other little boy or girl went through what he did.

I had no choice but go on, did I Jakie?

So, I continued to chase Shane Ross.

In the summer of 2016, I was asked to speak at the launch of a public consultation for Dublin City Council's plans to roll out a limit of 30km/h in residential areas that summer.

As soon as my role as a speaker was announced, I got a phone call from the Department of Transport. They assured me that I was down for a meeting with the Minister at some point.

I slammed Shane Ross to anyone who'd listen at the launch.

I said I'd been calling his office every day since he became transport minister but after months, I'd heard nothing.

"If the Minister changes, does that mean we've got to start all over?" I asked. "That's not how it should be. I didn't just work with one man; I worked with an office."

I explained that without support from the Minister, speed limits could never happen nationally as private estates were exempt from council guidelines.

"Our housing estate where Jake was killed is still 50km/h because the council can't touch it. We, like a lot of families in Kilkenny, live in a private estate," I said.

"This is why the Minister needs to get involved because no matter what Dublin City Council do – they could change the entire city – they still can't touch the private estates."

"Without a national rollout, we're basically saying some children's lives are worth more than others."

I said I'd lost count of the messages I had left with the minister's secretary.

"Not once did Ross pick up the phone," I said. "But then there's a press release about Dublin City Council's plan and my involvement, and suddenly I get a phone call. I just found the timing odd, and I'm hoping that I haven't just been spun a few lines to keep me happy."

It didn't take long before I got my meeting with Shane Ross. To my surprise, I got on well with him. He really seemed to believe in the aims of the campaign, and he supported it.

He also wanted to get things done. I was impressed by his vitality and passion.

He oversaw the passing of the Road Traffic Bill 2016 just before Christmas in December that year.

The bill created a new option for local authorities to impose a special speed limit of 20km/h in built-up areas. This is in addition to the existing possible speed limits for built-up areas of 30km/h, 40km/h and 50km/h.

"This is being done, after careful consideration, in response to the Jake's Legacy campaign," he said in the Seanad. "I pay tribute to the work of Jake's mother, Roseann Brennan, and all involved in the campaign."

However, he still hasn't made the new speed limits mandatory in housing estates nationwide. The Government still claims that there are "legal and practical complexities".

Shane Ross's department wrote to me in early 2017 saying that they have sought legal advice from the Office of the Attorney General and the Chief State Solicitor's Office on these matters.

The last meeting that I had with Shane, I started getting that feeling of deja vu. It was like being in Paschal's office again. Shane had a fire in his belly when I met him first, but now he seems to be getting comfy in his ministerial seat.

He says it's challenging to enforce mandatory speed limits as there is no legal definition of what a housing estate is. There are constitutional difficulties in applying speed limits in estates that have not yet been taken in charge by the local authority.

All I hear about is legal problems, constitutional problems blah, blah, blah. I believe that where there's a will, there's a way. I'm just not seeing much will anymore.

Making new speed limits mandatory is going to cost the Government money, and I believe that's the crux of the issue.

I've offered to bring an eminent legal eagle to our meetings. He's a partner in a top firm as well as a concerned father who supports our campaign. He's interested in examining these supposed obstacles to mandatory speed limits.

However, the Minister's office doesn't seem to be in any hurry to arrange that meeting.

But the Minister for Transport should know that we're not going away anytime soon.

We still have more to do, but the Jake's Legacy campaign has a lot to be proud off and has achieved a lot of success.

We have a magnificent amount of support from people all around the country, and today we have more than 22,000 followers on Facebook.

Thanks to Jake's Legacy and other campaigns, lower speed limits are becoming the standard in housing estates all around the country.

In 2014, when we started, only Cork City Council had applied the 30km/h speed limit in 135 of their estates. By the end of 2016, a total of 25 local authorities outside Dublin introduced lower speed limits in 2,590 estates around Ireland.

During 2017, councils reduced speed limits in a further 3,621 estates.

Dublin City Council introduced a 30km/h limit in residential areas in early 2017. I cried when the councillors told me that Jake had a direct impact on bringing in the new limits.

In October 2017, the Road Safety Authority kicked off Irish Road Safety Week by urging local authorities to introduce more 30km/h zones in Ireland.

When asked for my response, I said that I was glad to see that the RSA recognised that speeding in built-up areas is a problem.

I added that I would have loved to have had their support when I started calling for reduced speed limits back in 2014.

By 2018, I'm proud to say, all 31 local authorities have or are about to introduce 30 or 20km/h speed limits in residential areas.

We will carry on Jake's Legacy, but it's not what I want to do for the rest of my life. I want to get back to being a mammy, and I want to spend more time playing with my kids. I want to study, and I want to work in the community.

I want to make a difference, but I don't want to fight politicians for the rest of my life.

At the same time, I don't want another child to die as Jake did and I don't want another family to suffer the way we have.

We haven't finished our job yet. We haven't achieved our aims of a mandatory national speed limit fully; so, we're staying around until we do.

We need to get speed limits changed in all residential areas and housing estates, all over the country.

Above all, we need the Government to get the simple message:

The difference between a speed of 30km/h and 50km/h is the difference between a child with a broken leg and a fatally wounded child, lying in his mammy's arms, begging not to die.

16. 'MENTAL' PATIENT ROSIE

Within a few months of Jakie's death, I had a complete breakdown. I was exhausted. Even when I took sleeping tablets, I wasn't sleeping.

I still wore a brilliant smile for the kids as I tried to be the perfect mother. I was also working hard on the campaign at the same time.

The breakdown crept up on me gradually until I reached a stage where I was almost insane with grief.

All I know is that I wanted to kill myself. I kept thinking of that sharp, pointed kitchen knife, picking it up and sticking it in my chest and finishing it all. It seemed easy. Nothing else could hurt as much as I already did.

At other times I thought of jumping off John's Bridge in Kilkenny. I don't think I wanted to die, but I knew that I couldn't live like this anymore.

Early after Jake's death, my doctor referred me to the Department of Psychiatry (the DOP) in St Luke's Hospital.

Psychiatric consultant Dr Séamus MacSuibhne was over my case, but I hadn't been referred to any counselling at the hospital at that stage.

My head was filled with these black thoughts, and I knew I was going to do something to myself. I was very sick, but I had the sense to beg Catherine to bring me to St Luke's Hospital.

"I can't do this anymore, I can't do this," I cried. "I'm too tired, so tired."

I was inconsolable, crying, shaking, massively depressed and anxious. Catherine could see I was in a bad way, so she reluctantly brought me to St Luke's.

At the hospital, I had to beg them to do something for me. There was a delay of some hours in getting someone to see me, and by then I decided I wanted to go home to sleep. That was how it was then. I was alternatively manic and then catatonic.

But then the doctors said I couldn't leave the hospital. They said I was a risk to myself.

I felt a sense of hope for the first time in months. Maybe they could fix me.

My sisters and Chris were very upset that the doctors had admitted me to a 'mental' hospital. They couldn't believe that I wanted to be there either.

In some ways, the hospital was like the asylums that I'd seen in the movies. They took away my phone, my shoelaces, and removed sharp implements.

The unit was loud and noisy, filled with screaming and shouting and pain. All hell broke loose at times and the sounds of agonised patients echoed through the place, but it didn't bother me because it wasn't my noise.

They gave me a room to myself, and I slept like I hadn't slept in months. The bedlam outside had nothing to do with me, so I rolled over and slept and kept sleeping.

For four solid days, I stayed sleeping. I only woke to cry. I wasn't capable of talking to anyone. The girls and Chris visited, but I didn't want to see them.

When I wasn't sleeping, I'd sit on the floor as I did at home with my photo of Jake and rock and cry. I cried quietly like I always did at home so not to wake the kids.

I remember a nurse walked in and interrupted one of my crying sessions. She picked me up off the floor and let me ramble and rant. Then she put me back to bed, and I went back to sleep again.

I never thought I'd be a person who'd end up in a psychiatric hospital but there I was. My sisters were horrified by some of the people they saw in there.

They couldn't see, as I rocked in my bed, that I was just as troubled and as broken as anyone else there.

After four days, I started coming around enough to have a shower and get cleaned up. I went to the place where patients can make a phone call, and I rang Chris to ask about the kids.

After a week I wanted to go home. I wanted to be with my kids, but I found that you can't just pack your bags and leave.

The unit sets up a home-based treatment plan that involves supervision and counselling before a patient leaves. They gave me an excellent supervising counsellor called Ashley who called to see me every day until he was comfortable that I was coping.

I still have an entire team around me under Dr MacSuibhne including a social worker, and a counsellor. The team is not interested or involved in any way with my children because they know they're not at risk.

They have no communication with Chris, my family or anyone else. They are there only for me.

I've been in the DOP a few times since, during some of the lowest moments of my life. Each time, I've met some of the nicest people in there. They're all ordinary people trying to cope with their problems, their tragedies and their frailties like I am.

I came out feeling rested but not feeling any significant improvement. Instead, the months after my first psychiatric admission passed slowly and no less painfully than before.

I dreaded the approach of our first Christmas without Jake, and by then, I'd started self-harming by cutting my legs. I'd lock the bedroom door, take out a hair clip, take off the padded ends, and start scraping and scratching my thighs until they bled.

I knew that it was crazy behaviour, but I couldn't stop myself. It fulfilled some need to punish myself, and doing it gave me a few moments of relief.

I couldn't even bear to put up a Christmas tree in the house that I hated so much, so I focussed on making Jakie's grave look festive with lights, candles and flowers.

We went through the motions in the run-up to Christmas for Kaelem's sake. Savannah was still too little to know what was going on. We moved into my sister Pamela's house on Christmas Eve so that he'd have some sense of a happy festive season.

Kaelem and Savannah had a great Christmas, but all we had of Jakie was his photo on the dinner table and visits to his grave.

We stayed with Pamela for a week, and it was a relief to escape the dark house on Lintown Grove. I realised that Christmas and every other family event would never be the same for us again.

I tried to keep myself together, but everything went pear-shaped in the New Year. I felt like a failure where the kids were concerned.

Everyone was telling me that I should be getting over the worst of Jakie's loss by now, but I wasn't.

It was a new year, and they said I should be turning a new leaf and getting on with life. I only saw another year of misery, pain and loss.

They told me that I had to hold it together for the kids. I knew that, but I was struggling to do it. I tried to be cheerful and keep a smile on my face, but all I wanted was to sit on the floor of my room, and rock and cry.

I felt like I was letting down Kaelem and Savannah; like I was the worst mother.

I also felt alone. It seemed to me that I was on my own, doing everything and that Chris was no help. It was all getting too much for me. Suicidal thoughts resurfaced and took over my mind again.

I only got scared when I started having thoughts about harming the kids. I was drying Savannah after a bath one evening when I had a vision of putting her and Kaelem to bed, smothering them in their sleep and then killing myself by taking every tablet in the house.

My mind started to churn with vile thoughts like this, and I couldn't stop it.

I went to Dr MacSuibhne and confessed what I was thinking, what I was seeing and about the constant self-harming.

"Would you kill yourself?" he asked.

"Yes, I think about it all the time. Living is too hard. I don't think I can do it anymore."

"Would you kill your children?" he asked.

I was never surer about anything else in my life.

"I'd never harm a hair on their heads."

I couldn't sleep at night for thinking what went through Jakie's mind after I let him cross that road, and he was crushed.

"The guilt I feel about Jakie makes me want to die. Do you think I could handle my two other children's last thoughts being that Mammy was trying to hurt them?" I explained. "But why am

I thinking these horrible things? I want it to stop. Why can't I stop thinking these things?"

Dr MacSuibhne admitted me, and they took everything from me again apart from a hairclip in my hair. I was relieved when I found it. I sat in that bathroom in the DOP scraping and scratching my flesh until I bled.

The first time they admitted me, they let me sleep because the break down was the result of exhaustion.

This time they encouraged me to walk around the gardens, to go to art classes, to attend mindfulness classes and to engage with people. I spent a lot of the time jogging endless circuits around the garden.

This admission was the opposite of the last time. The last time I was exhausted, but this time my mind was racing, and this evil voice was taking over.

You're useless. Look at you in here in a mental hospital, and your kids are out there. Look at what you did to Jake. Look at what you're doing cutting yourself, you stupid woman.

The voice in my head was bad enough, but the sisters' voices were critical too. They decided it was time to apply tough love.

"This is not the solution. You can't hide away. You have two other kids to think about," they said. "How could you be so selfish to think about suicide? What would that do to those poor children left behind?"

At the same time, I had the evil voice nagging in my head.

You don't have to leave them behind. Sure, take them with you.

I tried to explain to my sisters that I was doing it for the kids; that I was afraid that I would hurt myself; that I was having these awful thoughts about harming them.

I admitted I wanted to die, and I begged them to let me go and give me their blessing.

"Please let me go," I pleaded. "Tell my babies that I love them, and I'm sorry. I'm useless to them."

I don't know how long I was in there, but when I came out, life was still a constant battle. I wanted to go back to the DOP. I guess I wanted to be fixed, but no one could find a cure.

I was a zombie; like the living dead. It took all my energy to pretend that everything was okay when I was around Kaelem and Savannah. I tried to make sure my kids never saw the real me. When I felt a bad day coming on, and I couldn't act anymore, I called Catherine, and she took them from me.

Sometimes, when I woke in the morning, I forgot about this nightmare. For an instant, I woke like I used to, stretching and happy. Then I remembered and felt the familiar stab to the heart again.

There were times I put Jake's favourite plate out for his dinner, and I wanted to scream when I realised he'd never use it again.

I still found myself picking up the little things that he liked to eat in the supermarket aisles. It felt easier to abandon the trolley and leave the shop than to return his favourite cereal or yoghurt to the shelf.

My birthday rolled around in March, and the girls brought me out for the first time since Jakie died nine months earlier.

I didn't feel like going out, but I got dressed up and went. I thought I'd be miserable. So I was surprised when I enjoyed myself. I had a few drinks and danced all night. I started going out every couple of weeks after that for drink, music and dancing.

It was like turning back the clock and returning to a time when I was single and carefree; a time before Chris and me. It meant I had a few hours of normality when I was party girl Rosie again.

But drink and grief don't go together, and I began to feel very low the day after. I realised that by trying to return to a time when I was single, I was also trying to wipe out Jakie's existence.

I decided I didn't like party girl Rosie anymore. I stopped going out. That escape route ended, and the depression continued.

I found a lump in my breast around that time and I know it's a terrible thing to think or to say, but a little bit of me hoped it was cancer. I was finding life so hard that a terminal illness seemed tempting.

By the summer of that year, I was heading into another episode of feeling very unwell. I started obsessing a lot about The Driver.

She cleared out of the estate about six weeks after Jakie died, but someone told me where she was working and living. I raged because she was getting on with normal life after wrecking ours.

I never wanted to waste a single minute thinking about her because she never gave a thought about my family. So, I despaired when I couldn't get her out of my head.

I went back to the Department of Psychiatry at St. Luke's Hospital in a bid to see someone, anyone. As usual, it takes a long time to see anyone, and I walked out exhausted. I knew I didn't want to go home.

I crossed the road and booked into the Kilkenny House Hotel.

I rang Samantha and told her where I was, so she could let Chris know, and he could mind the kids that night. I needed a quiet room and sleep.

The gardaí rang me at some stage, and I had to assure them I'd return to the DOP in the morning. The hospital admitted me again for treatment.

When I came out again, nothing had changed. I was still lost in a world of grief, and so was Chris. I'm not saying we were always unhappy together. Home life was very calm, and we worked well together for the kids' sake.

As I said, there was no screaming or fighting but also little feeling or connection between us apart from resentment and anger. We led separate lives. I stayed upstairs; he stayed downstairs, and we only met to look after the kids.

Chris finally moved out near the end of 2015.

By now I had, and still have, a great clinical psychologist called Dr Claire Regan. I felt I was making real progress in dealing with Jakie's loss and rebuilding my life. But Chris wouldn't go to counselling.

Through First Light, we tried group counselling for couples who lost children. We met once a month with three other sets of grieving parents, but I ended up going to one of the sessions with Pamela because he refused to finish it.

I felt very hurt that he wouldn't make an effort.

We tried marital counselling in the DOP with a counsellor called Sean. But Chris wouldn't open up, so that didn't help much either. No matter how much we wanted to, we couldn't seem to help each other.

I begged him to seek help on his own but he wouldn't.

"I'm grand; I'm dealing with it," he said.

Then sometimes he'd swear that he was going to seek professional help, and then he didn't. I had enough of false promises.

He didn't want to deal with Jake's death, and there seemed to be no point in trying to work on our marriage until he did.

Chris took everything with him when he moved back to his parents' place. He made sure he didn't have to come back for anything.

I know it sounds crazy, but my husband's departure didn't bother me. It was a relief to me that he was gone. We didn't fight, and there were no tears or recriminations. We were both hurting too much over Jake to hurt over each other.

I thought: "I don't miss him; I don't care that he's left, so it's obvious that I don't love him."

It was all very civilised, unemotional and easy. We agreed that Chris would take the children with him to Castlecomer for two nights and three days and I'd have them for the rest of the time.

I missed the kids moving out for three days, but it meant I didn't have to wear a smile for those days, and I could cry as loud as I wanted to. I didn't have to get dressed for three days; I didn't have to answer the door for three days, and I could go out for one night of the three if I wanted to. I could let go.

Two months after Chris moved out, the novelty wore off for Kaelem, and he started kicking up about the new arrangement.

"I'm not going to Comer!" he screamed. "I want Daddy home!"

The whole point of staying in Lintown Grove was to give Kaelem time to adjust to life without Jake. We realised that dragging him to Comer several nights a week was not in his best interests.

It was coming up to Christmas again, and we decided that Chris would move back downstairs for a couple of nights a week.

We agreed one of the grounds of his return was that he had to seek professional help. He said he'd get counselling if the marriage counsellor Sean would see him. Sean agreed, and Chris is now an outpatient with the DOP.

The truth is our marriage almost died along with Jake. There was nothing between us for a long time, and it's only since early 2017, that we started finding each other again. But we realise that we still have a long journey ahead.

When someone precious is lost, Christmas and other family occasions bring their own brand of heartache and pain. They become dreaded dates on the calendar that highlight Jakie's loss and the fact that he's no longer around.

A stabbing reminder of our second Christmas without Jakie came with the Late Late Toy Show in November 2015.

Like every child in Ireland, Jakie loved the Toy Show. His eyes were out on stalks as he watched all the toys and the children performing on TV. I remembered Jakie's last Toy Show as he curled up with Kaelem on their chair in front of the telly.

Chris and I laughed because, despite all their excitement, they both fell fast asleep long before it was over.

By November 2015, Chris was employed as a chef, and he was working the night of the Toy Show.

My sisters knew that I'd feel low that night and they offered to come over. But I insisted: "No, I'm grand. It's your kids' turn. It's a big deal to them, and they want you there with them."

I told myself I'd be fine. Without Jake around, Kaelem didn't know anything about the show, so I was able to put him to bed and forget about the programme.

Around 9.00pm, I found myself in my ensuite bathroom in a pool of blood after slashing the whole back of my thigh with a blade. I didn't plan it; I just did it.

I was there and not there. I slashed my leg three times, and I never felt a thing. I couldn't face casualty and the memories of Jakie there.

I waited until I heard Chris come home, then wrapped my leg in a towel and drove up to Pamela's because I knew she had a first aid kit. I should have got it properly stitched because it took a year for it to heal.

Chris found a blood-soaked hand towel, and he was livid.

"Roseann, you promised you'd stopped that!" he said.

I told my psychologist because I was as bewildered why I did these things to myself.

But I couldn't count the times that people have said to me since Jakie died: "You're so strong; if that was me I would have killed myself."

It was the kind of thing I said myself before Jake died. I remember Pamela and I watched some awful tragedy about the death of a child.

"God, Pamela, what would you do if that happened to you?" I said. "I'd kill myself."

"I wouldn't blame you," she replied. "I'd do the same myself."

Pamela recalled that conversation after Jake died. She was petrified that I'd commit suicide and that she had granted me permission by saying she wouldn't blame me.

Chris worried, my sisters and my mother worried about me killing myself. I worried about it. Suicide was on my mind a lot. I wanted to be with Jakie with all my heart.

The only thing that stopped me was my other two children. I love and cherish my kids, and I know the agony of losing a parent when you're very young.

I never thought I'd inflict the same pain on Kaelem and Savannah but a few months later, I very nearly did.

17. JUSTICE FOR JAKIE

"A road death is not like a normal death. It's a violent death – as violent as murder."

These words resonate strongly with me. They're the words of Brigitte Chaudhry, who set up RoadPeace for road victims in the UK after the death of her son.

Jake's death felt as traumatic and as savage as any murder to us. He died a violent, cruel and brutal death. He died in a way that no six-year-old child should die.

For six months after Jakie went to heaven, we didn't know if there would be any justice for his death. We were in a legal limbo.

We didn't know when or if the DPP was going to prosecute The Driver. We didn't know where The Driver struck Jake; or why she kept going after hitting him.

We were still searching for truth and justice for our baby.

During that time, the Jake's Legacy Campaign kept us going. For us, it meant that Jake's name and spirit could live on and that his death could have some meaning.

But at the same time, we needed answers, and we wanted justice for his senseless death.

For those six anxious months, we waited to hear the decision of the DPP. We felt we couldn't move on with our lives until we knew if we'd get justice for Jakie.

Very early after our baby's death, a bereaved parent, Tony Cullen, contacted us through our Jake's Legacy Facebook page. He lost his four-year-old daughter Clodagh when a car struck her in a housing estate in Thomastown, Kilkenny in September 2007.

Jakie was only in heaven a few weeks when I first met Tony, so I felt at death's door and in the depths of despair.

The first thing to that struck me about Tony was his undying love for his daughter and his passion for justice. He had buried his baby seven years earlier, but he was still so affected by her loss that her death might have happened the day before.

Chris and I were flailing around in the dark when it came to the legal and investigative process surrounding Jake's death. We hadn't much of a clue about the steps involved in a garda investigation. We knew nothing about the legal proceedings, the DPP, the post-mortem or the inquest.

An angel must have sent Tony to us because he brought us along the path and guided us through the maze. He became our go-to person who advised us through every turn and twist of the case.

He inspired us and pushed us to keep searching for answers and keep demanding justice for Jake.

For years, he fought over inconsistencies that he found in the investigation into his daughter's case. In our opinion, he made a better job of the inquiry into Clodagh's killing than the authorities.

He believed that the pathologist's report on her death contradicted the statements taken by the gardaí after the accident, and he tried to fight the DPP when they refused to press charges over his daughter's death.

He and his wife Anne Marie even took their case to the Garda Síochána Ombudsman Commission (Gsoc).

Gsoc agreed that the investigation lacked some avenues of inquiry and record-keeping. However, their report concluded, there was no basis to believe his daughter's death was "anything more than a tragic accident".

In the end, Tony and Anne Marie could only take a civil action against the driver. Families of road victims can still take a civil case even if the DPP decides that there won't be a criminal prosecution.

The standard of proof in a criminal trial is "beyond a reasonable doubt". The standard of proof in civil actions is that one party's case need only be more probable that the other.

Winning a civil case is a hollow victory for most bereaved family members. Yet, winning this action in the high court was the only sense of justice that Tony and Anne Marie received.

They never got the answers to questions they had over Clodagh's death, and they never got the justice that Clodagh deserved because they believe that the garda investigation was flawed.

From the start, Tony warned that we needed to take steps to stop the same thing happening to us, and he used to meet with us often to advise on our case.

He pushed us to ask every question and to try to ensure that everyone investigated Jake's death thoroughly. He warned that we'd never establish what exactly happened or have any hope of a criminal prosecution if we didn't keep on top of the case.

Tony was a rock of support and a font of information the first year after Jakie's death. He was always a phone call away when we needed him. When we learnt of his premature death in May 2015, we were very shocked and saddened.

As months passed waiting for the DPP's decision, we got less and less optimistic about them pressing charges. Through our work with Jake's Legacy, I'd met and talked to more and more parents who'd lost children in crashes on housing estates.

My hopes sank as I learnt there had never been a successful prosecution in such a case. We knew it would be an uphill battle for justice in any road death case where ridiculous speeds are legal.

I'd already met loads of parent who never got justice for their children because of this.

In my opinion, there were grounds for dangerous driving causing death or even careless driving causing death in Jake's case.

The charges sounded like a slap on the wrist after the death of our child, but it would have been something. It would have been an acknowledgement that drivers should not accelerate from parked to 47km/h within a few metres on a cul-de-sac where children play.

The timeline during those dark days is a bit vague, but it was near Christmas 2014 when I got a call from our garda family liaison officer, Frances Dunphy.

We were feeling low anyway with the approach of our first Christmas without Jake. We were trying to keep up a united, happy front for the children, but it was difficult because our marriage was over, and we were both very depressed.

Frances said Superintendent Padraig Dunne's office wanted to arrange a meeting to see Chris and me later that week. The meeting was about the decision from the DPP's office.

My heart started racing.

"Tell him I need to know now, not in a few days' time!" I said. "I want to know now. I'm not having this hanging over me a minute longer."

Frances was always kind to us, and she understood our urgency. She made a few calls and called me back within minutes telling me the Superintendent was going to wait at the station to see us.

We went straight to the station where they brought us to an office with tea and biscuits laid out on the meeting desk. I felt like getting sick as I faced a plate of Custard Creams.

Superintendent Padraig Dunne didn't give us much of a preamble.

"We have to inform you that the DPP has directed that there'll be no criminal proceedings," he said. "It means that we won't be pressing charges for careless or dangerous driving."

I let out a shriek of despair, and Christopher roared: "This is f**ing ridiculous!"

It was like the final kick in the teeth for both of us. The Driver, whose car killed our baby, was going to walk away without even a rap on the knuckles.

Chris's face was red with fury and suppressed tears. My heart thumped, and my stomach was a knot of anxiety again.

Tony had already explained to us that the Superintendent would have sent his recommendation to the DPP with the Garda Investigation File.

"Padraig, can I ask you what your recommendation was to the DPP?" I asked.

He tried to say that he had nothing to do with the DPP's decision and that it was the decision of the DPP alone.

"Padraig, can you be a man and tell me what you recommended to the DPP?" I said. "I will write away for all this information anyway, and I'll find out. Was your recommendation not to press charges?"

We left the station knowing little more than the DPP's decision.

Christmas was never going to be a festive season for us, but this news sent us into a spiral of despair. It was like another 'f**k you' from the world.

It seemed that we would never see any justice for Jake. Without a prosecution, it was like the death of our baby meant nothing. Anyone could speed up from zero to 47km/h within metres, smash into a child, cause fatal injuries and keep driving with impunity.

I was livid. I had to return to the station with our solicitor Tim Kiely a few days later. We also sent letter after letter to the DPP. I wanted the reasons behind the decision not to prosecute, and I demanded a review into the case.

We wrote to Kilkenny Garda Station and the DPP again and again over the following months. I wanted to know if The Driver had been breathalysed because no one on the road that day saw it happening.

I wanted to know why Superintendent Padraig Dunne kept repeating that he was advised by the DPP not to tell us anything about the investigation even after the DPP decided not to prosecute.

I sought help from voluntary organisations like the Irish Road Victims Association (IRVA) and PARC Road Safety Group in Ireland.

IRVA has been an excellent source of information and support for us throughout our ordeal. They offer free bereavement counselling, as well as assistance with garda investigations, the DPP and the inquest.

Donna Price, who founded IRVA after losing her 18-year-old son in a crash, and others in the association are always available for shattered families.

In April 2015, while we were still trying to fight the DPP's decision, I was invited to attend the National Road Safety Conference in Dublin Castle.

I listened to the speakers talking about more education for children and talking about training. They discussed how adult pedestrians could be a better example to children.

I got angrier as I listened to the endless victim-blaming. The message was that children can avoid road death if we educate them enough, and parents are to blame for not setting a good example.

They also made idiotic suggestions such as parents living in estates need to measure their roads and point out safe spots where children can cross.

"And what happens when we point out a safe spot for our children, and they find cars parked there the next time they want to cross the road?" I asked.

The speakers were only interested in what pedestrians could do to avoid being hit by traffic. We heard little mention of speeding or distracted drivers, the culprits behind most road deaths.

Fed up with the waffle, I demanded to know how they planned to reduce the speed limits that were killing our children in housing estates.

Another woman, Rita Ní Mhaoileoin, whose child Oran was badly injured by a car on a housing estate, was also annoyed by the Road Safety Authority's agenda that day.

She and I put our hands up, interrupted speeches and sessions, and contradicted a lot of blather at the conference.

"Education is great and so is being a good example to children," I said. "But what are we going to do about drivers who drive too fast in estates and residential areas?"

In the end, I told the conference that I had to leave because it was my son's 7th birthday and I needed to celebrate it at his grave. I'm sure they were glad to see the back of me.

An Irish Examiner reporter wrote afterwards that we "were about the most effective hijackers of a conference agenda" that he'd ever seen.

Being called a 'hijacker' was a first for me. He meant it nicely though.

"Every delegate ... found it impossible to do anything other than respect their determination to see their concerns dominate the discussion," he wrote.

The voluntary organisation IRVA presented me with an award on Road Victim's Day in November that year.

They hold a World Day of Remembrance for Road Traffic Victims on the third Sunday in November every year. The day is a public recognition of the loss and suffering of all those bereaved or injured in road crashes and also honours members of the emergency services.

IRVA founder and chairperson, Donna Price, made the presentation and addressed the audience.

"Anyone at the Road Safety Authority Conference this year in Dublin Castle witnessed that Roseann will not take 'no' for an answer," she said. "When road victims were not included or were not the main focus on the agenda, Roseann made sure that they were."

In our opinion, several short-comings in the garda investigation emerged at Jake's inquest in March 2016. Again, we requested a review of the DPP's decision not to prosecute.

But we learnt, like other families of road victims, that there is little justice for those killed on the roads.

Organisations like IRVA and Parc are doing great work fighting against the dismissive attitude by the authorities when it comes to road traffic deaths.

If someone is killed by a blow from a cudgel or the stab of a knife, it's a serious, criminal matter. But when someone is killed, and the weapon used is a car, it's regarded as "an accident".

A road traffic death is regarded as unfortunate but a misdemeanour at most.

To me, a road death should never be considered accidental when it's avoidable and preventable.

I still find it so hard to think of the shock and the fear in the face of my baby after that car struck him.

He was cruelly killed at six years of age when The Driver got behind the wheel of two tonnes of steel and accelerated to 46.3km or more in a matter of metres in a little cul-de-sac where children play.

She mowed our baby down right outside his own house, tossed him in the air and dragged him down the street.

She was going so fast she didn't even apply her brakes. We can only assume that she was accelerating at such speed that she couldn't stop. She wasn't speeding away from danger; she was going to Lidl.

That's no accident to my mind, but according to the justice system, it is.

Chris and I are not alone in our anger and frustration. There are many thousands of others who have discovered that the legal and investigative response to road deaths is inadequate.

Thanks to IRVA and PARC in Ireland and RoadPeace in the UK, victims are getting a voice at last.

Donna Price and fellow grieving parents in IRVA are calling for a proper forensic investigation of every road accident.

When IRVA started in 2006, in nine out of ten cases, the driver who survived a fatal crash was not even tested for alcohol or drugs.

The organisation is calling for sentencing that reflects the fact that the driver has killed someone. They've been campaigning for a fairer justice system, with more transparent investigations and prosecutions.

"Road deaths should be investigated and prosecuted like other homicides," says Donna who was also appointed to the board of the Road Safety Authority (RSA) in early 2018.

"Road crime is real crime, and road victims are entitled to the same support and protection as other victims of crime. Just because a death is caused by a car, it is no less of a death."

When relatives of road victims demand justice, we are often accused of being vindictive towards the driver.

When we insist that our relative's death or injury is investigated with the seriousness it deserves, some say we're vengeful.

A criminal conviction will never bring back our dead loved ones, and a jail sentence will never heal our broken hearts. What it may do is act as a deterrent to others who drive recklessly.

Until road crimes are treated as seriously as other crimes, there is no deterrent.

People will continue to speed or use their phone while behind the wheel. They will continue to drive carelessly because they can do so with impunity.

In the meantime, drivers, if they happen to kill or seriously injure someone in the process, are treated with sympathy rather than censure.

After all, accidents happen, don't they?

18. LOVE, LOATHING AND JAKE'S INQUEST

We continued fighting the DPP until every avenue into pursuing a criminal prosecution was exhausted. In the end, it seemed that the inquest into Jake's death would be our only opportunity to find answers to the many questions we had.

The coroner set a date for the inquest on Thursday, March 31, 2016. The date was two days before what should have been Jake's eighth birthday and the prospect of the day hung over us like a dark pall.

Chris and I were still sharing the same house a few nights each week, but we lived separate lives. The only ties between us were the kids, and we put up a great front for the kids when we had to.

In the early days, we made the mistake of spoiling the kids because of Jakie's loss. We let Kaelem away with a lot more than we should have in the year after he lost his big brother.

Kids are smarter than we give them credit. Kaelem learnt how to play the Jakie card, and we fell for it. It took a while, but we realised we were spoiling Kaelem and we had to rein him in again.

It was a difficult time with Kaelem, but Chris and I worked as a team for the kids' sakes. The problem was we forgot to look after ourselves and each other.

I won't deny there were occasions when we felt that old spark between us. There was never anyone else in either of our lives. We knew the love was still there somewhere, but there was too much heartache in the way.

Sometimes fell into our old ways and managed to laugh and joke like we once had. There was the rare night when we'd go out together, and it was like the old Rosie and Chris again.

We'd feel some of the old magic between us, but the next day, grim reality would hit. Then we'd slide back into our habits of living and grieving alone.

We reached our fourth wedding anniversary three days before the inquest. The day I married the man I loved was still fresh in my mind, but I couldn't feel the love I had for him anymore.

The memories of our wedding day were too painful. All I could think of was Jakie standing on the altar with us that day.

We made an effort and tried to make our anniversary a special day, but Jake and the inquest were at the forefront of our minds. We were sick, anxious and distracted at the prospect of this inquiry.

We had no idea about what an inquest involved at first. We learnt that the coroner, who oversees it, is either a medical doctor or else a solicitor or barrister.

Our family solicitor, Tim Kiely, turned out to be the district coroner for Kilkenny so to avoid a conflict of interest, Jake's inquest was moved to Carlow.

We learnt that the inquest would be our only chance to question witnesses like the gardaí and The Driver. We were told we could have legal representation to ask questions on our behalf, or we could ask questions through the coroner.

Another partner in our family solicitor's firm called Michael Lanigan represented us at the inquest. We had a lot of unanswered questions and concerns about the garda investigation, but Michael didn't sugar coat things.

An inquest does not find anyone guilty or innocent, does not allocate blame and does not determine liability. Instead, the aim of this public hearing is to establish the cause and circumstances of the death.

But with the help of the legal advice from Michael and grieving parents who had been there before us, we learnt how to achieve the most out of the inquest.

We were determined to have our say at this public hearing. We also hoped to get our first proper insight into the garda investigation.

Coroner Dr Brendan Doyle presided over the three-hour long inquest in Carlow District Court.

By law, an inquest into a death resulting from a road traffic collision must be held before a jury. The small courtroom soon filled up with the jury of about eight people, gardaí, witnesses, media and the family and friends who came to support us.

Chris and I, as witnesses, were required to take an oath on the stand like in a real court. Then our depositions or statements were read out, and the coroner, jury and our solicitor could then ask questions of us or any of the other witnesses.

Some interested parties, like the retired surgeon who pronounced Jake's death, were not at the inquest. Their depositions to the gardaí were read out to the court instead.

Of course, we wanted to address many of our questions to The Driver whose car killed our child, but she didn't appear. She was one of the most important witnesses, and she wasn't there.

Our solicitor informed us before the inquest that she said she wouldn't be there because she had to work. On the day of the inquest, however, the inquiry was told she submitted a doctor's cert to excuse her absence.

"Oh, she's sick? I heard she had to work," I said aloud.

"Now, now, Mrs Brennan," admonished the coroner.

It was one of many occasions that the ever-patient and very understanding coroner issued warnings that day.

The doctor's cert for The Driver said that she couldn't attend because she had commenced treatment for anxiety.

It was like another slap in the face. Did she think that we weren't suffering from anxiety? For the past two years I'd been in and out of a psychiatric hospital and had been prescribed a cocktail of drugs, yet I was at the inquest.

Instead, The Driver's signed statement to the gardaí, taken the evening after her car killed Jake, was used as her deposition at the hearing.

The statement appalled and enraged me. Her statement begged more questions than gave answers.

She said that she was travelling around 20-30km/h when gardaí estimated her speed at the time of the impact to be anything between 44 and 50km/h.

She said in her first answer that she saw Jake on the road and then in another response, she said she didn't see him until "he just flew up in the air a bit."

When asked how high he flew up, she said she didn't know.

Everyone gasped when they read the part of the statement where she admitted she didn't apply her brakes after hitting Jake.

She made some bizarre statement that she kept driving because she felt something under the car that was either 'a body' or a kerb.

Shortly after, we were to hear various witnesses say her car drove at least 40 metres and up to 70 to 80 metres after hitting Jake which is why Chris took off and chased after her.

The pathologist later said that Jake's injuries were consistent with being 'dragged' by her car.

For some reason, the garda who took her statement never asked for a proper explanation why she didn't apply her brakes.

Surely the first thing you do when you hit someone is apply your brakes? I still, to this day, can't understand why she didn't stop when she hit our child.

And because she had a medical cert for 'anxiety', we couldn't ask her at the inquest either.

She also claimed that she didn't speed because two years earlier she had another car accident in Lintown.

The gardaí failed to ask her anything about that accident while taking her statement. They asked her which supermarket she was planning to shop in the night her car killed Jake. But they never asked her to elaborate on her other accident in Lintown. So, we will never know more about that either.

I fumed when it got to the part where she said that our kids were always "on the street."

Our children were always under our watch in our front garden, or they asked for permission to cross the 6.2-metre wide road to the small green on the other side. They were never "on the street."

Her statement came across as cold, dispassionate and heartless. Taken 24-hours after her car killed Jake, I couldn't discern an iota of anguish or concern in her words.

She seemed more concerned with repeatedly informing the gardaí that her boyfriend didn't live with her.

Excerpt from Statement of evidence of Garda Michael Corcoran of Kilkenny Garda Station made on 23/09/2014.

...On the 13/06.2014 at approximately 17.45pm I was accompanied by D/Garda Brendan Walton when I took a cautioned statement from (The Driver) at Kilkenny Garda Station in the presence of her solicitor John Harte...

Excerpts from the cautioned memo of (The Driver) of No. 22 Lintown Grove, Kilkenny, DOB 10.07.1976 on the 13/06/2014 at 5.45pm. Read into the inquest record by Garda Michael Corcoran on Thursday, March 31, 2016.

Q: You are not obliged to say anything unless you wish to do so but whatever you say will be taken down in writing and may be given in evidence. Do you understand the caution?
A: Yea, I do.

Q: The reason we're here is we are investigating a road traffic collision at Lintown Grove yesterday evening 12/06/14. Can you tell us in your own words and as much detail as possible, tell us what happened?
A: I come back from work, when I drove the kids were playing outside so I just slowed down and parked my car beside my house. I then around 6.30pm I went out from home and I opened my car and I saw neighbour, he was reversing his car and I got into my car and waited till he moved. Then he move and I follow him and then just happened. I didn't even see this boy. I just saw him in front of my car. I didn't see him on right side, on left side. I didn't see him. I didn't use my brakes.

Q: Where are you originally from?
A: Poland.

Q: How long you in Ireland?
A: 10 years

Q: How long you living in Kilkenny?
A: 7 years

Q: What do you work at?
A: Accommodation department in Hotel Kilkenny.

Q: Is it a Polish driving license you have?
A: Yes, Polish.

Q: How long have you been driving?
A: Since 1995.

Q: Do you know the registration of your car?
A: 00D1275, silver Opel Zafira.

Q: How long do you own it, are you the owner?
A: Yes, I'm the owner, own it about 6 years.
I've NCT next week, every on car is perfect.

Q: When you came home, I will take it step by
step, did you drive to work yesterday?
A: Yes.

Q: Did you go home straight?
A: Yes, straight.

Q: What time was this?
A: Before 6 p.m.

Q: When you came into Lintown Grove, what did
you see? It's a cul-de-sac, is that fair to say?
A: Yes, few cars on there and there (shows us
on map).

Q: So you drive in, did you see children playing
you said?
A: Yes

Q: Where did you see them?
A: (Showed on map, on grass.)

Q: What number is that, do you know?
A: Other side of stairs [to duplex houses], they
always have door opened, always kids out. I
always slow down, I couldn't speed. 2 years ago
I had accident in Lintown myself so I never
speed, I always so careful, wear seatbelt,
everything. I also have a daughter aged 15 years
and she lives with me at 22 Lintown Grove, it's
not first time the kids are on the street.

Q: Did you have to slow down or stop?
A: Yes, slow down because kids everywhere. I always slow down and be careful. Yesterday his father say I speed and my boyfriend in blue car but my boyfriend have black car. My boyfriend never here, he lives in Dublin.

Q: You continue on, Is there a car park space outside your house?
A: Yes.

Q: Can you drive in?
A: Yes I drive from work and drive straight in.

Q: What happened next?
A: I put in pin in alarm box, went upstairs, had shower, changed clothes, went into my garden, I got new plants.

Q: Did you leave your house then?
A: 6.05pm

Q: Where were you going to?
A: To do shopping.

Q: Where?
A: Lidl or Aldi
[She says she let a neighbour drive out ahead of her before she pulled out]

Q: So ye travel on out of the estate, how far ahead of you was your neighbour's car?
A: I don't know.

Q: Could you see the car?
A: Ya.

Q: So were you directly behind him?
A: No, he move on, I told you I go slow.

Q: So you drive on, so do you know what gear you in?
A: I don't, between 2nd or 3rd.

Q: So you driving, what do you remember?
A: I saw him. I don't know. I didn't see him on the right or left, he just flow up in the air a bit.

Q: Did something distract you?
A: No I just driving. I look straight ahead, when I start my car radio is automatically on so I didn't start radio, it automatically on.

Q: You say flow up, could you see his face, back or side?
A: I don't know, it was seconds, I didn't see him. I didn't touch my breaks. It happened so fast.

Q: How far you think he flow up?
A: I don't know.

Q: Did you see the boy before you hit him?
A: No, I didn't see him on right or left, just up. I don't know where he came from.

Q: When you say the boy flow up, what happened then?
A: I don't know, it like a black out, it's like he disappeared.

Q: Can you remember if the boy went underneath the front of your car?
A: I don't. I couldn't think. I couldn't see where he was, that is the worst part.

Q: Did you stop your car at this stage?
A: No, I try turn my car to the right because I think he was on the left, I think, I was in shock.

Q: Did you stop or did you stay going?
A: No, I stay going because I thought he was behind my car so I turned right to the kerb, I felt something, I not sure body or I think it was kerb, I don't know, I just wanted to park my car and see.

Q: So you kept over to the right so you think it was the kerb or little boy, what do you think you hit it with tyre, front or back?
A: No, front, my side I think. I don't know I can't remember everything, I was in shock, I just wanted to get out and check everything.

Q: Where did you leave your car?
A: Just where I stopped (showed on map), then someone tell me move because the ambulance, so I pulled into space here (shown on map).

Q: So you parked your car on right hand side, did you get out?
A: Ya, sorry, I didn't sleep today. I so tired. I didn't take my keys out, I just got out to see if boy was breathing.

Q: Where was the boy?
A: On the right, two men were with him, so they moved him on his side and put blanket under his head so they moved him. Can I take tablet?

Q: Do you take medication?
A: Just the one you saw yesterday for the under active thyroid gland.

Q: Is that Eltroxin?
A: Yes, I took tablet at 8.00am before I eat.

Q: Just before you stopped car, did you see or hear anyone?
A: Just after I hit him, I hear someone call his name.

Q: Did anyone come up to you when you were in the car?
A: No.

Q: After you hit the boy, did you see him get up?
A: No, I told you, he disappeared.

Q: So you didn't see the boy till you got out of the car?
A: Yes.

Q: What speed do you think you were travelling at?
A: 20 - 30. My car is old, so it doesn't start that fast.

Q: Is that km or mph?
A: I don't know.

Q: When the boy flew up, what part of the car did he fly up to? Was it high as the windscreen?
A: No. No, it wasn't.

Q: Do you wish to add or change anything?
A: Just that my boyfriend stays in Dublin during the week but stays in 22 Lintown Grove at weekend.

Q: Anything else?
A: Just that when you asked me my speed, I answered 20 - 30, I mean 20 or 30 km/h.

Q: This has been read over, is it correct?
A: Yes.

I don't know what I expected to hear from her or her statement. After all, this was a woman who hadn't even sent so much as a sympathy card to our family in the two years since she ran Jake over.

All I can say is that I would have expressed more concern and exhibited more distress if I had run over a stranger's cat, never mind someone's child.

19. GARDA BLUES

Hearing The Driver's statement was bad enough, but things didn't improve when the gardaí started giving their evidence.

The inquest confirmed, in our opinion, our long-held suspicions that our son's case wasn't properly handled.

We heard from several witnesses who claimed that The Driver was driving too fast and had a history of fast driving on the estate.

The coroner also heard from several witnesses, including The Driver, who said Jake was thrown in the air on impact. Then the garda forensic collision investigator got up and gave evidence that this didn't happen all.

We have to assume that the garda believed that all the witnesses who reported seeing Jake go up in the air, imagined it.

I might have laughed if I wasn't crying so hard.

Excerpts of Deposition of Michael O'Keefe, an eye-witness living in Linton Grove:

I was at home on the evening of the 12/06/2014. I was in my sitting room which is the front room in my house… The television is positioned just at the side of the front window with looks onto Lintown Grove.

At around 6.00pm/6.15pm, roughly that time. I was watching TV and happened to glance out the window.

I saw a child going up in the air after being hit by a car. The child then came down in front of the car and then the car went out over him.

241

I could see that when the child went underneath the car, the car was still coming forward. It stopped then and I remember some person banging on the driver's window. I can't say it if was a man or woman.

I didn't actually see the child run out in front of car or walk out. I just saw the child on the road seconds before the car hit him.

The child hit the front driver's side and was thrown up in the air…when the child went underneath the car and the car had stopped, the child got up again and ran back towards his parents.

He then fell down. He ran down a small bit, then collapsed. I then went out to see could I help…I just want to add that I felt she was driving a bit fast from what I can remember.

Excerpts of deposition from Patrick (Pakie) O'Hara:

I parked slightly after their driveway so I could put the lawnmower onto the driveway.…I was parked on the road and they had their car in the driveway…

I got out of the car, Karl stayed inside, he wouldn't know the family. Rosie was standing at the door holding her baby…Chris was standing around the car and the kids were in the garden…

I was actually asking him to go play soccer. He said he had to bring Jake to some Jesters thing. I just said see ya anyway…

I went around the driver's side door and I got in and I went to press the start button and close the door and I remember seeing a biggish silver car.

When I started the car I remember thinking in my head she's going fairly fast… Then I had just clicked my seatbelt on and I heard a bang. Straight away Karl went "Oh my God, look.'' …

I looked in the driver's side mirror and I saw the car go the left a little bit and then saw the child Jake, hit the ground. ..I got out of the car…I seen Jake staggering back towards his mother, He was wobbly, he was having fierce trouble walking.

I used to do first aid so I remember trying to get him to lie on his side, he was fighting, very agitated and shaking and screaming for his mother…

It was Rosie that was with me first. Then Chris ran by me, I was trying to hold Jake down and calm him down a bit, he was trying to speak he was turned a very unusual colour. He was talking for the first few minutes, he said "am I gonna die mammy" and she said no…

I remember the lady that was driving the car got out of the car when me and Rosie were with Jake. I remember somebody said she was speeding and she said no I wasn't. I think Chris shouted at her, you were fucking speeding.

I remember another man, bald like myself, came along and said yeah you were, you were speeding. She just kept saying "no, I wasn't''… she didn't sound Irish...

I would approximate that we were waiting for about 10 minutes, it seemed like that anyway. …about two minutes in from getting to him, his breathing was getting worse and worse, he was spitting blood out of his mouth and then he got very unresponsive, his eyes kind of glassed over.

I think Rosie left then, she was so worried, she was hysterical. When the ambulance got there, I remember holding his hand. He was still trying to gasp for breath, then the ambulance took over. His colour was a kind of greeny/grey…

Excerpts of Deposition of Karl Gleeson (passenger in Patrick 'Pakie' O'Hara's car):

Pat had gotten back into the car… I seen a blonde woman drive past in a 7 seater, silver car, it could have been beige. I had my eye on the car going by and she came up towards Jake on the road, at that stage I didn't know it was Jake.

I could see the back of her car when she came towards him. I noticed the child, He was kind of on her side and I heard a bang. Jake came from behind [her] car then.

At that stage I turned around I was looking over my shoulder, I seen Jake running back toward his house to his mother. I knew it was Jake at that stage, I recognised him. Both my window and the driver's side window was open…

Pat got out of the car then and ran towards Jake. I think Chris ran over to the woman in the car and started shouting. Jake's mother ran over to him as well. I stayed in the car the whole time…

I remember when the lady drove out past me, I thought to myself she was going a bit fast for an estate…

When Chris was finished ringing the guards he gave me his younger son to mind. I don't know his name, he's about 3 or 4. I didn't really seem much after that because I had to make sure his son wasn't watching as well.

Excerpts of deposition from John Renehan, passerby from Kilkenny taken on 13.06.2014:

I was walking on the Lintown Hall side of the road. ...I heard a bang in the estate. It was the bang that resembled a car accident.

I looked into Lintown Hall estate. I saw a silver 5 seater car heading parallel with the Johnswell Road.

The car was driving in the estate. The car was travelling fast and a male was screaming after the car to stop. This male was tall, blonde hair, tight haircut. He had an Irish accent. I think the car was an Opel Zafira.

I saw a child lying on the ground shaking, I thought the child had a navy blue top. I heard persons say to the child to keep breathing... I was looking at this through the railing. I was in shock. I stayed about 2 or 3 minutes

I left before the ambulance and Gardaí arrived. I went back later into Linton Hall and have [gave] my details to the Gardaí. I have read this statement over and it is correct.

It was when we started hearing gardaí evidence and our solicitor started asking questions, that we discovered a complete mess.

It wasn't so much that there was a problem with their depositions. The problem was the amount of information that was missing from the depositions and their reports.

There were no measurements or accurate notes made of where the car stopped after hitting Jakie.

Our solicitor ascertained that there were two gardaí on the scene shortly after the accident and they didn't take any measurements of how far she drove after hitting our child.

And the forensic collision investigator, Garda Maurice Mahon, did not take any measurements either.

Instead, they noted the spot to where she reversed and parked after the accident.

During his evidence to the coroner, Pakie stated that he told Garda Mahon several times that the car was moved and was not in the position that the guards placed it in their investigation.

I told the guards the same thing myself on several occasions. The forensic collision investigator, Garda Maurice Mahon's conclusions stated that after hitting Jake, the car 'came to rest' in a space opposite 12, Lintown Grove.

It didn't. The Driver reversed the car back to 12, Lintown Grove, closer to where she hit Jake and parked there when the neighbours asked her to move out of the way.

Yet, the gardaí never noted the position or measured where she'd actually stopped.

The gardaí, under oath, said they were under the instruction of the DPP not to take measurements.

Everyone looked at each other in disbelief.

Then we heard from the forensic collision investigator who wrote in his initial report that Jake could have been thrown up in the air by the car.

In Garda Maurice Mahon's original report, he said a throw was possible, and speed tests indicated The Driver was going at 46.3km/h.

There were several eyewitness accounts to confirm that Jake was thrown.

However, even the DPP got confused when in a later report he said 'a pedestrian throw' didn't happen. For good measure, he later told the DPP, that in his opinion The Driver was going at 18km/h.

Our solicitor, naturally enough, enquired why he didn't take eyewitness statements into account.

The collision investigator claimed that the DPP directed him not to read them.

The whole thing was totally crazy. We all threw our hands in the air in despair. There was a huge rumpus. The coroner tried to keep some order and warned me several times to refrain from interrupting.

But it was difficult in the face of all the mistakes and the contradictions in the garda statements.

I think the coroner gave us a lot of leeway because of the mess.

One garda gave evidence on the stand that he spoke with Pakie for example. Pakie looked at me, and he was adamant: "I never spoke to that guard."

Of course, I had to let the inquest know this very loudly, and the garda just spluttered and stumbled on regardless.

Anything they got wrong, I was like a dog with a bone and either I nudged our solicitor to interject or I interrupted myself.

At one stage, our solicitor asked the coroner who was in charge of the case.

"There seems to be a lot of errors in the garda evidence," he said.

The gardaí were rifling through files and were going off rooting for papers all the time.

Superintendent Padraig Dunne said he was in charge.

I couldn't help scoffing aloud.

The poor coroner had to warn me again, but I wasn't going to stay silent. Someone had to speak up for Jake.

There were more gasps and expressions of annoyance when another garda pointed out that the DPP had decided there would be no prosecution against The Driver. Nearly everyone at the hearing was angry at this stage.

Excerpt of Deposition from Garda Maurice Mahon:

I am a Forensic Collision Investigator and am called upon to attend and examine the scenes of fatal or potentially fatal road collisions and to conduct a forensic reconstruction of the incident...I have detailed my findings in the accompanying report and drew conclusions.

Excerpts from Garda Mahon's report:

The width of the road is 6.24m from hard shoulder to hard shoulder. When the Renault Scenic [Pakie O'Hara's car] was positioned on the roadway, there was approximately 4.24m of clear roadway.

...There was no physical evidence of the point of impact ...or physical evidence of the landing or resting position of the pedestrian. There was a small amount of blood on the road way and I was informed that this was from where the ambulance personal took a tube out of the pedestrian.

...The distance from where Roseann Brennan pointed out the point of impact to where she stated she held him [Jake] is 17.02m. The car would have to travel between 44.6km/h and 53.46km/h at the point of impact to project a pedestrian this distance.

…On Sunday 24/8/14...I met Michael O'Keefe. He informed me that he did not see the point of impact but pointed out to me where he saw Jake Brennan on the bonnet of the car… The point of impact that Roseann Brennan stated to this point is 21.38m. The car would have to travel between 50km/h and 59.9km/h at the point of impact to project a pedestrian to this distance.

The pedestrian was 1.26m in height…the height of the bumper of the car was between 0.23 and 0.55m. This is below the centre of gravity of the pedestrian and therefore a Pedestrian Throw was possible.

Conclusions:
…It was not possible to calculate the preimpact speed of the car involved in this collision from physical evidence at the scene. After the collision the car came to rest in a car parking space opposite 12 Lintown Grove.

…The pedestrian left the footpath of 15 Lintown Grove prior to the collision. There was no physical evidence to locate the point of impact between him and the car or the post impact landing or resting positions.

Using Sergeant Baldwins speed test the maximum speed to travel from the car's starting position to the point where Roseann Brennan stated the point of impact was is 46.33km/h.

The absolute minimum speed that the car was travelling to throw a pedestrian from the point that Roseann Brennan stated was the point of impact to the point where she held him is 44.6km/h.

The absolute minimum speed that the car was travelling to throw a pedestrian from the point that Roseann Brennan stated was the point of impact to the point where Michael O'Keefe saw him on the bonnet is 50km/h.

Our solicitor highlighted a letter dated May 2015 sent from the DPP to Kilkenny Garda Station. The DPP pointed out that in the original collision report, Garda Mahon said that a 'Pedestrian Throw' was possible.

The letter from the DPP added:

"During the consultation he indicated, on the basis of his findings, that there was no Pedestrian Throw. Garda Mahon should confirm this opinion in an additional report."

The DPP also asked:

"Garda Mahon should also be asked for his opinion on what inferences can be drawn from the damage to the car and the location of the damage on the car."

Garda Mahon's written response:

While a pedestrian throw was a possibility all material evidence collected in this instance indicate that a pedestrian throw did not take place...

In my opinion it did not occur in this incident as:
(1) The damage to the car was too slight and non existing on the bonnet of the car.
(2) The speeds involved to throw a pedestrian would have been too high not to cause injuries.
(3) There was no evidence of a landing or resting position visible on the roadway...

...The evidence suggests that the pedestrian was knocked over. This would indicate that the point of impact was not where Ms Brennan stated.

The damage to the car is very slight as outlined above and this is consistent with a low velocity at the point of impact.

So, it seemed that Garda Mahon was of the opinion that the nature of Jake's injuries and the damage to the car were so minor that our baby couldn't have been thrown and that the car couldn't have been going fast.

The injuries sustained suggest a low speed? The mind boggles. I'm pretty sure that Jake couldn't have sustained an injury more severe than death.

The autopsy report, which Garda Mahon would have seen, listed 33 separate injuries on Jake's body including a lacerated liver, a lacerated lung, eight broken ribs and severe internal bleeding.

The medical expert at the inquest, the deputy state pathologist, gave evidence that suggested that if The Driver had driven at 20km/h, Jake would have been uninjured by the collision.

Yet, despite hearing the witness testimony at the inquest and all the medical evidence about Jake's injuries, Garda Mahon was adamant that he was still right: the car was going at less than 20km/h, and Jake wasn't thrown by the car.

We received a letter from the DPP the following year saying:

"Garda Mahon has now read the witness statements [about Jake being thrown] and confirmed that they do not affect or change his conclusion."

The letter also said:

"The injuries sustained and lack of damage to the car suggest a low speed at the point of impact. Garda Mahon is of the opinion that the suspect may have been travelling at 18km/h or less."

His evidence confirmed everything we had feared all along about the investigation.

We had already made enquiries to Kilkenny Garda Station and the DPP to see if The Driver was breathalysed on the scene. No one on the road saw it happening that day.

However, Garda Michael Corcoran, who took a statement from The Driver the day after Jakie died, said in his statement that he asked for a breath specimen on the scene.

He also said that he 'checked' The Driver's phone. That was of little comfort to us. We would have hoped for a proper forensic examination of the phone after a fatal road collision.

Excerpts of deposition of Garda Michael Corcoran:

At approximated 18.30pm, we received a call from Garda Eddie O'Reilly to attended Lintown Grove, Kilkenny as a young child had been knocked down. At the scene I observed a young boy lying on the ground, I now know this boy to be Jake Brennan of 15 Lintown Grove…

I then made a lawful demand for (the driver) to provide a breath specimen under Section 9 Road Traffic Act 2010. Result was negative…

She stated that she was just driving out of the estate when Jake just ran out in front of her. She stated that she didn't see him till the last second…

I then seized (The Driver's) Samsung Galaxy S4…as evidence under Section 7 of the Criminal Justice Act 2006. I viewed the information on the phone and I could see that no calls incoming were received or no calls out-going were taken in the last few hours from the phone. I also checked the text message and again I could see no evidence of any text received or sent in the last number of hours from the phone…

Deposition from Garda John Moloney:

On the 12/06/2014 I was detailed as the driver of the official patrol car along with Garda Corcoran as observer. At approximately 18.30p.m. As a result of a call from Kilkenny Garda Station we attended the scene of a road traffic collision at Lintown Grove….

On arrival I observed a young male…lying on the ground. I saw two paramedics, one of whom I know to be Mick Kavanagh, and the other I now know to be Peter Reynolds. They were administering first aid to the young male. I also saw two other males assisting the paramedics. I know them to be Patrick O'Hara… and Adrian Bouros of … Lintown Grove…

Also at the scene were Christopher Brennan of 15 Lintown Grove… and Roseanne Hayes. I learnt that they were the parents of the child… Garda Corcoran stayed with the driver while I went and spoke with the paramedics.

Mick Kavanagh requested that I organise a Garda escort to St. Luke's Hospital for the ambulance. After a short time, the paramedics placed the child in the rear of the ambulance. Garda O'Connor went ahead and cleared traffic on the route to the hospital. The ambulance left at approximately 18.50 p.m. and I followed it to St. Luke's A&E Department.

Excerpts of deposition of Sergeant Patrick Baldwin:

…I carried out a detailed examination of the alleged impact area and found: the offside headlight was slightly pushed back with one of the supporting brackets snapped off. The offside faring panel below the offside headlight had been displaced. There was a scuff mark on the bumper below the offside headlight, also a slight scuff mark on the underneath bumper skirting on the offside...

I also carried out a speed test on the vehicle over a distance of 50.7mls [metres] as was supplied to me by forensic collision investigator Gda Mahon, the speed was measured by laser equipment.

The fastest I achieved over 4 runs was 53km/h with the average being 47km/h. Normal acceleration of the vehicle over this distance was 25km/h approx....

From my examination I determine that the vehicle was in good condition and not defective at the time of the incident on 12/6/14.

Second deposition from Garda John Moloney:

On the 13/06/14 at approximately 13.00 pm I attended the mortuary at Waterford Regional Hospital. While there, I met with Dr. Curtis. At 13.59p.m. I formally identified the deceased to Dr. Curtis as Jake Brennan...

I was present when the post mortem took place. I was present at 16.28 p.m when Dr. Curtis determined that the cause of death was crush injuries to the chest and abdominal areas.

Excerpts of deposition by Garda Tom Jones:

I am a trained Scenes of Crime Examiner... On 13/6/14 Gda Mohally and I attended the mortuary at Waterford Hospital where Dr. Curtis carried out the post mortem examination. Gda Mohally photographed the examination.

During the examination Dr. Curtis took the following samples from the body: a visceral (eye) sample which placed in a sealed tamperproof evidence bag … a head hair sample which I placed in a sealed tamperproof evidence bag… a nail scraping sample, both wet and dry, taken from his… fingernails which I placed in a sealed tamperproof evidence bag…. samples of a grease like material were also taken from his right hand and forearm which I labelled… and placed in a sealed tamperproof evidence bag…

While on duty on the 20/6/14 I conveyed one blood sample and one vitreous sample in sealed bag … to the State Laboratory at Young's Cross, Celbridge, Co. Kildare.

Excerpts of deposition from Garda Tadgh Mohally:

On my arrival the scene was being preserved by Garda Aoife Gubbins. I entered the scene at 8.15pm. Also present was Garda Mahon who was conducting the Forensic Collision Investigation. Also present was Sgt Pat Baldwin PSV Inspector,

The two members requested me to take certain photographs of the scene for them for the investigation. I also took a swab from the ground which had an appearance of blood which I labelled …

The following day I was requested to go to Waterford Hospital where Dr Curtis was to carry out a post mortem on the deceased Jake Brennan…I carried out the photography side of the PM and Gda Jones carried out the swabbing.

Chris was called to the stand where his deposition was read into the record too. Many of us were in tears when he admitted that Jake was the rock of the family, but by the time the ambulance arrived, he knew that Jake was too far gone to be saved. We gave our statements separately, and we hardly talked about that day, so this was the first time I realised that Chris knew so soon after the impact that there was no hope for his child.

Excerpts of deposition of Christopher Brennan:

...Kaelem and Jake were playing outside with Sophia [Siofra] who is a friend's child...they were playing outside and they were as happy as Larry.

At about 5.45pm, Paddy O'Hara my brother-in-law called to drop back the lawnmower. We were bantering on and I was saying "you broke my lawnmower'' because it wasn't kind of working... I brought the lawnmower back to the front gate and I said I would bring it in later. The kids were just playing away and the wife just let a big roar, she said "my baby, my baby''. I don't know what it was. I turned quickly.

I didn't even hear the car coming out. I could see...my child up in the air. He came down straight away and she rolled over him. I made a run and I banged on the right driver's side or back window. She kept going. She rolled over him. I said "what do you think you're doing'' or "what the f*** do you think you're doing.'' I hit the window real hard. I said to her "you're always doing it, you're driving up and down this road real fast,''

I think Jake went under the left tyre of the car back and front. I think it was a Citroen or Renault, greyish colour like a Space Wagon. When he came out from under the car, he got up and he came down along fast enough for a young lad who was after getting knocked down... I was looking for a phone and I rang the ambulance on 999 on my phone...

She got out of the car and she said 'I wasn't speeding, I wasn't speeding.' I said I'm going to ring the guards, I said 'you're always doing things like this in and out, up and down.'' I heard my wife "don't worry about the guards, I just want my child.''…

I kept saying is he ok, he is ok. I think I rang the ambulance again and I said I was just on the phone to you a few minutes ago. The man said the ambulance is on the way, be calm if you can…Then a third time I rang them. I was panicking.

I was on the phone or Adrian up the road took the phone and he was talking to them, He said he was a paramedic. He talked to him for a few minutes…

Then all I know the ambulance was there and I knew myself at that stage that he was gone. I knew he was trying to get up but trying to find a comfortable space to let go. He was moving left, right, trying to find comfy place to let go…

I was in the back of the ambulance with him. I knew myself they were only trying to keep him breathing. I kept saying "Jake I know you're strong, please don't leave me.'' He was like the rock of this family that kept us together…

I got up on the stand, took an oath, and they read out my deposition to the inquest.

I gave them the details of Jakie's last day and what I'd witnessed, all of which I've detailed in the previous chapters.

A second statement that I'd given to the gardaí that concerning other incidents on the estate involving The Driver was also read out.

Maybe about 6 weeks or 2 months before Jake was knocked down…Chris was out fixing up the garden when the man from number 21 was passing… Chris was asking him if there was any change in getting speed ramps and the man said we have been trying for years.

Chris said because that one in the silver car and yer man at the end are just flying in all the time. That they are speeding in their cars, driving in carelessly and not caring. This man is on the Residents Committee…

After Jake's accident, the girl in number 17 came up to me. She said that …the lady that knocked your baby down, we were out and two girls were playing on their bikes …and I had to put up my hand to stop her.

She said that "she'', the driver, didn't even give them a chance to bring in their bikes, that she rolled her eyes and drove around them. I said that I had the same problem with the driver last summer.

She said "Rosie, 30 minutes before she knocked down your baby, she drives fast all the time but this day she flew into her house. I was shocked."

I was also given the opportunity to add any comments to the inquest. I was already a mess of snots and tears, but I was infuriated by what I'd heard.

I slammed the gardaí investigation and questioned their competence. I said, in my opinion, they made a mess of the case.

"Why would the DPP say that you shouldn't measure the crime scene? Would someone answer my question? Would someone be truthful here? Don't you know that lives have been ruined here? Do any of you even care?"

In the end, I got so distraught that my brother Darren came up and took me from the stand.

All the family were upset and galled at what we heard. Jake never stood a chance of justice.

The gardaí seemed to dismiss all our eyewitness testimonies as worthless. Their whole attitude just made me despair.

Even in the condition that I was in that day, I still remember one member of the jury, a woman, who was crying with us.

I see her face clear as day. She was sobbing as much as we were.

It was a terrible day for all of us, and more horrific details of Jakie's death were yet to come.

20. MY BROWN-EYED BOY

The Driver's statement really upset me while the garda evidence was bewildering, frustrating and troubling.

However, we found the medical details and the list of injuries inflicted on our baby very distressing

The Deputy State Pathologist Michael Curtis, who wrote the autopsy report, was one of the last to go on the stand as far as I remember.

His deposition started by describing Jake's physical attributes - his height, his dark hair, his eyes:

```
The body was that of a young boy, the appearance
of whom was consistent with the stated age of 6
years. Height 4ft 1in or 126cm and of average
build. He had dark brown hair measuring up to
2.5cm in length... The eyebrows were brown. The
eyes were natural and greyish/blue...
```

Some of our family gasped, and others cried when they heard the pathologist describe the colour of Jake's eyes. Everyone who knew him knew he had brown eyes.

I'd told them all that I'd seen the colour leave his eyes. I don't think anyone believed me until they heard those details read out at the inquest.

Before we heard the autopsy report details, we heard that the emergency services had trouble finding our cul-de-sac.

It took the ambulance crew four minutes to drive across Kilkenny city to the estate, but almost the same time again to find Lintown Grove

Paramedic Mick Kavanagh from the National Ambulance Service said the estate was a 'nightmare' for gardaí and ambulance crews. He said it was built as a 'Celtic Tiger' estate and the lack of signage made it 'a maze.'

"It took us twice driving around the estate to find the location," he said. "It's nigh on impossible to find anywhere in these places."

I interjected to say that the council won't erect proper signage in estates that are not in public ownership or as they refer to it, "taken in charge".

I said the lack of funding for proper signage was ridiculous in the light of the controversial building of the St. Francis Bridge in Kilkenny. Many of the locals had been trying to block the development.

"Yet the council can find millions of euro for a new bridge in the city that no one wants," I said.

The paramedic, Mick Kavanagh's deposition, reports that Chris was in the front of the ambulance while I was in the back when, in fact, it was the other way around. But hearing his medical evidence and the details from the doctors at A&E was traumatising.

The paramedic's report said that when he arrived on the scene, he had a GCS of 3. In the Glasgow Coma Scale (GCS) of brain injuries, you cannot score lower than a 3. Our poor child never stood a chance once two tonnes of steel slammed into him.

Deposition from Paramedic Mick Kavanagh:

On the 12th of June 2014, I was detailed for duty from 7 a.m. until 7 p.m. as a paramedic, accompanied by Peter Reynolds, an advanced paramedic.

261

Regional Ambulance Control Centre received a call at 18.28pm to a 6 yr old child hit by a car at Lintown Grove, Kilkenny.

The child was conscious and alert according to control and we went mobile, as in the ambulance crew, at 18.30 p.m. We arrived at Lintown Hall at 18.34 p.m.

And it took us twice driving around the estate to find the location of Lintown Grove and arrived at scene at 18.37 p.m.

On scene I observed a child lying on the ground being comforted by three adults, one that I know now to be his mother. We noticed the child to be unconscious and very waxy looking so we immediately put the res. Team on standby in the hospital.

We got out our equipment from the ambulance and the child was having a heart rate of 35 (the normal heart rate would be 100+) Respirations were very shallow and pupils fixed and dilated. He had, the child, a GCS (this is a scale used to describe a level of consciousness) of 3, which indicates a deep level of unconsciousness.

The child had a mark over its left flank (left side of his abdomen). I sheared off his clothes to examine and the only thing noted other than his left flank was his pants were full of faeces. There was no obvious injuries noted at this time.

Shortly after he went into respiratory rest, we suctioned his airway to remove fresh blood and tried to place an advanced airway but this was not possible due to the volume of blood.

We ventilated the child normally with a BVM and the child went into a cardiac arrest and it was (the rhythm) was a systole, aka flat line. We started CPR on the child and I asked the group of bystanders was anyone trained in CPR and an Eastern European man said he was so he took over CPR.

At this stage we got other equipment (neck collar/spinal board) from the ambulance to prepare for transport.

I asked Garda J. Moloney to make sure Greens Bridge was clear for us and arranged for us to be escorted by Garda motorbike from the scene.

We placed the child on the spinal board and placed him on the stretcher on the back of the ambulance and the child's mother accompanied in the rear of the ambulance with Peter Reynolds and the father sat in the front of the ambulance with me.

Back at the scene we were transfusing fluids into the child via IO access (interosscous) through the left shin.

We left the scene at 18.57 p.m. By Garda escort and while en route I confirmed that a full resuscitation unit would be awaiting us and we arrived at St Luke's Hospital at 7.01 p.m.

There was three doctors waiting on us for our arrival at the back door of the hospital. We offloaded the child who was still in cardiac arrest and handed over the child to the resuscitation team in the A&E department...

This statement has been read over and is correct.

At the scene I asked the bystanders which car had caused this incident so I could figure out the mechanism of injury and the bystanders pointed out an Opel Zafira, silver in colour, to me.

Deposition of Dr George Nessim read into the record by Insp G Redmond:

I am a retired surgeon, My last job as a consultant general surgeon was in St. Luke's Hospital, Kilkenny until I retired on the 29/8/2014.

I qualified from Alexandria University in Egypt in 1974 and I have been practicing general surgery in Ireland for over 30 years.

On the 12/06/2014 I was surgeon on duty at St. Luke's Hospital, Kilkenny. At around 19.00 p.m. I was called by a member of surgical that they were expecting a child in that was in a traffic accident.

When I arrived in A&E we were told that the child was on route in the ambulance. On arrival I spoke with the paramedics and I was told the child was knocked down by a car.

On examination the child was not breathing, there was no palpable pulse and the blood pressure was non recordable.

It was during this examination I became aware that his name was Jake Brennan and he was 6 or 7 years old.

We commenced resuscitation the child immediately with a multi disciplinary team. This involved intubating the child and IV fluids. Clinically, we suspected the child sustained multiple rib fractures and internal abdominal bleeding.

Despite the intensive resuscitation which lasted more than 25 minutes, as best I can remember, there was no response to indicate that he was going to survive.

After consulting with my colleagues and the parents of the child, during which I informed them that Jake was not going to make it, we decided not to carry on the resuscitation any further.

At approximately 19.19pm I instructed one of the team to document that this was the time of death. I then spoke with the family, with the medical team to convey our condolences.

Police Statement from Mr Frank O'Dwyer, Consultant in charge of Accident and Emergency, St Luke's General Hospital, Kilkenny. Dated 29/09/14:

I can state from records at my disposal that a Jake Brennan attended the Emergency Department of St Luke's hospital on the 12.06.14 @ 19.02pm. When he arrived in the Emergency Department he was unconscious. He was not breathing and he did not have a palpable pulse. His heart tracing did not show any sign of cardiac activity.

He was intubated and ventilated. Chest drains were placed on either side of his chest. He was given fluid and blood. Despite resuscitation he never regained a pulse or blood pressure.

Resuscitation efforts were stopped at 19.19pm and he was pronounced dead by Mr George Nessim, Consultant Surgeon. A post mortem was performed to determine the full nature of his injuries.

The Deputy State Pathologist Michael Curtis, who performed the post-mortem, gave evidence that Jake's death was caused by "crush injury to the chest and abdomen". He said the injuries were consistent with being "run over and dragged by the front body work of a vehicle."

The ambulance paramedic had earlier noted in his evidence that Jake had a mark on the left side of his abdomen. I saw the same mark myself and identified it as a black rubber tire mark. Witnesses said they saw Jake come out from under the back wheels of the car.

The Deputy State Pathologist also noted on his autopsy report a large mark on his lower left side:

```
Over the back of the left shoulder blade and
extending down to the lower rib level on the
left side there was discontinuous stippled
purplish/red bruising in a total area of 16.5cm
vertically by up to 10.5cm across.
```

So, I was stunned when the pathologist said that Jake was "run over" but "there was no clear evidence to indicate that he had been run over by a wheel."

I was cross at that stage. As far as I was concerned, here was another expert making liars of all the witnesses. When I get annoyed, my sisters tell me my face is something to be afraid of. I can be a bitch in the moment.

"Sorry, I'm distracted by the look I'm getting from Mrs Brennan," said the deputy state pathologist at one stage.

The pathologist listed 33 different areas of cuts, marks, bruises and abrasions to his head, limbs, abdomen and back. On the right side of his chest, his 1st, 4th, 5th and 6th ribs were fractured, and on his left, his 1st, 2nd, 6th and 7th were fractured.

When asked about the correlation between injuries and speed limits, the pathologist agreed that lower speed limits would reduce fatalities.

He said road collisions at 50km/h had a fatality rate of more than 80%. In contrast, if the Opel Zafira car that hit Jake was doing

20km/h, the speed limit that we've been campaigning for, Jake would probably have been uninjured.

Extract of report of post-mortem examination on Jake Brennan by pathologist Dr Michael Curtis: Conclusions:

```
At postmortem examination, this 6-year-old boy
appeared fit and well. There was no evidence of
any natural disease. He appeared well-nourished
and well cared for.

His death was the result of a crush injury to
the chest and the abdomen resulting in
laceration of the upper lobe of the left lung,
laceration of the left lobe of his liver and a
superficial tear of the spleen.

There was considerable bleeding into the chest
cavities and also into the abdominal cavity.
The pattern of injuries would be consistent with
his being run over and dragged by the front body
work of a vehicle. There was no clear evidence
to indicate that he had been run over by a
wheel.

Cause of Death:
Crush injury to chest and abdomen (pedestrian
struck by car)
```

At the end of the inquest, the jury delivered a verdict that death was due to a crush injury to the chest and abdomen, consistent with being struck by a car.

We requested, through our solicitor, that the jury recommend that speed limits be reduced from 50km/h to 20km/h in housing estates.

Our solicitor Michael Lanigan explained that we wanted this to be "Jake's Law" and our son's legacy.

We also asked that the jury recommend the installation of proper street signage in housing estates.

The jury decided to call for a mandatory 30km/h speed limit which was an improvement on the default speed of 50km/h.

They also recommended improved signage after hearing how the emergency services had trouble finding our cul-de-sac.

The coroner ended the proceedings saying that Jake's death had left "a huge space in the lives of a lot of people", particularly his parents and family. But his legacy would serve as "a beacon to his memory".

Dr Brendan Doyle was very kind and patient that day considering that we were overwrought at times and constantly interrupting his hearing.

The day after the inquest, he wrote to the Department of Transport. He told the Minister that the jury attached two riders to their verdict. They recommended lower speed limits and traffic calming measures in all housing estates along with proper street signage.

Two weeks later, he received a lengthy reply from Paschal Donohoe's office listing reasons why he was going to ignore the jury's recommendations.

The long-winded, three-page reply to the coroner can be summarised as follows:

1. The application of 'Special Speed Limits' rests with the local authorities, not with us.

2. There's an issue with legally defining what exactly constitutes a 'housing estate' anyway.

3. Traffic calming measures are the responsibility of the relevant local authority too.

4. Appropriate street name signage in housing estates is nothing to do with us. Please see the "Minister for the Environment…Alan Kelly TD whose Department is responsible for this area."

The inquest into Jake's death was a rollercoaster of an emotional day. There were times that I cried and shouted, and there were parts where I just felt like a zombie that hardly heard what was going on around me.

I was furious at times, distraught and numb at other times. I felt battered and bruised leaving Carlow District Court.

Speaking to the media afterwards, I said we were demanding a new examination of the case because we felt the inquest threw up more questions than it answered. We felt the gardaí had mishandled the entire case.

On a personal level, I left feeling so hurt about the pathologist's description of my brown-eyed boy. In the overall scheme of things, his eye colour might seem so trivial to most people. The pathologist was not wrong; he described the colour of Jake's eyes as they were when he saw him.

But for me, I felt it was the last description of Jake, and 'greyish-blue' is now on the record as the colour of his eyes.

Everyone who knew him knows that his most distinguishing facial feature was his soulful brown eyes. It was one of the things that set him apart from everyone else.

Remember, Jakie, how I used to tell you how I loved your big brown eyes, and you'd laugh and say: 'I love your blue eyes, Mammy'?

As far as I was concerned, many so-called 'experts' presented a lot of inaccurate evidence at the inquest.

It seemed like another injustice that Jake's big brown eyes were consigned to posterity as 'greyish-blue'.

21. SUICIDE ATTEMPT SHOCK

Two days after the inquest, it was Jake's eighth birthday. The rain was so torrential that it seemed like the monsoon season had arrived in Kilkenny; it hardly let up all day.

I was still getting over the inquest, but I wanted to mark my baby's birthday.

I had planned to bring all the kids to the grave where we'd have a birthday cake celebration, but there was no way I could take any of the children out in this weather.

To my troubled mind, it was like another kick in the teeth from the universe.

I asked my niece Donna and her friend to fix up the house, give it a bit of a party atmosphere with balloons and candles and to arrange indoor games for the children.

I always explain to the kids that Mammy and Daddy were so happy when Jake was born that we'll always celebrate his birthday just like theirs.

We tell them that Jakie celebrates his birthday in heaven and can't be here for the cake but that he's watching over them, and he loves them to blow out the candles for him.

With Donna in charge, we left the children, their cousins and friends enjoy their party in the house. I met with all the adults at Jake's grave with a smaller cake, and we sang 'Happy Birthday' under our umbrellas.

I kept the smile on my face all day until I got the kids to bed that night, and then I crashed as usual.

Two more birthdays had passed since Jakie went to heaven and still, I begged God to give me back my baby.

A journalist from The Kilkenny People newspaper had let us know that they were doing a piece on Jake's inquest that week. They were focussing on the short-comings in the garda investigation.

The reporter said he was shocked at what emerged at the inquest and told us the story would be a front-page splash.

I was glad that the truth was coming out at last. I looked forward to the next edition of the paper published six days after the inquest, on Wednesday, April 6.

I met my sisters in a local cafe to read it.

I thought I was ready for it, but it was difficult to see Jakie's little face on the front page of the paper and to read the rehashed inquest details.

Still, I felt glad that the whole of Kilkenny was hearing the full truth in front page headlines:

Excerpt from Kilkenny People, Wednesday, April 7:

JAKE'S PARENTS CALL FOR REVIEW BY DPP AS INQUEST THROWS UP MORE QUESTIONS

The family of the late Jake Brennan were left bewildered after the inquest into his death held in Carlow on Thursday after being told that the woman who drove the car that hit Jake would not be prosecuted.

The woman who hit Jake was driving at between 44 and 47km/h when she hit him, and she didn't brake with the car travelling on another 40 yards at least and possibly double that.

During the course of cross-examination by the Brennan family solicitor, Michael Lanigan said that if the Opel Zafira car that hit Jake was doing 20km/h, he would have walked away uninjured.

Following the inquest, Jake's parents instructed their solicitor Michael Lanigan to raise a number of issues that emerged at the inquest with the DPP in an effort to have the entire matter reviewed.

1. No measurements taken at the scene in relation to where the car started from and ended up after the fatality.

2. Gardaí saying, under oath, that they were directed not to take measurements.

3. Direction by the DPP that the forensic collision investigator not to read eye-witness statements.
Especially in the light of the fact that position of the car that hit Jake Brennan was moved after the accident to allow the ambulance through.

They want a fresh, new examination of the case because the inquest threw up more questions than it answered.

Mr Lanigan established that despite the presence of two gardaí shortly after the accident, they did not take any measurements because of a direction from the DPP.

And the forensic collision investigator with the gardaí did not take any measurements either, it emerged…

I sent a message to the reporter Sean Keane to thank him for his work on the article and he admitted that he felt under pressure because the gardaí were not happy about the story.

The next day was Thursday, the day of the week that Jakie died, and the day I always go to his grave.

After returning from the grave, I started getting calls to say the piece was up on the newspaper's website. I went on to the site and began reading all the comments. I was happy to see how many people were sharing it and felt glad that people were reading the truth.

I knew the guards wouldn't be happy about it especially with all the critical comments that were flooding in below the article. But it was time that people knew what was going on.

I got the children ready for bed and let them settle down for the last of their television shows. As I started cleaning up after the dinner, I opened a can of Coors beer. I thought it might calm me. It wasn't a great idea because I hadn't eaten much since the day before.

Chris put the kids to bed. He had plans to meet friends of his, but he knew I was still hyper about the newspaper article, so he asked me if I wanted him to stay.

"I don't have to go out," he said. "I'm just as happy staying home if you don't want to be on your own."

In the years since Jakie has died, I've become very good at disguising my true feelings even from myself. Anyway, when I feel bad, I want to be on my own. The last thing I wanted was Chris asking me every five minutes: "Are you sure you're okay?"

It's very tiring concealing your real feelings all the time.

"I'm grand, really I'm grand, Chris. Go out and meet the boys," I insisted.

I probably would have been okay that night, but shortly after Chris left, people started calling and sending messages.

"Why is the article on Jake's inquest not online anymore?"

I checked the Kilkenny People website, and the entire piece had disappeared. I suspected straight away that the newspaper had removed it because the gardaí weren't happy about it.

I got very worked up about the removal of the story. I remember pacing up and down the bedroom, up and down, for a long time. During that time, I drank two more cans of Coors. I was anxious, very upset.

I decided to express my fury over the removal of the article by recording a video and uploading it to the Jake's Legacy Facebook page.

I don't think I'd have any real memories of recording the video at all except that I've watched it since.

Using my phone, I focussed the video camera on a photo frame that contains four family pictures. It's a photo that I often hold while I'm sitting on the bedroom floor grieving for Jake.

I gaze at it and remember the happy times that we had in each of the pictures, and I cry knowing that we'll never have them again.

One of the four photos is of Jakie and me on a fairground roundabout. There's also a black and white photo of the three kids and me. The third picture in the frame is of Jake and Kaelem wearing shades as they perform their songs in the back garden and there's also one photo with Jakie, Savannah and me.

They're all smiling, happy photos of Jake with his family. You can only hear my voice on the video as the camera focuses on the photo frame.

"This is a little boy, this gorgeous, gorgeous boy that was taken from our lives," I said. "He loved his family, loved his family. He was all about family."

I explained: "The article in the Kilkenny People went up on their Facebook page today. It was being shared and being commented on."

I spoke very slowly and clearly with the video camera focussed on the photos of Jake and our family for the duration of the recording.

I concluded the video by addressing the gardaí and the DPP with the words: "We're going nowhere" before adding: "Love you, my baby, love you, my Jakie."

I don't remember recording it but more than 36,000 'liked' and shared it afterwards. I don't even recognise my voice on the video - it's so calm and precise.

After I posted it, I can see my responses in the comments section, but I don't remember writing them.

All I can remember is the shock of hearing that the article had disappeared from the website. To me, it was like they were spitting on my child's memory again.

Then, all I can say is that it was like someone else took over.

Chris had collected all my prescriptions that day. I have medicines for depression, sleeping and anxiety. They're all foil packed, and I had to work every one of them out of their packaging, but I have no recollection of that either.

I do remember washing the pills down with the third can of Coors. The reason I remember it is because the taste was so bad, that I couldn't forget it. I had no idea how many I took.

I remember lying down with a sense of relief. I was just getting drowsy when I woke with a fright.

Oh, my god, the kids. They're on their own if I'm not here.

I called Chris. I knew he was only five minutes away, and I said: "You need to get home now and look after the kids."

I fell asleep afterwards. I don't even think it was the pills; I was just emotionally and physically drained.

Christopher knew how many tablets were missing because he'd picked up the prescriptions. He saw that more than 50 pills were gone.

The next thing I remember is waking with a terrible burning feeling in my chest. Some of the tablets hadn't washed down properly, and some of them had stuck in my throat.

The hospital gave me activated charcoal to stop the drugs in my stomach being absorbed. Chris also said they injected me and they also put me on a drip, but I don't remember any of those details.

When I realised I was in hospital, my immediate reaction was: "Oh no, what have I done?"

I felt a sense of burning shame.

Before Jakie died, I never liked even taking an aspirin. I never took tablets for anything if I could help it. I hated having to take prescription pills, but after Jake, I had to accept that I needed medical help.

But I've always respected drugs, and I'm very careful about following the instructions and taking them properly. I have a fear of accidentally overdosing and ending up brain damaged and a burden on my family.

The sense of shame was awful, and to add to the misery I also felt very unwell. My legs couldn't hold me up afterwards, and I felt nauseous all the time.

I've learnt that it's a horrible thing to have that many drugs in your system, and it took weeks for me to feel normal again.

Coming down from that episode was rotten, but I'd inflicted it on myself and felt I deserved everything that happened.

As soon as I was able, the hospital brought me to a psychiatrist. The first question he asked was "Are you feeling suicidal?"

"No, no, I never planned this!" I insisted. "I don't know what happened. I don't remember even doing it!"

I desperately wanted people to believe me. I was more shocked than anyone else that I'd done this.

I'd thought about suicide lots of times, but this overdose was not deliberate. It wasn't a conscious decision. I was shocked at myself. It almost happened without me knowing it.

I didn't want to be admitted to the Department of Psychiatry. I told them I wanted to be back in my own bed, in my own home but I had to spend two nights there. The home-based team from the DOP descended on me again.

Even Chris knew by my reaction that I didn't mean this to happen, and he blamed himself even though I pushed him out the door.

"I should have stayed home that night, I knew it," he said.

There were other repercussions because of that moment of madness. The hospital said that the child protection agency Tusla would have to be alerted because I had alcohol in my system. I had three beers, I tried to reason, but there was no point in arguing.

I got a letter from Tusla shortly after to say that they had opened a file on me. They said as part of their risk assessment, they would contact the school and day centre that Kaelem and Savannah attend.

They added that if there was any place that I didn't want to be contacted, I had to write to them and let them know.

I didn't write back, but I knew I had to alert the kids' schools to the fact that they would be contacted by the child protection agency.

Kaelem attends Johnswell School in Kilkenny, and so I went in early next day to talk to his former teacher, Ger Patterson, on her own.

It was sunny outside, and I had sunglasses on my head. As I began to try to explain what happened, I pulled the dark glasses down from my head because my eyes were filling up.

"There's no easy way of saying this, but I took an overdose, and now Tusla are now involved, and they may contact the school as part of their assessment," I said trying to hold back the tears. "I just wanted to let you know why."

I was mortified having to tell her about the overdose. It was bad enough knowing what I'd done without confessing it to Kaelem's teacher.

I'll always be grateful to Ger because she made a very humiliating situation as easy as she could for me.

"They can contact here, and all I can say is that Kaelem is a well-cared for and happy child and comes in here with the best of lunches," she said, her eyes filling up too.

It's funny the things that stick in your mind, but I always remember her saying: "the best of lunches." It made me feel a little better about myself.

I had to go to the Newpark Family Resource Centre where Savannah went to preschool and do the same thing there.

I know them all in there. It's where Jakie was for years, and I worked there myself at one stage. I went to the office of the childcare manager, Perle Leahy, who has a photo of Jakie on the wall behind her desk.

I just broke down as soon as I tried to tell her. She got as upset as I was, but she assured me that Tulsa would only hear good things about my children and my parenting.

I had started seeing clinical psychologist Dr Claire Regan once a week by that time. From the start, Claire was wonderful, and I couldn't have found a better person to work with.

She cried as much as I did in the sessions, but she was building up my confidence again, and I started seeing a light at the end of a tunnel.

I felt that I was making huge progress with her, so I couldn't explain how this overdose had happened. I told her about recording the video and how I didn't even recognise my voice on it.

She explained that I had experienced a manic episode. My stress levels had built up over the previous days starting with the trauma of the inquest and reliving the awful day we lost Jakie. Then there was the agony of Jake's birthday and then the controversy over the front page newspaper article.

I had just become overwhelmed by the stress, and it triggered this break from reality. She said I really didn't know what I was doing.

Now I was stressed out by the Tusla investigation. I had already lost one child, and suddenly I was living in fear of losing my two surviving children.

"I don't mind them coming to my house, they can visit anytime; it's just the thoughts of them taking my children, I can't deal with," I sobbed.

Claire asked if I had her permission to contact Tusla on my behalf.

"I need to explain what went on that week and how you ended up in that frame of mind," she said. "I'll tell them that we've never had a concern about your children."

Dr Séamus MacSuibhne in the Department of Psychiatry in St Luke's also assured me that I didn't need to worry and that he would write to Tusla to support me too.

The weeks rolled on, and I didn't hear another word from Tusla, but I was so worried about the case that I ate and slept even less than usual.

I felt like I was looking over my shoulder the whole time. After Jake died, I lost all confidence as a parent, and this investigation sent me into a spiral of even more self-doubt.

It was about three months later that I received a letter from them saying that they had closed the case. I never physically saw anyone from Tusla the whole time. They never interviewed me; they never talked to me once.

But I had to wait those three long months not knowing if they were going to take my kids from me. It was inhumane treatment. Only for my doctors, I think Tusla could still be on my back today.

The overdose was the lowest point of my life after the loss of Jake. I got a massive fright when I realised I could have died and I could have left Kaelem and Savannah without a mother.

I could have lost everything, and it would have happened without me even thinking about it.

Since then, I do every therapy that they suggest. I'm doing counselling; I'm taking sleep therapy courses and meditation courses; I accept every treatment that they offer me. I apply myself to everything, and I'm doing everything in my power not to end up in that state again.

The overdose was a wake-up call. I haven't self-harmed or thought about suicide since.

Do I still miss Jake and want to be with him? Yes. But do I want to leave my two other babies? No, never.

It terrified me. I came so close to suicide and ending it all without even meaning to.

I'm still shocked and appalled at what happened that night; I almost sleepwalked into killing myself.

22. TEARS, TRAUMA AND THERAPY

After all this time, I wish I'd discovered a secret formula or technique to magically help people recover from the grief of losing a loved one.

For the longest time, I was caught in a trap agonising over the reasons for Jake's death. I was frozen in a state of despair and anger. My anxiety levels were still sky high, and flashbacks and panic attacks plagued my life.

People told me that it was time to 'move on' or 'get over it' or to accept that 'it was part of God's plan.'

All I can say is that people are all unique and so is grief.

People process grief at their own pace, and for me, it is taking years. From talking to other bereaved parents, I don't think any mother or father ever really recovers from losing a child.

Some are better at putting on their masks and facing the world than others, but it's not something anyone gets over.

However, the overdose came as a massive scare to me. It rattled me to my core, and I knew that I had to take every treatment offered.

Before I had Jake, I never took any prescription medication. I hated even taking an aspirin for a headache. At one stage after Jake died, I was swallowing over 20 different pills a day. I'm still on far too much medication.

I'm on Lyrica pills for anxiety, Dalmane to sleep, Rivotril as a relaxant to help my sleeping pill. I'm taking pills for depression, palpitations, blood pressure, and for my stomach.

For a long time, I didn't pay attention to how I took the medication. I swallowed pills on an empty stomach even when the instructions specified they should be taken with food.

I couldn't eat a lot of the time, and I attacked anyone who suggested taking food with the medication.

"Get off my case!" I'd growl. "I'm taking the bloody tablets, aren't I?"

Now, I'm paying attention to how, when and what I'm swallowing. I'm taking the medication seriously.

I've also talked with Dr Séamus MacSuibhne in the Department of Psychiatry (the DOP) in St Luke's about being weaned off some of the medication.

"This was always meant to be short-term," I said to him recently. "I never expected to be still on so many tablets."

He has assured me that as soon as I have 12 months without incident that we'll start removing the medication. I'm hoping that this process will begin very soon.

I know that nothing is going to fix me. I'm never going to wake up a day and not miss Jakie. And anyone who has lost a child will know there is nothing that can heal profound loss or grief.

But some things can help, and counselling is one of them.

In the immediate aftermath of Jake's death, we got some counselling. The early therapy sessions were organised by Ger O'Brien of First Light which supports suddenly bereaved parents. It's an incredible organisation. They threw us life buoys when it felt like we were drowning in grief.

I talked to therapists at a time when my life felt over, and I couldn't understand how everyone else's life was going on. I don't even remember the counsellors' names, but I remember they were lovely people and they did what they're supposed to, which is to listen.

I needed to rant, to talk about Jakie, to try and process out loud what had just happened to us.

I started the more intensive help I needed after they admitted me to the DOP in St Luke's. Dr MacSuibhne began managing my case, overseeing my medication and referring me on to other specialists.

Through him, I attended day support services like sleep therapy and classes on confidence and self-esteem. Professionals taught me how to cope with anxiety and panic attacks. I learnt so much.

It's not magic, but I used to think that if I scrolled through my phone long enough at night, I'd tire myself out. Of course, I know now the opposite happens.

Any time that I felt anxious, I used to head straight for the coffee pot, which sent my anxiety levels to new heights.

I learnt breathing techniques, mindfulness and other tools to deal with panic attacks. It's good to understand what's going on in your body and what you can do to help yourself.

One of the best things that Dr MacSuibhne did for me was to refer me to clinical psychologist, Dr Claire Regan.

Claire was very interactive in her approach from the beginning. She believes in a lot of intervention and feedback.

She turned my worldview on its head and pointed out so much that I couldn't see. She cries with me, she laughs with me and brings a fresh perspective on everything.

Often she says something that makes me stop and think: "God, she's right; why didn't I ever think that?"

Sometimes it's a simple thing like telling her about a bad day when I didn't get out of bed. I admit that I feel guilty about it; it's like I've failed Kaelem and Savannah again.

"Here we go, there's Rosie's blaming herself for everything again," she says. "Didn't you tell me you spent all day bringing them to that park and having a picnic on Sunday? And how many days in the past month have you looked after them? Are you not entitled to take a day off like everyone else? I think you're doing a damn good job!"

She's like an angel sent to me. I had zero self-confidence when I met her. I second-guessed everything I said and did. I worried whether I could ever be a good enough mother to my two surviving children. She rebuilt me, piece by piece, from the ground up. I couldn't praise her enough.

She also worked on my panic attacks, which could strike at any time.

The first panic attack I experienced was when they brought Jake's body back to the house after his autopsy. I didn't know what was going on then, but that incident turned out to be the first panic attack of thousands.

It happened every time I got distressed over Jake. I'd rant and cry; my heart would start beating faster; my shoulders and back would tense, and I'd feel rigid with distress.

Then I'd find it difficult to breathe, my throat closed over, and those around me would say my eyes rolled back in my head. At times, I thought I was going to die. Then I'd wake gasping, and I'd find people holding me at an open window or a door to give me air.

Claire taught me to recognise the panic attack coming on. As soon as I start getting worked up, I break the cycle by not talking. I go away to a quiet place and wait for the feeling to pass. Before, when I felt anxious, I went with it and worked myself into a frenzy. Now I know to be silent.

I was also worried because I knew I was experiencing moments of complete memory loss. I was out one evening, and my friends started discussing a fight breaking out in a chip shop. I had just been in there, but I didn't know what they were talking about.

The girls stared at me oddly.

"What are you on about, Rosie? You saw it yourself. You were there."

Claire reassured me that I wasn't going mad. Instead, I was unconsciously blocking out memories associated with a high level of stress.

She said that I couldn't cope with more traumatic events, so my mind's coping strategy was to repress all memories of it. The brain is a strange thing.

Claire also started tackling the flashbacks that I was experiencing. They could strike while queueing in a supermarket. A vision of Jakie staggering to me on Lintown Grove would appear in front of my eyes.

It was as real as the day it happened. My legs would almost buckle under me with the shock, and the trauma might then send me into a full-blown panic attack. It was a vicious circle.

She decided that conventional therapy for the flashbacks was not working fast enough. They were still too frequent and too disturbing. So, she referred me to Senior Clinical Psychologist, Martin Doohan, who specialises in a therapy called EMDR.

EMDR stands for eye movement desensitisation and reprocessing. It's now a very standard treatment for trauma. American and UK military chiefs use it to tackle post-traumatic stress disorder in the forces.

If anyone told me a year ago that a therapy that involves moving your eyes from side to side could help change your life, I'd have laughed at them.

The easiest way to explain the process is to compare it to laundry. The brain files memories in the same way we wash and store clean clothes.

Martin told me that sometimes if we experience something very traumatic, the brain fails to process or store the memory properly.

The traumatic memory sits in the front of the brain, behind the eyes, so it's never far from the front of our minds.

It's like having a broken-down washing machine with a laundry basket full of dirty socks in front of it. The socks sit there because you can't wash them and put them away in a drawer.

The longer you leave it, the worse the smells gets, and soon the whole house starts to stink.

You must fix the washing machine before you can wash the socks and store them away.

EMDR therapy fixes the brain by helping it process the disturbing memory. Then the trauma can be stored away in another area of the mind.

This sort of counselling isn't easy because it entails reliving every detail of the experience. While doing this, you follow the therapist's instructions to move your eyes left or right according to his or her hand movements.

The eye movement is supposed to replicate the rapid eye movement (REM) stage of sleep which helps process memory.

There have been times that I feel I can't face it; like when I haven't slept the night before. I text Martin at 6.00am to say: "My head is all over the place and I haven't slept so I can't do this today."

He doesn't look at his phone often, so I know I won't wake him.

Ten minutes later, I start regretting that decision.

You're wide awake anyway; what else are you going to do? You might as well go and get it over with.

So, I text him back.

"Sorry Martin. Ignore that last message."

Every EMDR session starts with the memory we want to work on.

We identified my worst flashback as the one where Jake reaches for me on the road and saying that he doesn't want to die.

Martin instructed me to bring the picture up in my mind and follow his hand while keeping the image in my head.

We label each flashback, and that one is, 'Mammy, I don't want to die.'

Afterwards, he told me to clear my mind again to discuss other things. Then he told me to bring back the 'Mammy, I don't want to die' image again.

He tries to uncover the primary emotion in every traumatic memory.

"Look at yourself in the scene now, what are you feeling about yourself?"

"I'm feeling angry."

"Why?"

"I knew he was dying and I didn't cradle him and rock him like he wanted me to."

I denied Jake the last thing he ever wanted from me. That guilt and regret haunted me from the time he died. It made my life miserable.

"Step back and look at the scene, what do want to say to yourself?"

"Stupid f***ing woman. He's dying for God's sake, pick him up!"

"So why aren't you picking him up?"

"Everyone's telling me to put him in the recovery position."

"You aren't putting him in the recovery position, are you?"

"No."

"Why?"

"Because I think that moving him that way would be too painful."

"What are you doing?"

"Asking him to lie down."

"Why are you asking him to lie down?"

"I can see that he's in pain when he's raised up."

"So, what are you doing by making him lie down?"

"Trying to make him more comfortable."

"So, you don't cuddle him because you don't want to inflict pain on him and instead you're trying to make your child comfortable. Why are you calling yourself stupid?"

It hit me that he was right. Up to then, I had tortured myself for not cuddling my child as he wanted. In reality, he was in too much pain.

In my heart, I knew that Jakie was going and I was trying to let him go as comfortably as he could.

Yet, I'd called myself stupid and focussed on the negative for so long that I believed it. I berated myself over and over for not cuddling my child when he was dying.

Once Martin made me realise that I hadn't done the wrong thing, I cried and cried until I was exhausted. All the flashbacks I suffered were regrets, anguish, remorse and guilt over things I felt I should have done differently.

*Why didn't you f***ing hold him?*

Martin made me realise that I did my best. Everything I did, even if I did it without understanding it at the time, was in Jake's best interests.

EMDR therapy doesn't wipe the memory away. I won't forget it; I can't forget it. Recalling anything about that day still makes me feel sick to my stomach.

But the memory of my child reaching for me and saying that he doesn't want to die no longer sends me to my knees when I'm pushing a supermarket trolley.

We also went through some memories that haunted me of Jake's funeral. I fixated on the coffin and that dark hole in the ground. Through EMDR he brought me back to the funeral, and I remembered so much more. I remember a whole community grieving and all the love that was there for Jake.

It was like watching everything through a small portable TV before and now I see it through a 50-inch widescreen. It was all there before, but I couldn't see it.

It's tough therapy. I'm exhausted after it, and my eyes are red and raw, but I leave with a feeling of hope that I've never had before.

Once I started to feel less angry with myself, I started feeling angrier with The Driver.

A lot of what I felt since Jakie died was anger in myself. I let him cross the road. If only I have done this or done that.

Now I was starting to accept that I was watching him, and it was a little cul-de-sac. I didn't do anything wrong; Jake had every right to be able to cross that road. It could have been five kids that stepped out to cross that street, and she would have struck them all.

So next, we dealt with my growing obsession and anger over The Driver. I don't want to speak her name. I don't know her name, and I won't spare the memory space required to learn it. I never will. Martin's not going to change that.

But I was always worried that I'd bump into her on the street. She still works in Kilkenny. I didn't know what my reaction would be if I came face to face with her again.

Martin brought me back to the day, and suddenly I remembered seeing her as I was getting into the ambulance. I felt furious looking at her talking to a man and a woman on the green. I wanted her. I wanted to get her.

He brought me right back, remembering things that I had forgotten. It felt like I was there, and she was there right on that green.

Martin said to me: "Okay, walk over to her, go on, walk over to her. What do you want to do to her?"

"I want to hit her; I want to hurt her badly."

"Go on, do what you want and hit her."

In my mind, I went for her. I threw myself at her and started belting her, pulling her hair, smacking her.

"What's she doing?"

"Nothing. She won't look at me."

"So, what are you going to do now?"

I started shouting at her, roaring in his therapy room.

"Tell me why you didn't hit your brakes and stop, answer me! Just explain why you didn't brake when you hit my child?"

I was crying and screaming and saying all the things I wanted to for years.

"What's she doing?"

"She's looking down. She won't answer me."

"You can keep hitting her."

"I don't want to. There's no point. She still won't answer me."

I was really there, back on the green on Lintown Grove and she was there in front of me. I screamed everything I ever dreamed of saying to her, but I got nothing back. She looked away or looked down.

Then it came back to me. I remembered that she drove her car down Lintown Grove a week or so after Jake died. I saw her, and I ran to the side of the road and screamed at her, "Why didn't you hit your brakes?"

And she put her head down and kept driving. She refused to even look at me. I had forgotten that until then.

It all made sense.

When she kept telling everyone, "I wasn't speeding, I wasn't speeding,' she was reassuring herself. She can't go there. She can't accept what she did."

"So why is she looking down or looking away?"

"Because she wants to pretend it didn't happen. She can't go there."

For all these years, I kept directing the anger I felt at her, towards myself. I beat myself up every day for years for things I never did, about things that weren't my fault.

She has never had to accept any responsibility at all. I took anger out on myself instead. I now know there's no point in being angry with her either. It takes more energy and effort than loving someone. She's not worth that to me.

I used to be afraid that I'd meet her or that I'd see her. Now I couldn't care less.

The truth is that I could have forgiven her if I'd seen some human reaction. If she'd shed a tear that day seeing Jake lying there, I could have forgiven her.

But at least now she doesn't matter anymore.

It's not all about EMDR with Martin. We have worked on coping techniques to handle the emotional distress that comes up during and between sessions.

It's always at the back of my mind that I could overdose again. It happened once, what if I had a manic episode again?

Martin helped me identify the precursors to getting manic and has helped me develop useful ways to calm myself.

Usually, when I start to feel anxious, I start cleaning, running around and keeping myself busy. Martin made me realise that only serves to make me even more manic.

Now if I have a bad day and feeling anxious, he's taught me that I need to distract my mind by engaging all my senses. I have to light a candle with a strong scent. I get something tactile and comforting like a blanket or like Ruby, Jake's teddy. I play my favourite tape of calming water sounds turned up loud in my earphones.

The whole idea is to use your senses to distract and soothe yourself until the anxious stage passes. By getting all your senses working, it gets you out of your head.

So, whenever anxiety hits me, I have my favourite things ready, and I step out of the situation for 30 minutes.

He also has quick fixes if I find I'm already in the manic stage. If music, candles and quiet don't work, there are other tactics.

Putting your face in a basin of warm water automatically slows down your heart rate. Placing a bag of frozen peas on your brow and bridge of your nose can work too.

Some people keep a hot chilli pepper in the fridge and bite it when they're getting manic. The shock can often distract you long enough to get out of your head.

It gives you time to refocus, turn on your music, get your candle lit and wind down again. You use whatever works for you.

I'm not as scared now that it will happen again because I have the coping techniques to nip anxiety in the bud.

He's made me drop my old coping strategies. In the past, I'd hold negative feelings in until the kids went to bed. Then I'd go to my room and try to let it all out. He said what I was trying to do was schedule my grief. It wasn't working.

"If someone tells you a funny joke, do you say, 'I'll store that laugh for later'?" he asked. "Of course, you don't. You can't."

But that's what I was trying to do with my grief. Now if I'm sad today, that's it, I'm sad today.

I also felt that I didn't deserve to be happy. I'd feel guilty for smiling and for living. He taught me to go with my emotions. If I feel like laughing, crying or whatever, he says, do it.

He must be getting through to me because I saw something stupid on Facebook the other night and I laughed and laughed. Christopher looked at me oddly, but I couldn't stop.

Since these sessions with Martin, I'm breaking down in tears all the time too. The last months of this therapy have been challenging but very revealing and worthwhile.

The more I cry and scream, the happier I make Martin. As far as Martin is concerned, he's doing excellent work because it means I'm grieving properly.

When I started seeing counsellors and when they admitted me to the Department of Psychiatry (DOP), I didn't want everyone to know about it. It embarrassed me. I'd tell my sisters not to mention it to certain people.

Now I don't care. I know there's a whole stigma about being 'mental', but I regard working on my mental health the same as going to the gym.

The professionals are there to help and always have my best interests at heart. Séamus, his secretary Maria and Claire are always a phone call away. Martin has turned my life around as have all the counsellors and therapists I've seen since Jakie died.

I'm a different person now because of the work I've done with these people. I've learnt something from every professional I've seen, and I know now that I'm never finished learning. They've all helped me, and they're all teaching me things.

Most of all, they are trying to stop me blaming myself for what happened.

I'd say to anyone who's thinking of going for counselling, don't go in thinking anything's going to fix you. I know nothing can fix me, but I also know that there are a lot of things that can help, and therapy has been a life-saver.

Thanks to the dedication of mental health professionals, I'm feeling a little bit lighter these days.

23. TRUE FRIENDS

Everyone tells us that grief gets easier as time passes, but it doesn't always feel like that to Chris or me. We'll never 'move on' from this, and we'll never live long enough for this gaping wound to heal.

We'll always miss our child, and we won't get over the loss, but we know we have to live with it.

In the last year, thanks to counselling, I'm learning to do that. I've improved dramatically, and I'm starting to see the light at the end of a tunnel.

Still, there are days when getting dressed seems impossible and when every step is an effort.

And it's not the constant ache in my head and in my heart that hurts. All the stress, grief and longing for Jake seems to manifest itself in physical pain too.

I get so anxious and tense that it results in terrible back and shoulder pain. I never had a back problem before, but now some days, I've got to be helped out of bed.

The worst times are significant events like birthdays, Christmas and other family milestones. Those days are a special form of torture for every bereaved parent.

That empty seat at Kaelem and Savannah's birthday parties and the Christmas dinner table is never less empty. Our baby was part of Christmas past, but he's missing from Christmas present and every Christmas in the future.

Every family event is a reminder of the enormous gap in our lives that will always be there.

We know that Kaelem's seventh birthday this year, like every family birthday, will be a happy day. At the same time, the birthday will be difficult because Jake was the big brother in the family when he died at age six.

It's wonderful to watch Kaelem and Savannah grow up, healthy, happy and strong. But each birthday is another stark reminder that time and people are moving on without Jake.

There's an ever-present feeling of guilt too. It feels wrong because Chris and I are the parents and we are alive, but Jake isn't. Shaking off that huge sense of failure is difficult.

We feel guilty for enjoying things like pushing the kids on a swing, lighting the candles on a birthday cake or going to see Santy. It feels wrong being happy when Jake's not around to enjoy those things with us anymore.

These days, every big family day begins at Jake's grave. It's all we can do to include him now. Then there's more guilt because we know we shouldn't feel sad around Kaelem and Savannah.

After all, they deserve to feel happy and know they have a happy Mammy and Daddy with them on their big family days.

Memories of Jake coming flooding back to me during all these family occasions. As I get Kaelem and Savannah ready to go out at Hallowe'en, I can't help seeing an excited Jakie bounding around the place.

He was in his element at Hallowe'en because he loved dressing up. He went out as Ghostface for his last Hallowe'en, wearing a Scream mask, and a big black cloak and hood. He was allergic to face paint, so he could never wear any make-up like the rest of the kids.

My sisters and I split the children into an older and toddler group to go trick-or-treating. Jake was delighted when we allowed him to go two doors ahead with the 'big boys' who were all around nine and ten years old.

He thought it was great even though we were right behind, and we warned his cousin Bradley to hold onto him.

"Kaelem, you have to stay with Mammy, but don't worry because I'll be just up ahead," he proudly told his little brother.

Like every child, he loved Christmas. We always made a big deal of the annual visit to Santy. For his last Christmas, we went to Rancho Reilly in Carlow with all his aunts, uncles and cousins. My sisters and I enjoyed the Elves Workshop and the Magical Christmas Carriage as much as the kids.

Watching Jake and Kaelem's faces light up in all the build-up to Christmas was magic itself.

Peace and goodwill were in short supply sometimes, even at Christmas, as Jake and Kaelem were always killing each other. But at least we could rely on Santy to help control our boisterous boys.

I never needed a fancy phone app to contact the North Pole as my brother Darren is a personal friend of Santy. Many of Jake and Kaelem's rows broke up as soon as I thrust the phone at them.

"It's Santy from the North Pole, and he's looking to speak to both of you."

Kaelem would recoil in horror from the phone, but Jake would take the phone reluctantly.

"This is Santy!" his big voice would boom down the line. "I'm calling because I hear that you and your brother are fighting again. Do I put you on my naughty list?"

Jake's face would drop with the shock and shame.

"No, Santy! I'll be good from now on Santy, I will!" he'd gasp, while Kaelem nodded frantically in agreement behind him.

Peace reigned for at least ten minutes after Santy's calls.

Christmas wasn't all about Santy for Jake. He loved the traditions, the routines and the whole social aspect of the festive season.

The official start of Christmas for Jake was the arrival of his nanny, Ann, and her daughter, Channy, from Carlow. They'd come down armed with presents the day before Christmas Eve. He knew once they arrived that Santy was on the way.

"When are Nanny Ann and Aunty Channy coming?" he'd keep checking.

Darren brought Santy to our house for what turned out to be Jake's last Christmas. At this stage, Jake was five and agog with excitement about Christmas.

Shortly after we got him to bed on Christmas Eve, Santy arrived in full red-suit and beard regalia.

Chris woke Jake whispering, "You'll never believe it, but Santy's downstairs. Shhh! Be really quiet, so Santy doesn't hear you out of bed."

He led Jake on tip-toes to the top of the stairs. Jake's eyes were the size of golf balls when he saw 'Santy' coming down our hall. He was afraid to breathe despite all the excitement.

"Quick! Let's get back to bed before Santy sees you!" Chris whispered.

The poor child probably didn't sleep again for hours. Jake's breathless tale about seeing 'the real Santy' was the big story at all the houses we visited the next morning. Everyone loved watching him tell it with all the wide-eyed wonder of a child.

Jake's favourite thing after opening all their toys was visiting family and friends on Christmas morning. He and Kaelem met all their cousins, aunts and uncles as they dropped in at Nanny Joan and Granddad Mickey's house.

Then we'd visit Daddy's grave and go on to Nanny and Granddad Brennan's in Castlecomer. There would be more people coming and going there and children showing off their new toys. Jake couldn't be happier.

When all the visiting was over, we'd return home and have dinner back in our own house. Jake monitored the situation to ensure that no gravy touched his plate on Christmas day. Tomato ketchup was the only acceptable sauce in Jake's world.

We still ensure Jake is part of our Christmas day routine. We open Santy's presents with the kids first, and then we go to Jake's grave which we always decorate for Christmas.

Our family and friends who are part of 'Jakie's crew' come to the grave with us. We sing songs like Winter Wonderland with altered lyrics so that it becomes Jakie Wonderland. The kids know that Christmas is about them, but we want them to remember Jake too.

For the first time since Jake died, we hosted Christmas for all the family in our new house last year. It was our fourth Christmas without Jake, and yet it was the hardest yet.

Chris bottled up a lot of his grief, but it all hit him hard two nights before Christmas. He broke down and was so upset that he could hardly explain what happened. While dozing on the couch, he felt Jakie breathing against his face as he used to when he fell asleep in our arms. When Chris woke, the realisation that Jakie was gone was like a punch in the gut.

We have to accept holidays and birthdays are never going to be the same for us again and that it doesn't get any easier.

Campaigning for Jake's Legacy helped me enormously. In the early days, it was a way to channel my anger. I could have spent my life pursuing justice for Jakie, but it was never going to bring him back. At least pursuing changes in the laws will stop what happened to Jake happening to other children.

It feels good to know that we've achieved a lot in Jake's name. The speed limits are being reduced in estates all over the country, so I know his death is making a difference. His death has been instrumental in saving the lives of other children.

I miss him so much but all I can do is honour his life through this campaign, and I couldn't have done it without the support of so many friends and family around us.

The thousands of messages of support that we've received from complete strangers through Jake's Legacy has been so therapeutic.

Recently, I asked people to share Jake's picture, and within a day it had 45,000 views and was shared across England, all over Europe and the world.

That feels like an achievement in itself. It means that people are reading Jake's story and a few of them might change their behaviour when they're behind the wheel of a car.

No one wants to be the person who accelerates from five doors down the road to 47km/h and can't stop their car when they hit an innocent child. To see 45,000 people sharing Jake's photo means that many people care.

It has also helped that Jake's Legacy makes me feel emotionally closer to our little boy. I never miss the nightly ritual of posting his bedtime kisses on the page.

When he was alive, we gave Jake kisses for his Nanny Joan, Granddad Micky, his Nanny Nolan, Nanny Brennan and Grandad Brennan and from Chris and me.

Thanks to Jake's Legacy page, he's still getting those kisses every night. It sounds bizarre, but every time I press 'publish' on the page, it feels like I'm sending the messages and kisses directly to him somehow.

I do it every night without fail. It's a routine that I find comforting and helps me feel a little more connected to him.

Religion has also been a consolation because I believe in God and an afterlife. My faith has sustained me even though it's tested me too.

I don't know why God let this happen and why he chose to inflict more pain on us than I could have believed possible. But I don't know where I'd be if I didn't think that I'll be reunited with Jake someday. I have to believe, or I don't think I could cope with the loss.

We were raised as good Catholics and my sisters, and I used to serve at mass as altar girls while my brothers were altar boys. I lost the habit of going to mass, but I'm getting more involved in the church again.

I took part in the nine-day annual parish novena last year for the first time. I attended all the masses and confessed to my overdose and self-harming and I felt better because of it.

Now whenever I get the urge to start cutting myself, I remind myself that I've made a vow to God that I'll never commit that sin again.

We sometimes go on family pilgrimages to Mount Melleray on the slopes of the Knockmealdown Mountains, in Waterford in memory of Jake. We walk with flowers and photos of Jake to the Holy Year Memorial Cross up the hills about 5 km from the monastery.

Despite this, I'm not what people would call 'religious'. I like to visit a church once a week, but I don't go to mass.

Jake went to church for christenings, communions, confirmations and weddings but not for Sunday mass. I brought him into the church to sit and pray and light a candle. Since I was a child, I've talked to Daddy in the church.

Now I talk to Jakie all the time too. I dream of the day that we'll meet in heaven again. I know that he is up there, our angel child, watching over Kaelem and Savannah and his mammy and daddy. And I'll always have the comfort in this life of knowing that I'll be with Jake again in the next life.

Thursdays, the day that Jake died, is now a special day in the week. I had to make it special or else I might never have got out of bed on Thursdays. That's the day I visit his grave with three roses - a red rose for Daddy and two white ones for Jakie.

I mark it down in a notebook that I call my 'bill book' which I use for appointments, reminders and payments. The book used to be full of reminders like "Jake's Jesters', 'Jake's new runners' or 'Jake's doctor appointment'.

After June 12, 2014, Jake's name no longer appeared in the book. I didn't realise it at the time, but now I see it was comforting to add 'Jake's flowers' to my book every Thursday.

Religion, routines, counselling, therapy - there are lots of ways we've tried to cope. But what has really got us through the worst of times has been the support of our closest family and friends. We feel so blessed because we couldn't have made it as far as we have without them.

Family and friends rallied around us when Jake died. They gathered with us at his graveside on the anniversary of his death on the 12th of every month. Everyone promised that they'd stand by us and that they'd always be there with us.

I was sceptical. Give them a year, I thought, and they'll be gone, and it'll be Chris and me in the cemetery on our own. I never expected that nearly four years later, Jakie's crew, as I call them would still be turning up every month on the 12th. We can never feel alone thanks to this incredible group of family and friends.

Jakie's crew is my mam Joan Hayes, my step-dad Mick Nolan, my sister Mary Hayes, her partner PJ Costello and her two kids, Cassie and Bradley. My sister Pamela Costello is always there with her husband Robert and their three kids, Sherice, Kayla and Mason.

There too without fail is Angela O'Hara who's married to Pakie and their three kids Sasha, Kai and Jaida.

Also showing up every month is my sister Catherine Hayes and her two kids, Donna and Megan. Her partner Brian O'Sullivan goes up to see Jake most days rather than the 12th of the month, but he's still a member of Jakie's crew.

My girlfriends are always there with their children. Mary Conroy comes with her daughter Shanice while Nicola Dunne arrives her two girls, Alanna and Ciara. Samantha McCullagh shows up with her partner James Hurley and their two kids Kyle and Amelia.

Hail, rain or sunshine, there are always 20 to 30 of us who gather on the 12th.

Part of the ritual involves ordering and collecting a bouquet of twenty roses for the grave. From the start, our florist has been Jonathan Clement, of Forget Me Not Florists, in Newpark Shopping Centre.

The first time I'd ever met Jon was when he delivered flowers for Jake's funeral. There were so many flowers he had to lay them out all over the front garden.

Jon has the roses wrapped and ready for me every Thursday and every 12th of the month. To mark the big occasions of the year, Jon and I pour over the flower catalogues and try to find themed roses.

For Easter, we had roses that looked like they were dipped in chocolate. I think Pakie tried to have a bite of one, but they were made of chocolate-coloured wax. For Hallowe'en, we had pumpkin-coloured roses with witches and goblins mixed into the bouquet. At Christmastime, we had white roses with sparkles and glitter which were mixed with frosted pinecones and festive holly.

Jakie's crew all know the routine inside out by now. The monthly anniversary gatherings start at 6.25pm - the exact time our lives changed forever.

I know there were so many different times mentioned at the inquest, but I was clock-watching, so I know that Jakie was fatally struck at 6.25pm.

We start by reciting six prayers. We adapt the prayer, There are Four Corners to My Bed, to include all our family members and friends who have died:

There are four corners to my bed
There are loads of angels overhead,
Daddy, Jake, Angela, Nicola, Bocky and Tyler.
Bless the bed that we sleep on.

We all sing my song, Hush Little Jakie before his Nanny Joan and my nieces Cassie and Kayla recite poems and sing a song that they wrote for our little boy.

Teenagers Sasha and Sherice switch it up by performing a new song for us every month.

Sometimes they rewrite the lyrics to make them more personal like the Wiz Khalifa and Charlie Puth song, See You Again:

It's been a long day without you, Jakie
And I'll tell you all about it when I see you again
We've come a long way from where we began
Oh, I'll tell you all about it when I see you again
When I see you again

At other times, the songs are perfect as they are like the Caissie Levy song, With You, which brought tears to everyone's eyes recently:

You took my days with you
Took my nights with you
Those unfinished conversations
We used to have, still speak to me
And I write you letters every day
That I'll never send and you'll never see…

We pray, sing, laugh, cry, bring our roses and duck and dive from showers on the 12th of every month. Then we all go our separate ways, and everyone continues to surprise me by always showing up four weeks later.

I love how all those that promised to be here for us are still here after nearly four years. It matters to me that the people I'm closest to care still. The worst thing for me would be to think that Jake could be forgotten.

It helps me to know that he's remembered so fondly; that he meant this much to so many other people that they come out month after month and year after year.

Chris and I had this beautiful child for six years, so we do our best to keep his spirit alive. It's so heartening that people still turn up to celebrate his life every month.

When we were consumed with grief, it was easy to take for granted the people that we have around us. But we realise that we are lucky to have had the love and support of so many wonderful family members and friends.

These people stuck with us and kept us going when we were more the living dead than the walking wounded.

They listened to us, held us, cried with us, prayed for us and filled a treasure chest of memories and stories for us about Jake.

We couldn't have survived without our families and friends. We can never repay their love, support and kindness. They held our heads above troubled water on so many occasions when we were nearly swept under the tide of grief.

24. A NEW START

Moving house in the first week of January 2017 was far more emotional than I expected.

At first glance, the house in a new housing estate off the Kells Road seemed perfect. It has a large back garden for Kaelem and Savannah, and it's a comfortable, new-build family home flooded with light.

For the two and a half years since June 12, 2014, I wanted to leave our house on Lintown Grove. I kept the curtains drawn at the front of the house all day and night to avoid seeing the road where Jake died. I hadn't started EMDR therapy at that stage, so I felt panic when I saw that street.

I'd experience the screams, the noise, the smells of the day we lost our baby. I'd have flashbacks of Jake reaching up or staggering back to me each time I set foot on that road. I had to brace myself every time I went out the front door of that house.

The prospect of moving to a new home far away from these reminders seemed to be the answer to all our problems.

It took far longer than I expected to find a new home. Now that the day was upon us, I found myself having second thoughts.

The new house was all I could have asked for except it never had Jake in it. It struck me that he'd never be in our bedrooms, play out the back garden or sit at our kitchen table. He'd never splash in the bathtub or stomp up and down our stairs.

I wanted to leave Lintown so badly, but then it hit me that I was also leaving all the memories of Jake behind. My head was all over the place as the move approached.

Chris and I were still limping along and cohabiting for the sake of the kids. Still, things were better, and he spent fewer nights in

Castlecomer. The resentments and anger that had built up between us were fading. There was a glimmer of hope between us, and we spoke about trying again when we moved to a new home.

Some of the girls volunteered to come over for a 'packing party' as we got ready to go.

The move was a positive thing for us, and it was also Nicola's birthday. The plan was to clear out a few rooms and then have a few drinks to celebrate.

Everything was fine until we got to Jakie's room. Pulling out furniture, we started finding little pieces of paper filled with his childish scrawls and drawings.

We found notes reading 'I love my Mammy and Daddy' and crayon drawings of his house and his family. We unearthed so many little reminders of him that it broke my heart.

I started to believe this move was the worst mistake ever.

The celebratory mood disappeared, and we were all red-eyed and sobbing as we got through the work.

It all got too much for me. I went into the downstairs bathroom to dry my eyes and blow my nose. Then I took a deep breath, and I used a hand-soap container to smash the mirror in front of me. The glass shattered into the sink below and scattered all over the floor.

I screamed my head off.

This is f***ing ridiculous! Why did I think that moving is going to make any difference? It's always the same. Here we are, all crying again. My baby is gone, and it's impossible to be happy anymore.

When the girls reached me, I had a shard of the glass mirror in my hand. I don't know what I intended to do with it. I don't know what I intended by smashing the mirror.

310

It was frustration and rage and grief rising to the surface again.

"Please just give us the glass," said one of my sisters.

I was staring at the small jug which I had been using to measure Jake's urine every day. It was on a shelf in the bathroom ever since the day he died.

It made me even angrier looking at that stupid measuring jug.

"I did everything I was supposed to do!" I roared at the top of my voice. "I did what they told me to do, I did everything, and still, he was f***ing taken from me!"

I was in full rant mode, and my sister Mary said she couldn't deal with it.

"I'm going; I'm leaving; I'm not listening to this anymore," she said grabbing her coat.

I yelled: "Go, go, get out, get the f*** out! You can all walk away. I can't walk away from this!"

Mary screamed back: "Shut up, just shut up! I don't want to hear this anymore."

Pamela was shouting: "Don't listen to her lads, she's upset, and she wants us to fight with her. She's trying to pick a fight."

She was right. I was picking a fight so that I had the excuse to scream even more.

Then I saw Catherine sobbing, on her knees, as she cleaned up the mess I'd made. I was filled with remorse. Pamela persuaded Mary to come back, and I apologised for the outburst.

"I just want him back!" I cried.

Then we all ended up hugging and bawling and getting nothing done.

I looked in on Jake's room before we left forever. There was only an empty bed and bare mattress left. It was a stab in the heart because it was like Jake had never been there at all.

Moving is hard to do anyway. But this was harder than I ever dreamed because it felt like I was losing him all over again. It was like a second bereavement.

The first night in the new house, I thought I'd made the worst mistake ever. I was a tumult of regret, anxiety, loss, sadness and fear. I thought I could never make this new house a home.

Then as the days passed, I felt myself exhaling a little. I woke in the morning, and for the first time in years, I could draw apart the bedroom curtains and let the new day in.

There were no memories outside that made my stomach churn, or my heart beat faster. I went downstairs in the morning, and the sun streamed into the kitchen. I had daylight in my life again, and I felt brighter.

I realised that Jake is in our heart wherever we go. I know now that the house in Lintown lost all its lovely memories for me after June 12, 2014.

There's still a park bench that commemorates our little boy on the estate, but we had to move on. I still shudder when I pass near the road where we lived. There will always be that darkness there.

We made a special bedroom for Jake in the attic, and it was a relief to be able to unpack all his possessions from boxes and black sacks. Once Jake had his own space, it felt like he was with us again in our new house.

His room is never off limits. Kaelem has his room and Savannah has her own too, but the kids can come up and play with Jake's toys anytime. I know that's what Jake would want and it's what I want too.

There's no doubt in my mind it was healthy for our family to leave Lintown and all the terrible memories associated with it.

The back garden of our new house was a sodden mess from the construction when we arrived. So, we laid new grass and had a path made down the centre of it in the shape of a long "J" for Jake.

Last summer, Savannah was old enough for the first time to go out and play with Kaelem in the garden. I felt a surge of happiness as I saw each of them on their bike, flying down the J-shaped path, legs in the air.

Age six and three, they were the same age as Jake and Kaelem were when they last played together. And they fought over that bike the same way Jake and Kaelem used to too.

It was bittersweet looking out at the two of them and remembering how it was three years earlier.

Still, it was wonderful to see the two playing together and hear them squealing with delight as they speed down the slope of Jakie's "J".

I don't know if I've imagined it, but the new house seems to make the children happier too. The move was the hardest thing to do, but it was also the best. It seemed to bring a warm shaft of light into all our hearts.

It has been the new start that Chris and I needed, and we're starting to find each other again. I don't know if it will ever be the way it was. He's not the same man anymore, and I'm not the same woman. We're different people now, and we have to learn about each other all over again.

It's no secret that a high percentage of marriages end after the loss of a child. We don't want to be another statistic but we've both lost someone precious to us, and somehow we lost something precious between us.

There's a piece of our hearts missing now. We laugh and say that we're trying to beat the odds, but we know how close we've come to splitting up forever and know it can happen again.

When Chris moved out the first time, I believed our marriage was over. We were finished, and I felt relieved.

We had so much going on as individuals that we weren't able to deal with each other's problems. We knew that we were better off away from each other. When the tension levels rose between us I said "Just go!" and thankfully, he could, and he did.

When he moved back a few nights a week for Kaelem's sake, there was less of a pressure cooker environment in the house. Looking back now, we broke up to avoid any potential conflict. It was one thing less to worry about and allowed us to turn our focus on the kids.

We didn't have the words or the clarity of vision to know that at the time but in hindsight I can see that's what we were doing.

For a long time, there was no feeling between us.

Then gradually, there was a thaw, and then we realised that we don't want to break up. The move to the new house came at the start of a new year, and it was the fresh start we needed.

We never said Chris was moving back full-time. Nothing was definite. We needed to have the safety valve of a spare room in Castlecomer. These days I don't want him gone anymore, and he doesn't want to go.

We've taken the advice of couple's counselling, and we talk to each other about the future and not about the past.

I know I could live without him, but I don't want to. I never want to see him with anyone else, and he says he feels the same way about me. We still want each other, so we have a good chance of beating the odds.

It feels a lot of the time that Jake is keeping us together. We have Jakie's name on our wedding rings, and he's holding our original rings, so it's another reason not to give up.

We know he's watching us and it makes us want to be better people.

We've said that if we beat the odds, we will renew our marriage vows even if it's just for ourselves and the kids. It's not that we don't love each other, it's that we're still learning a new way of living.

It's the same as when I had to learn to be a mother again after Jake. I lost all my confidence as a mother after he died. It took time for me to accept that I could be a proper mammy to Kaelem and Savannah.

I wasn't good at it in the beginning because I overdid it. I watched them too much, fretted over them, spoiled them.

I also had to find myself again and learn to be kinder to myself.

Now we have to learn to be a couple again. I know I love Chris and that I never stopped loving him behind it all.

It helps that I don't let things fester like I used to. I don't get upset if he falls asleep on the couch and doesn't come to bed. I'd like him to accept more counselling and take it seriously instead of going to one session and missing the next two.

But I give him his space and concentrate on working on myself. We're both more understanding of each other.

I was looking at him the other day in a new light because he shaved off the beard that he'd been wearing for a long time.

He grew it at a time that he was tired and depressed, but he's shaved it all off, and now he looks ten years younger again.

Last Friday night, we found ourselves laughing a lot again. It brought me back to a time years ago. "That's still MY chin," he said at one stage. It seemed like another lifetime when he used to say that.

We're much better together, especially in the past six months. I still feel like killing him occasionally, but that's good because at least I'm angry. I have feelings again.

I know too that we'd be lost without the kids. Kaelem and Savannah make us laugh so much. They make us pull our hair out at times too, but mostly they make us laugh.

For a long time after Jake died, I didn't cook. I couldn't cook in that house. The smells and the thoughts of eating turned my stomach. Dinner was always something we did as a family. I thought we couldn't sit down to a family dinner if one of us were missing.

Luckily Chris is a good cook, and my sisters all rowed in, so Kaelem and Savannah always ate well. Since we've moved house, I'm getting back into the routine of family dinners, and last week I decided it was time we resumed grace before meals.

"We're going to say our thanks before dinner today. I'll go first," I announced.

"I'm grateful because I have three wonderful children and even though one is in heaven, he's still mine, and I have two mad yokes with me here. I'm thankful for my lovely husband, and I'm very thankful that he's able to cook."

Chris said he'll always miss his little boy in heaven but thanked God for the food before us, the family around him and the love between us.

Kaelem got into the swing of things quickly and was brief like his dad.

"I'm thankful for me mammy, for me daddy, for Jakie in heaven and Savannah."

"Good boy Kaelem!" I said.

We looked at Savannah. She's still only turning four, and she seemed a bit doubtful about this new dinnertime event.

"I don't know if I want to," she said.

"If you don't want to Baby, that's fine; maybe you'll do it the next time."

We were about to serve dinner when she piped up again.

"Okay, wait," she said. "I'm grateful for the food, for my family, for Jakie in heaven, for the dessert and ice cream, for Mammy, Daddy and Kaelem…"

"Good girl!" I enthused.

"No wait, I'm not finished. I'm grateful for Nanny and Grandad and my other Nanny and Granddad and Betsy the dog and my dolls and all my toys and my teacher and, and…"

"Good girl!" I said. "That's a lot of thanks for today!"

"No wait, I'm grateful for my best friend and all my cousins and…"

Chris and I looked at each other, and he shrugged as if to say, 'Don't blame me'.

Savannah has the gift of the gab like her mother and her 'thanks' went on so long I ended up having to reheat my dinner.

I forget they're growing up so fast. Kaelem and Savannah are both developing such strong personalities that they astonish me at times. Kaelem is just like his dad, quiet, sometimes moody but a real boy who loves sports and is full of energy and mischief.

Unlike Jake, he has no time for girls, dressing up or anything he considers 'girly'. Savannah is a loveable little madam, who is aged four going on forty, and a doyenne of fashion and all things 'girly'.

But she's well able to stand up for herself and can still give Kaelem as good as she gets in a row.

I'm still working on being the best mother that I can be, and therapy is certainly helping me, but it has been tough.

My psychologist, Martin, had me in tears during our last session when he asked me if I'd ever said goodbye to Jake.

"You'd say goodbye to Jake if he went off to school, wouldn't you?" he asked.

"Of course, I would."

"So why haven't you said goodbye to him now?"

He also made me realise that subconsciously I've known all along that I had to release him.

"Why else did you insist on letting a hundred balloons fly off into the sky at his funeral? Why else did you release those doves?"

It was true. I had never let a balloon fly off in my life before Jakie's funeral. The kids used to cry if their balloons got away.

But throughout the whole ordeal, from the time that Jake died, throughout his funeral, and in the years since, I realised I had never said goodbye to Jake.

It's only recently that I've been able to say the words 'Jakie's dead'. I couldn't get my mouth to form those words before. I knew that Martin was right. I was shocked to realise that I hadn't ever thought to say goodbye to my baby.

Martin was concerned about me driving after the session, but I insisted I was fine. I was a woman on a mission. I was determined that I was going to say goodbye to Jake.

After the session, I went straight to my sister's Mary's house. I knew that if I went home, I might not do it.

I was in tears, but I rang my sister Catherine who lives around the corner from Mary.

"Will you come over to Mary's?"

"What's wrong?"

"Nothing, nothing but I had counselling, and I have to say goodbye to Jakie."

Catherine was adamant.

"No, you don't! No, you don't! That's stupid. I'm not saying goodbye to Jakie."

She came straight over, and she and Mary agreed.

"No, you don't have to say goodbye! Here, have a cup of coffee."

I would have poured coffee into myself before I got all this advice to stay away from it when I'm already anxious.

"Look, Martin's right. When Kaelem went off to school this morning, I said goodbye. Jakie's gone three years, and it is goodbye until the day when I have him back again. Until then, I'm holding him back by never saying goodbye to him."

Mary admitted that she had been discussing the same thing with her partner PJ. She asked him if he thought we were all keeping him here, refusing to let him go.

The three of us were all crying in the end, but they agreed that I should do what I thought best.

I said I was going to write a goodbye letter to Jake. I scribbled my heart out in minutes, and my notebook was damp and tearstained by the time I finished.

I read it out on video and posted it on Jake's Legacy along with his usual bedtime kisses. It always feels more real, like I'm sending messages straight to Jake when I post them on his page.

I felt sad and drained afterwards. I expected that I'd feel even more depressed as the evening progressed. I normally do after a heavy therapy session with Martin.

Instead that night, I started feeling better, a bit brighter, relaxed and more self-assured. Christopher and I sat down in front of the television, and in minutes he fell asleep.

I recalled how Martin also asked me if I was starting to feel like the old Rosie again yet, and I'd replied that I didn't want to be the old Rosie again.

"It was much easier being the old Rosie, but she never knew how to appreciate how much she had," I said. "I'm starting to feel like a new Rosie instead."

That night my letter to Jakie lay in my notebook on the coffee table in front of me. Chris dozed beside me, and Kaelem and Savannah were safely asleep upstairs.

I looked around me and, for the first time in a long time, I realised that I felt content.

My Goodbye Letter to Jakie

I love you so much Jakie. This is one of the hardest things your mammy will ever have to do. My heart is broken.

I'm sorry I didn't hold you in my arms when you were passing, but I just wanted you to be in less pain.

If I could change anything of that horrible day - like me stepping in front of that car instead of you - I would Jakie.

I would give my life for yours in a heartbeat, but I can't, my little man. No matter what I do, I can't change places with you.

And it hurts, but your Mammy has got to accept this even though she doesn't want to.

I want you to love; I want you to love and grow in heaven, but how can you do that if I keep you stuck here worrying about me?

So, I have to leave. You've got to live, love and grow into that wonderful man I know you'll be.

I know I will get to hold you again, my beautiful boy, but till then I have to say goodbye Jakie.

I love you so much, but I've got to let you go so that you can live on in heaven.

I know you're not here on earth with us anymore so until I see you at heaven's gates, goodbye my beautiful boy.

Even though your mammy is saying goodbye, this doesn't mean I stop being your mammy, or you stop being my Jakie.

This is just goodbye, my beautiful son, my Jakie, till we meet again in heaven.

Until then, I want you to rock heaven with Grandad, and always remember you're loved and missed every minute of every day.

I love you. Goodbye, my beautiful.

Always, your Mammy.

Epilogue

Night time is the hardest, Jakie. I have no chance of sleep without a sleeping tablet and that second pill to slow my over-active mind.

Even with these, there's no guarantee of a full night's sleep; but without them, I'll pace the floor all night.

My anxiety levels go through the roof in the black of night. That terrible day repeats in my head like hell on an endless loop.

I crave sleep, unconsciousness, an escape from real life. More than anything, I crave dreamtime with you.

I've many dreams about you, Jakie, often fleeting and disjointed. Sometimes they're nightmares of that terrible day.

At other times, wisps from the past come to me during sleep; happy, hazy memories of days we had when you were here with us.

But the dreams I crave are the rare times when you visit me. Then everything is so vivid, so clear, that it's hard to believe they're not real.

I remember everything; I know I'm dreaming and I know you're in heaven, yet you appear right in front of me.

I see you as clear as day. Sometimes there are other people in my dream. I call out in excitement to Chris or my sisters, 'Jakie's here! Can you see him?' but no one can.

I say, 'I'm not going mad, I'm not! Jakie is right here!'

Sometimes you stand watching me, and you have that mischievous smile on your face, dimples dancing. Your brown eyes sparkle, and you laugh because they can't see you.

I'm afraid to move, to do anything, in case you disappear. So, I ask, "Can Mammy hold you?"

You have no idea how I long to hold you in my arms. Your light comes towards me, and everyone else fades into darkness.

It's just you and me again.

I reach out, my fingers trembling with hope and yearning. My heart leaps when I realise that I can touch you; you're solid flesh and blood again.

I feel the agony of our long separation and fight the urge to grab you to me. I touch you gently first; cup your face in the palm of my hand and caress the warm, soft skin of your cheek.

Then I can't resist anymore. I wrap hungry arms around you, pull you to me and squeeze you like I'll never let you go again.

I can't stop sobbing. It's the relief of feeling you in my arms at last; of filling that aching void in me. I whisper in your ear how I miss you, but I thank you over and over for visiting Mammy in her dream.

You don't speak, but you hug me back, and then you pull back from me and stand there before me, smiling. I stroke your cheek and tell you how I miss this perfect, perfect, little face.

Then you step back again, smiling, still smiling, and then you fade right in front of me, and you're gone again.

I sit there, sobbing, bereft, alone. I know that I'm dreaming. But still, I thank you for visiting me. I plead with you to come back soon; to relieve the agony of that forever-hole punched through my heart.

When I wake, a torrent of fresh tears unleashes, but I close my eyes and cherish the memory of the dream, the feel of you, your warmth, your scent. I let it wash over me and fill my aching heart and head.

This isn't the life I picked. People tell me it's part of God's plan, but it was never part of my plan. I never wanted to be the mammy of an angel child. So please Jakie, try to come back soon again.

Even if I only see your lovely smile in my dreams, maybe I can face this future that I never wanted. If I can hold my little man in a dream world, then maybe I can exist in this nightmare world without you.

So please, please try and visit Mammy soon again. Dreamtime is all I have, my darling baby. I have nothing but dreams until you're back in my arms forever…

The Driver

Dear Reader,

One of the main reasons I wanted to write Jake's story is in the hope of changing the driving behaviour of even a few of the people who read it.

There are several references to The Driver in this book, but the grim truth is that you, or I, or anyone could be The Driver once we sit behind the wheel of a car.

The Driver, in Jake's case, accelerated from parked to 47km/h in a matter of metres. Her car stuck Jake within seconds of leaving her driveway and dragged my beautiful boy's body along the road.

Admittedly, there are many ways to turn our cars into lethal weapons. Talking, texting, phoning, fixing hair or make-up in the mirror, reaching under the seat, turning around, or driving while under the influence of drink, drugs or prescription medication can result in tragedy.

Yet, the easiest, surest way to turn our cars into lethal weapons is by driving too fast.

The faster we drive, the more likely we are to kill.

We can still kill a person by hitting them at 30km/h, but according to the World Health Organisation, pedestrians have a 90% chance of survival when struck by a car travelling this speed or lower.

If The Driver's car hit Jake at 30km/h, the stopping distance would have been about half that at 50km/h. The car might not have dragged him, and Jake might still be alive today.

A pedestrian has less than a 50% chance of surviving an impact at 45km/h which means a child, like Jake, has less chance again.

Most collisions, including the one that killed Jake, are preventable. No other child should die like our little boy died, and no other family should suffer likes ours did.

Remember, the most important thing we can do to protect ourselves and protect others while in control of a car is to drive slowly.

As I've said, the difference between driving at 30km/h and 50km/h is the difference between a child with a broken leg and a fatally wounded child, lying in his mammy's arms, begging not to die.

Jake's Legacy is about trying to save the lives of children so telling Jake's story only has value if it can inspire people who hear it to slow down and drive with extra care.

So, dear Reader, in the name of Jake and all the other thousands of children who have been needlessly killed and injured on our roads, please slow down, and be mindful of vulnerable road users when you turn the key in the ignition.

It only takes a minor distraction or a few seconds of carelessness for any of us to become The Driver who smashes into a life and shatters another family.

Nobody wants to be that driver.

Roseann Brennan.

Life Without My Morning Sun

You were once my morning sun, rising early and
greeting me with your dazzling smile.

Now mornings are dark clouds and relentless rain
that will not leave me.

I'm lost without my morning sun who loved me
unconditionally, and I you.

Because when you looked into my eyes, I knew you
truly loved me.

But I know you left me with the light of two
brilliant stars so that I could live without my
morning sun.

So, I live forever knowing that I have three bright
flames burning within and around me, and I shall
love and cherish you all for all eternity...

Roseann Brennan

About the Author

Roseann Brennan is 34-year-old wife, mother and campaigner who was born and raised in Kilkenny.

She is the daughter of Joan and the late Michael Hayes and is the fourth youngest of a family of seven sisters and four brothers.

She attended Saint John's Junior and Senior School before completing her leaving cert in Kilkenny City Vocational School in 2002.

She went to Ormonde College where she received a Fetac level 5 in Nursing Studies which focussed on health and safety at work, early childhood education as well as anatomy and physiology.

She received a Fetac level 6 in Special Needs Assisting and is currently a studying Health Care in Kilkenny.

She married Christopher Brennan from Castlecomer in Kilkenny on March 28, 2012. The couple has three children, Jake born on April 2, 2008, Kaelem born on May 1, 2011, and Savannah, who arrived on February 9, 2014.

Roseann founded Jake's Legacy road-safety campaign after her six-year-old was killed by a car outside his home on June 12, 2014.

She has successfully campaigned to have speeds reduced in housing estates and residential areas in every county around Ireland in her beloved son's name.

She likes to spend her free time with her family, socialising with friends or working out in the gym.

Roseann's ambitions are to work in her community and to make a difference, however small, whenever she can.

Praise for This Book

"After the tragic death of her son Jake, Rosie Brennan would have been forgiven if she had closed her door and pulled the curtains.
Instead, she channelled her grief into campaigning to make our estates and developments safer for our children. I've no doubt that her efforts and this book will help save young lives."
Ray D'Arcy RTE TV and radio presenter.

"To lose a child is every parent's most dreaded nightmare. It is the nightmare that came to Roseann and her family with the loss of their beautiful, beloved Jake.
The journey Roseann has travelled, dealing with her pain, and campaigning for road safety to ensure that no other mother suffers her loss is extraordinary.
Her story is heartbreakingly sad and uncompromisingly honest. Roseann is driven by a determined love for her lost son. She is an inspirational woman, and I'm so glad she knocked on my door."
Mary Lou McDonald TD and Sinn Fein leader.

"This book documents the tragic loss of a child, its impact on a mother and father and the courage and bravery they found to turn such a horrific, life-changing event, into a campaign that would save lives and help prevent other families from suffering the same loss.
It's heartbreaking, gripping, inspiring and will leave every reader with a greater appreciation of just how fragile life is and how easy it is to lose something so precious."
Andrew McGuinness, Councillor & Mayor of Kilkenny 2014/15

"No mother should ever have to endure pain like Roseann Brennan. Her young, happy and vibrant family were shattered by little Jake's death. Roseann's description of holding her six-year-old as he slipped away will never leave me.
Every time I drive into a housing estate, I can picture Jake's perfect smile. This is the power of Roseann's road safety message and her incredible energy after Jake's death. She didn't allow us to forget him, but she made

everyone stop and think about how quickly everything can change. Roseann is an extraordinary woman who never gives up on her family. Her story is one everyone should read."
Eimear Ní Bhraonáin, Presenter on KCLR (Kilkenny & Carlow Local Radio)

"A truly heartbreaking and harrowing account of her little son's tragic death, by a very brave bereaved mother. Roseann describes in vivid detail the shocking death of her beautiful little boy Jake in what was a totally preventable road traffic collision.

Losing your child is every parent's worst nightmare. To lose them to an incurable disease is one thing, to lose them in circumstances where their death could, and should, have been avoided is absolutely soul destroying and leaves families such as Roseann's destroyed forever.

We cannot wind back the clock. Nothing will ever bring back our children. We are now compelled to try to do something to try to make our roads safer and to prevent our needless pain being visited on other families. We do this to help save lives and prevent injury and in honour of our children. It helps us to keep their memory alive and to ensure that at least lessons are learnt, and their untimely and unnatural deaths have not been in vain.

Roseann's soul-destroying account of her very personal experience, written from the heart and in her own down-to-earth fashion, is a must-read for anybody interested in keeping our roads safe for our families. It's the story of one family's tragic loss, their fight for justice, and little Jake's legacy.

I cried from start to finish, reliving the nightmare that no parent should have to experience, of the sudden and very violent death of their child in a road crash. Roseann's strength is to be much admired, and I'm sure little Jakie is very proud of his Mammy - a very inspirational lady. I know that all of the bereaved families in IRVA are. I was honoured to preview some chapters for Roseann (9,10,15 & 17).
Donna Price, Founder & Chairperson, Irish Road Victims' Association, www.irva.ie